Early Greek Alchemy, Patronage and Innovation in Late Antiquity

CALIFORNIA CLASSICAL STUDIES

NUMBER 7

Editorial Board Chair: Donald Mastronarde

Editorial Board: Alessandro Barchiesi, Todd Hickey, Emily Mackil, Richard Martin, Robert Morstein-Marx, J. Theodore Peña, Kim Shelton

California Classical Studies publishes peer-reviewed long-form scholarship with online open access and print-on-demand availability. The primary aim of the series is to disseminate basic research (editing and analysis of primary materials both textual and physical), data-heavy research, and highly specialized research of the kind that is either hard to place with the leading publishers in Classics or extremely expensive for libraries and individuals when produced by a leading academic publisher. In addition to promoting archaeological publications, papyrological and epigraphic studies, technical textual studies, and the like, the series will also produce selected titles of a more general profile.

The startup phase of this project (2013–2017) was supported by a grant from the Andrew W. Mellon Foundation.

Also in the series:

Number 1: Leslie Kurke, *The Traffic in Praise: Pindar and the Poetics of Social Economy*, 2013

Number 2: Edward Courtney, *A Commentary on the Satires of Juvenal*, 2013

Number 3: Mark Griffith, *Greek Satyr Play: Five Studies*, 2015

Number 4: Mirjam Kotwick, *Alexander of Aphrodisias and the Text of Aristotle's Metaphysics*, 2016

Number 5: Joey Williams, *The Archaeology of Roman Surveillance in the Central Alentejo, Portugal*, 2017

Number 6: Donald J. Mastronarde, *Preliminary Studies on the Scholia to Euripides*, 2017

Early Greek Alchemy, Patronage and Innovation in Late Antiquity

Olivier Dufault

Berkeley, California

© 2019 by Olivier Dufault.

This work is licensed under a
Creative Commons Attribution-NonCommercial 4.0 International License.

California Classical Studies
c/o Department of Classics
University of California
Berkeley, California 94720–2520
USA
http://calclassicalstudies.org
email: ccseditorial@berkeley.edu

ISBN 9781939926128 (paperback)   9781939926135 (PDF)

Library of Congress Control Number: 2019934642

CONTENTS

Acknowledgments vii
Abbreviations viii

 Introduction   1
1. Client Scholars   9
 1.1 Illiberal Scholars   10
 1.2 The Scholar and the *Magos*   19
 1.3 Client Scholars in Late Antiquity   23
2. *Mageia* and *Paideia*   26
 2.1 The Term *Magos* and Cognates in Early Greek Texts   27
 2.2 The Later History of *Mageia*   37
3. Representations of Scholars as Learned Sorcerers   51
 3.1 Anaxilaus of Larissa   52
 3.2 Apion   59
 3.3 Simon   63
 3.4 Pancrates   66
4. Patrons, Scholars and the Limits of *Paideia*   70
 4.1 Plutarch   70
 4.2 Heliodorus' *Ethiopica*   79
 4.3 Julius Africanus   84

5. Zosimus of Panopolis and Ancient Greek Alchemy — 93
   5.1 References to Alchemy in Late Antique Literature — 94
   5.2 Gold Transmutation in the Non-Alchemical Literature — 100
   5.3 The Soteriology of Zosimus of Panopolis — 108
6. Zosimus, Client and Scholar — 118
   6.1 Theosebeia's Household — 119
   6.2 Rivals and Scholars — 122
   6.3 *Mageia* and *Chēmeia* — 138
   Conclusion — 142

Bibliography — 145
Index of Passages — 159
General Index — 166

ACKNOWLEDGMENTS

Many thanks to Coralie Arntz, Peter Brown, Elizabeth DePalma Digeser, Mary Hancock, Cornelia Hartmann, Donald J. Mastronarde, Christine Thomas, Christopher Waß and anonymous referees for commenting on previous versions of this book or individual chapters. I have also greatly benefited from discussions with Renaud Gagné, Heidi Marx, Paul-Hubert Poirier, Joseph Sanzo and Jay Stemmle.

I would also like to give special thanks to Michèle Mertens and Matteo Martelli, whose efforts provided a very useful basis for my research. Many thanks to California Classical Studies for affording the opportunity to publish peer-reviewed books in open access and more particularly to Donald J. Mastronarde for his initiative and generosity.

Work for this book would not have been possible without the financial help of the Fonds de Recherche du Québec, Culture et Société, the UCSB History Affiliates and the Graduate School Distant Worlds at the Ludwig-Maximilians-Universität, Munich.

Olivier Dufault
Montreal, February 2019

ABBREVIATIONS

A   *Parisinus graecus* 2327.
B   *Parisinus graecus* 2325.
CAAG   Charles-Émile Ruelle and Marcellin Berthelot. 1887–1888. *Collection des anciens alchimistes grecs*, 3 vols. Paris.
DK   Hermann Diels and Walther Kranz. 1974. *Die Fragmente der Vorsokratiker*, 3 vols. Berlin.
FGrH   Felix Jacoby et al. 1923–1999. *Die Fragmente der griechischen Historiker*, 5 parts. Berlin and Leiden.
Lampe   G. W. H. Lampe. 1961. *Patristic Greek Lexicon*. Oxford.
L   *Laurentianus graecus plut.* 86.16.
LSJ   Henry George Liddell et al. 1940. *A Greek-English Lexicon*. Oxford.
M   *Marcianus graecus* 299.
MA   Michèle Mertens. 1995. *Les alchimistes grecs, Tome 4.1: Zosime de Panopolis. Mémoires authentiques*. Paris.
PGM   Karl Preisendanz et al. 1973. *Papyri Graecae Magicae*, 2 vols. Teubner.
P.Holm.   *Papyrus Holmiensis*. In Robert Halleux 1981. *Les alchimistes grecs, Tome 1: Papyrus de Leyde. Papyrus de Stockholm. Fragments de recettes*. Paris.
P.Leid.   *Papyrus Leidensis X*. In Robert Halleux 1981. *Les alchimistes grecs, Tome 1: Papyrus de Leyde. Papyrus de Stockholm. Fragments de recettes*. Paris.
PLRE   Arnold H. M. Jones et al. 1971–1992. *The Prosopography of the Later Roman Empire*, 3 vols. Cambridge.
SH   *Stobaei Hermetica*. In Arthur D. Nock and André-Jean Festugière 1954. *Corpus Hermeticum*, vol. 3–4. Paris.

Early Greek Alchemy, Patronage and Innovation in Late Antiquity

Introduction

The appearance of alchemical commentaries between the first and the fourth century CE provides us with an opportunity to study a striking example of innovation in ancient Greek scholarship.[1] Contextualizing the alchemical commentaries of Zosimus of Panopolis (c. 300 CE)—the oldest extant alchemical author—can help us understand how this form of scholarship came to be considered worth studying and copying by ancient scholars, i.e. by professionals of *paideia*. The term will be taken here to mean the sum of social interactions that lead at any given time to the production and reproduction of scholarly works written in Greek and of the legitimate dispositions toward these works. As I show in this book, the legitimation of alchemical commentaries can be partly explained by the fact that Zosimus was a client scholar, i.e. a person who was informally hired by a patron to teach or expand upon Greek or Latin literature and/or to produce new works.

Greek, or Greco-Egyptian alchemy, spelled *chē-*, *chu-*, *chi-* or *cheim(e)ia*, can be succinctly defined as the art and science of "tinctorial processes" (*baphai*) meant to color metals into gold or silver, to give stones or glass the appearance of precious stones and to dye textiles. This fourfold division, found in the fourth-century CE *papyri Leidensis X* and *Holmiensis*, was already present in the first-century CE books of alchemical recipes attributed to Democritus.[2] Some commentators presented alchemy as the art of "producing" (*argurou* or *chrusou poiēsis/arguro-*, *chrusopoiia*) or "preparing" (*kataskeuō*) gold and silver. Zosimus also described processes of transformation (including the making of gold) as a "turning" of matter "inside out." It is still unclear what Zosimus exactly meant by this but—to anticipate the argument developed in chapter 5—it can briefly be said that this

---

[1] For overviews of ancient Greek alchemy, see Berthelot 1885, Lippmann 1919, Lindsay 1970. For introductions to alchemy, see Schütt 2000, Principe 2013, Joly 2013. Ruelle and Berthelot (1887–1888 = CAAG) is dated and incomplete but is still the best edition for many alchemical works. See also Letrouit 1995: 11–93.

[2] See Mertens 1995, Martelli 2013: 13–18.

formulation was relevant to the soteriology he adopted, which he described as the extraction of the "luminous pneuma" from one's body.[3]

Zosimus is the first known commentator of alchemy and the most famous name in the Greek alchemical corpus, a group of codices dated c. 1000 to 1500 CE containing the vast majority of Greek alchemical texts.[4] Authors of alchemical texts can be divided into three groups. The first comprises the so-called "ancient authors" of recipes. All of these appear to be pseudepigraphic (e.g. Hermes, Agathodaimon, Chumēs, Maria, Moses, Democritus, etc.). Except for the remaining fragments of the *Four Books* attributed to Democritus, *P.Holm.* and *P.Leid.*, recipes attributed to the ancient alchemical authors are known only from citations found in the work of the second group of authors, the commentators (Zosimus, Olympiodorus, Stephanus et al.). This second group includes many different texts dating from the third century CE to the tenth century CE—the point at which the oldest alchemical compilation was written (the *Marcianus graecus* 299). Authors dated after this point can be classified in a third and last category (Michael Psellus, Nicephorus Blemmydes, the "anonyme de Zuretti," etc.).[5] These subdivisions are somewhat arbitrary but have the advantage of distinguishing between authors who are sometimes separated by a thousand years and who most probably wrote under very different circumstances, e.g. working on Greek translations of Arabic,[6] or Latin[7] recipes, assuming different theories concerning the transformation of metals,[8] etc.

In contrast to the majority of names found in the Greek alchemical corpus, "Zosimus of Panopolis" (or, "of Alexandria," according to the *Suda* Z 168) does not appear to be pseudepigraphic. Zosimus can be dated roughly between 240 and 391 CE[9] and his work provides more sociological details than any texts from the Greek alchemical corpus. This relative wealth of information makes Zosimus an interesting and underexploited source for the study of early Christianity and Hermetism. We know unfortunately little about Zosimus' cultural background and

---

[3] See MA 1.13–14.

[4] The chief manuscripts are M = *Marcianus graecus* 299 (c. 1000 CE), A = *Parisinus gr.* 2327 (fifteenth century) and B = *Parisinus gr.* 2325 (thirteenth century). See the introductions to Halleux 1981, Mertens 1995 and Martelli 2013 (a revised and translated version of Martelli 2011, ch. 2–3).

[5] See the introduction of Henri Dominique Saffrey to Halleux 1981, Letrouit 1995, Colinet 2000a, 2010.

[6] See Colinet (2000b: 165–190) who demonstrated that an alchemical text found in a Greek alchemical compilation of the fifteenth century CE had been translated from an Arabic text dated c. 800 CE.

[7] Colinet 2010.

[8] See Mertens 2001, Dufault 2015.

[9] All Greek works attributed to Zosimus are contained in the four families of manuscripts. On dating Zosimus and the Greek alchemical corpus, see Mertens 1995: i-cxii. As noted by Mertens, Ruelle and Berthelot attributed some works to Zosimus by error. To trace these false attributions, see Mertens 1995: 263–267. Note that Mertens also developed an argument against the attribution of MA 8 to Zosimus. See Dufault 2017.

his education. The fact that alchemical commentators normally referred to each other as philosophers does not help us in locating them in a specific tradition. This is also true of Zosimus, who considered Democritus of Abdera as the most authoritative author of alchemy. In contrast to many philosophers, however, Zosimus was not systematic in his use of terminology.[10] Some of his works show more than an inkling of Gnostic and Hermetic notions.[11] However, that is not to say that describing him as a Gnostic or a Hermetist would help us to understand his social context. I refer to the modern concepts of Gnosticism and Hermetism simply to provide readers with a rough idea of the importance of Zosimus' work for the study of the *Hermetica*, early Christianity and the Christianization of the Greco-Roman elite. These two terms are used here as shorthand for distinct (although related) types of texts rather than for coherent ideologies, sects or philosophical groups.[12] To my knowledge, studying the work of Zosimus as a "Hermetist," an "alchemist" or a "Gnostic" cannot provide us with an explanation for the fact that he is the first known author of Greek alchemical commentaries. Following the evidence found in letters Zosimus addressed to his patroness Theosebeia, I chose to study Zosimus from the perspective of scholarly patronage. The following argument is consequently concerned with ancient scholars, *paideia* and their representation. Considering that Christians and non-Christians were all schooled in Greek letters and that they sometimes met in the same schools or scholarly circles, I have not made a distinction between descriptions of scholarly patronage coming from Christian authors and those coming from non-Christians.[13]

[10] See Dufault 2015. It has been recently argued that Zosimus' use of the term pneuma was influenced by Stoic cosmology. See Rinotas 2017.

[11] In his edition of the treatise *On the Letter Omega* (= MA 1), Reitzenstein (1904: 105 n. 4) removed passages referring to Christ. I see no good reasons to deny that Zosimus saw Christ as a savior. See the arguments of Mertens (1995: 6 n. 80) and ch. 5 below. For a discussion of Hermetic or Gnostic imagery in the work of Zosimus, see Verbeke 1945: 338–348, Festugière 1950: 260–274, Stolzenberg 1999, Charron and Painchaud 2001, Mertens 2002, Charron 2005, Fraser 2004, 2007, Burns 2015, Bull 2018a. See also the notes to Zosimus' *On the Letter Omega* in Jackson 1978 and Mertens 1995. On alchemical imagery in the Κόρη Κόσμου (SH 23), see Festugière 1967.

[12] For a concise treatment of the methodological problems linked to the concept of Gnosticism, see Poirier 2004. Scholars attempting to describe what was specific to gnostic groups (i.e. Gnosticism) are almost invariably bound to use ideological rather than sociological characteristics. See, e.g., Rudolph 1977: 308–312. For a rebuttal of this position see Williams 1996: 96–109. See also Filoramo 1990: 171–178. We are not in a better position when we want to confirm the existence of Hermetic circles. Garth Fowden (1993: 155–195) argued that the difference seen in technical and theoretical treatises imply the existence of a curriculum, which in turn implies the existence of a Hermetic "school" or "circle." Anna van den Kerchove (2012) studied the master-disciple relationship and several other aspects of Hermetic liturgy thus demonstrating the existence of a "hermetic circle" and also prudently abstained from locating it in a late antique social context. Christian M. Bull (2018b: 224–225) and Fraser (2007) argued that Zosimus and Theosebeia formed a "Hermetic ritual community." Bull (2018c) recently argued that the *Hermetica* was the work of Egyptian priests.

[13] For studies dealing with the shared intellectual baggage of late antique Christians and non-Christians, see DePalma Digeser 2012, Elm 2012, Urbano 2013: 32–79, Burns 2014: 8–31, Marx-Wolf 2016.

Zosimus played an important role in valuing, adapting and diffusing metallurgical recipes in the world of Greek-educated scholars by claiming that Democritus was the last available source of true alchemy. While other alchemical authors certainly wrote before Zosimus, he is the first known author of alchemical commentaries. Other candidates to this title are nonexistent: the table of contents of the *Marcianus gr.* 299 attributes a work to a certain Neilos, which is the name of one of his rivals. Whether they were the same Neilos is impossible to determine since the quire that contained the work was lost; Bolos of Mendes is often credited as the first author of alchemy but this theory is no longer tenable;[14] the fragments attributed to Anaxilaus of Larissa (first century CE) and Julius Africanus (third century CE) include recipes that would later be recognized as alchemical but these scholars did not write alchemical commentaries;[15] fragments from the "ancient authors" are invariably concerned with recipes or identifying substances. While the texts from which the fragments were taken might have included interpretations of recipes, there is nothing in the extent material that comes close to the intricate allegories of Zosimus' *Lessons on Virtue*—the so-called *Visions* popularized by the work of C. G. Jung. In terms of methods, however, Zosimus' work was not innovative. Like Porphyry of Tyre and other late antique scholars, Zosimus sought to retrieve ancient wisdom through allegorical interpretation. While they both agreed that sacrificing to *daimones* should be avoided, they would have disagreed on the choice of texts worthy of interpretation. Zosimus not only drew inspiration from the prophet Nicotheos, who was read by the Christians whom Plotinus and Porphyry sought to refute, Gnostics and Manicheans;[16] he also turned to texts that must have passed at best for technical literature (and at worst for forgeries). Ignored by almost all known Greek textual traditions and commentators by the time Zosimus wrote, these recipes, it is reasonable to assume, would not have received much attention from the average scholar. Zosimus being the first known alchemical commentator, we can hypothesize in retrospect that the way he chose to frame his work played an instrumental role in legitimating alchemical commentaries in the eyes of late antique and Byzantine scholars.

Legitimation of Zosimus' work came in part through an appeal to the antiquity of alchemical texts. Following the Enochian narrative of the fallen angels, Zosimus wrote that a race of divine beings (whom he described both as a *daimonōn genos* and as *angeloi*) had originally brought alchemical recipes to humans along with "all

---

On the importance of *paideia* in nurturing bonds of *philia* among students (whether Christian or non-Christian), see Cribiore 2007b: 100–110, 165–169. See also Poirier and Schmidt 2010, who argue that Porphyry characterized the γνωστικοί from Plotinus' school as a group of Christians who branched out not from Christianity but from the παλαιὰ φιλοσοφία, which Poirier and Schmidt interpret as referring to Greek philosophy.

[14] See, e.g., Martelli 2013: 36–48.
[15] See *P.Holm.* 12–14 and 866–871 with Halleux 1981: 69–72.
[16] See MA 1.4, 10 and Porphyry, *Life of Plotinus*, 16. On Nicotheos, see Jackson 1990.

the arts of nature." A book called the *Chēmeu* (or perhaps, the "book of *Chēmeu*") had originally been written to record all their knowledge but it was later divided, damaged and "hidden."[17] In another treatise, Zosimus explained that the knowledge of the true and original alchemical techniques had been almost entirely seized by divine beings who promised alchemical success to those who would offer them sacrifices. Zosimus, however, also believed that Democritus had kept the wisdom of the *Chēmeu* alive. By attempting to tease out the divine tradition of the *Chēmeu* from the works attributed to Democritus, Zosimus effectively brought alchemy into the ambit of Greek philology. Just as his history of alchemy legitimated his own practice, it discredited the work of his rivals. Following Zosimus' narrative, these individuals sacrificed to *daimones* in the hope that they would grant them success in their alchemical practice. Zosimus rather enjoined his readers to keep away from *daimones* as much as possible. Only *paideia*, he implicitly argued, could bring one to discover the secrets hidden in the works of Democritus.

All this is known from treatises that Zosimus offered to his patroness, a certain Theosebeia, and in which he cast discredit on another form of alchemical practice. It is also legitimate to ask whether scholarly patronage had anything to do with Zosimus' positioning and, consequently, with the writing of the first known alchemical commentaries. The notion that patronage could introduce innovation in ancient scholarship has been recently defended by Rolf Strootman (2017) in *The Birdcage of the Muses: Patronage of the Arts and Sciences at the Ptolemaic Imperial Court, 305–222 BCE*. Strootman argued that competition played a key role in the production of innovative scholarship in the third century BCE. While competition must have influenced the evolution of ancient scholarship up to a certain degree, Zosimus' legitimation techniques also suggest that collaboration between aristocrats and scholars could change the makeup of *paideia*. Unlike scholars, whose standing depended on their status within the scholarly community, patrons could afford unscholarly tastes (both literally and figuratively), i.e. tastes that did not correspond to a legitimate disposition toward *paideia* or tastes for scholarly products that could simply not be squared with *paideia* at all. On the assumption that client scholars could tap into their patron's interests so as to adapt them to *paideia* and legitimate them, causes of change in ancient Greek scholarship should also be looked for where scholarly norms were most likely to be breached.

As argued in the first half of the book (chapters 1–4), certain Roman patrons c. 100–400 CE offered the necessary support as well as a motive for scholars willing to breach scholarly norms. Taken as a whole, the four first chapters show how second- to fourth-century CE representations of sorcerers (*magoi* or *goētes*) and scholars implied the existence of a form of scholarly patronage that provided an advantage to client scholars professing expertise in the so-called "barbarian"

---

[17] This part of Zosimus' narrative comes from a quotation from George Syncellus (*Chronography*, 18–19) and a Syriac text, which was edited and translated by Martelli 2014b.

philosophies of the eastern part of the Roman Empire and beyond.[18] *Mageia*, i.e. "Persian philosophy," comes out most prominently among them and sometimes appears as a byword for foreign philosophies, for common ritual techniques or for both at the same time.

Chapter 1 is devoted to the study of the kind of scholarly patronage that was likely to give consideration to scholars interested in *mageia*, whether one understood the term positively, i.e. as an eastern philosophy, or negatively, i.e. as the practice of illegitimate rituals such as curses and personal divination. Arguing against the practice of scholarly patronage in *On Hired Companions*, Lucian of Samosata (c. 180 CE) claimed that client scholars were likely to work for Roman patrons who expected scholars to act as *magoi* or *manteis*.[19] Assuming that Lucian's satire distilled his experience and beliefs as well as those of scholars and patrons he knew, we can infer that some client scholars were offering scholarly products that did not correspond to the official standards of *paideia*. His satire also suggests that Roman patrons, who did not necessarily have stakes in maintaining the boundaries of *paideia*, could lend support to those willing to cross them.

In chapters 2, 3 and 4, I follow the trace of these "boundary-crossing" scholars by looking at figures of client scholars who were represented as *magoi*. The authors of the texts analyzed here usually chose to represent certain individuals as scholars, clients and *magoi* for reasons specific to their polemical aim. The very fact that these texts were polemical and sometimes attacked specific doctrines suggests that their use of the figure of the *magos* reflected tensions among client scholars. In this, I build upon the work of Arthur Darby Nock, who emphasized the connection between figures of *magoi* and "house philosophers" in "Paul and the Magus." His point of departure, the following episode of the *Acts of the Apostle*, captures the commonplace I study in chapters 3 and 4:

> When they [i.e. Barnabas, Simeon called Niger, Lucius from Cyrene, Manaen, Saul and John] arrived at Salamis, they proclaimed the word of God in the synagogues

---

[18] The expression "eastern philosophy" occasionally used below tries to capture a tendency among Greek-speaking authors to focus on the Near East and Persia when discussing the writings of "barbarian philosophers." The search for a primordial philosophy combined with patriotism or the pressures of Greek scholarly norms (as I argue here) are also likely to have produced accounts that were deceptively ethnocentric. This is true of the *Phoenician History* of Philo of Byblos. See Dufault forthcoming b. It is worth pointing out here that the "Greek alchemical corpus" is Greek in as much as it was written in ancient Greek. It might be more fruitful to consider it as a product of Greek-educated scholars: Zosimus associated the practice of alchemy with Egyptian institutions and made use of Egyptian imagery (see ch. 5). Greek-Egyptian bilingualism was not uncommon in Hellenistic and in Roman Egypt (see Moyer 2011: 29–32 and Dieleman 2005: 104–110). See also Colinet, who argued that an Arabic text translated into Greek found its way into a Greek manuscript dated to the 15th century CE. It would certainly be useful to consider if other parts of the corpus came from different language spheres. This is the goal set up by Matteo Martelli with the AlchemEast research project (https://alchemeast.eu/). For a description of a similar research program, see Mavroudi 2006: 57–64.

[19] Lucian, *On Hired Companions*, 40.

of the Jews. And they had John also to assist them. When they had gone through the whole island as far as Paphos, they met a certain *magos*, a Jewish false prophet, named Bar-Jesus. He was with the proconsul, Sergius Paulus, an intelligent man, who summoned Barnabas and Saul and wanted to hear the word of God. But the *magos* Elymas (for that is the translation of his name) opposed them and tried to turn the proconsul away from the faith. But Saul, also known as Paul, filled with the Holy Spirit, looked intently at him and said, "You son of the devil, you enemy of all righteousness, full of all deceit and villainy, will you not stop making crooked the straight paths of the Lord? And now listen—the hand of the Lord is against you, and you will be blind for a while, unable to see the sun." Immediately mist and darkness came over him, and he went about groping for someone to lead him by the hand. When the proconsul saw what had happened, he believed, for he was astonished at the teaching about the Lord.[20]

To understand the meaning of the word *magos* in this passage, Nock combed sources for occurrences of the word starting in the fifth century BCE and ending in the fifth century CE. M*agos*, he concluded, must have had two mutually exclusive meanings. It would have originally meant a "Persian fire-priest." Very shortly thereafter, Nock argued, *magos* would have acquired a new sense similar to the one given to the word *goēs* and to the English "sorcerer." In the passage of the *Acts of the Apostles*, however, he sensed that Elymas must have had something more to offer to have earned a position in the household of a proconsul. Nock suggested that he must have been "a man of religious potentiality" with a status "not unlike that of the domestic philosophers whom men of rank kept."[21]

As shown in chapter 2, the last half century of research on the idea of ancient magic can be used to give more strength to Nock's observation while also qualifying it. Since the meanings given to *mageia* accrued through time but did not all pass out of use, I argue that the term *mageia* became ambiguous by the fact that it came in certain quarters to be seen as intellectually appealing, if not as the source of Greek philosophy itself. Doing so, the term *mageia* also continued to exist as a by-word for a host of illegitimate rituals. This is the "derived" sense identified by Nock, which I will call witchcraft for the purpose of this study. The ambiguity between these two large groups of uses also produced situations in which the legitimate form of *mageia*, i.e. Persian philosophy, could be equated with witchcraft. This, in turn, made it possible for scholars to polemicize against other scholars who demonstrated an interest in *mageia*.

Chapter 3 turns to the representations of Apion, Simon "Magus" and Pancrates, who were all described as scholars, sorcerers and clients—figures I call "learned sorcerers." I show that these polemical representations build upon the kind of images already found in Lucian's *On Hired Companions*. The polemical uses of the figure of the learned sorcerer reflect tensions that existed between

[20] *Acts of the Apostles*, 13.5–12 (trans. NRSV).
[21] Nock 1986: 325–326.

client scholars who competed for scholarly patronage.

In chapter 4, I finish providing evidence concerning figures of learned sorcerers with two special cases. In Heliodorus' *Ethiopica*, a work of fiction, the interaction between a Memphite priest and a Greek aristocrat recalls that of a client scholar as Lucian imagined him. Depicted as a wise man and a trickster in the novel, Calasiris is shown taking advantage of the stereotype of the learned sorcerer that attached to Egyptian priests. The social background implied by the interactions of Calasiris and Greek aristocrats is still that of scholarly patronage and reaffirms the argument of the preceding chapters, namely, that the repeated use of the stereotype of the learned sorcerer in the context of patronage was a symptom of competitions for scholarly patronage. I then turn to the work of Julius Africanus, whose self-representation emphasized his status of client as well as his special knowledge of eastern doctrines. The resulting image offers a striking resemblance with what Lucian decried. As could be expected from a client scholar, however, Africanus did not depict himself as a learned sorcerer and he did not make any specific mentions of *mageia* in his work. On the contrary, he alluded to his eastern knowledge while keeping within the bounds of *paideia*. As with the satires of Lucian and Juvenal, which implied that scholars could attract the attention of patrons with illegitimate scholarly products (e.g. erotic poetry, curses, divination), the figures of Calasiris and Africanus suggest that client scholars could attract the attention of patrons by showcasing their knowledge of eastern wisdom or *mageia*.

In the second part of the book (chapters 5–6), I present evidence pertaining to Zosimus' social context and argue that Zosimus was a client scholar and that the addressee of some of his treatises was his patroness, a rich woman named Theosebeia. Chapter 5 describes the appearance of alchemical ideas in late antique literature. An analysis of the relevant terms shows that authors of alchemy did not normally use a specific name for themselves and that the concept of the alchemist cannot help us understand how Zosimus was perceived by his contemporaries. Rather, looking at passages describing his social environment, his ethical concerns and his interpretive techniques suggests that Zosimus was a client scholar engaging with several scholarly debates of his day: Where does divine/cosmic evil come from? How can it be avoided? Are traditional sacrifices a solution? How can an eternal life, with or without the body, be acquired?

Chapter 6 turns to Zosimus' presentation of alchemy, which emphasized the importance of Greek scholarship in the correct performance of alchemy. Pushing for the study of an Egyptian tradition through the study of Greek texts, he made clear that alchemy had to be undertaken within the context of traditional *paideia* and that it was unrelated to *mageia*. Zosimus profited from the positive stereotypes given to eastern philosophies: he gave his work the trappings of *paideia* and projected negative stereotypes onto his rivals. His demotion of the ritual traditions of his rivals and his promotion of Greek texts in the practice of alchemy, I argue, helped legitimate Greek alchemical commentaries in the eyes of contemporary scholars.

CHAPTER 1

Client Scholars

Many of Zosimus' works were written for a certain Theosebeia, whom he simply addressed as "lady" (*gunai*) or as "purple-clad" (*porphurostole*).[1] This Theosebeia, as I will show in chapter 6, was an aristocratic woman who led a group of like-minded students of alchemy and who asked Zosimus for advice on alchemical issues. Theosebeia was not just Zosimus' student and perhaps his "sister" (*adelphē*, i.e. a partner in an initiatory group), as written in the *Suda*,[2] she was also his patroness. Figuring out Zosimus' social context inevitably brings us to look at scholarly patronage in late antiquity.

To understand the business of scholarship in late antiquity, however, one needs to go back at least to the early second century CE. One reason for this, as I will show in this chapter, was that the Greek-educated scholar was expected to be self-sufficient. There was consequently something of a self-contradiction in a scholar whose life (and perhaps livelihood) revolved around the exchange of scholarship for gifts or wages. We can consequently expect that client scholars would have referred to their patrons only when necessary. In fact, scholarly patronage was generally alluded to but not explicitly mentioned. One exception to this rule is Lucian, who captured the malaise around scholarly patronage in *On Hired Companions* by describing the different ways in which a client scholar could be humiliated. The client scholar, Lucian concluded, was no better than a slave.[3] This text will be examined here in detail. Part 1 introduces the concept of client scholar and describes the different images that were used to represent it. Part 2 turns to the figure of the client scholar in the work of Lucian. Part 3 looks at evidence on scholarly patronage in late antiquity. I conclude by noting that Lucian and Juvenal's descriptions of scholarly patronage in Rome imply that genuine or interested misunderstandings about the nature of *paideia* led patrons to expect

---

[1] CAAG 2.246.22.
[2] *Suda* Z 168. On this group see ch.6, n. 16.
[3] On the *De mercede conductis potentium familiaribus*, see now Hafner 2017.

that certain scholars might agree to play the role of *magos*. For the purpose of this study, the term scholar will be used to describe individuals who were recognized for their expert knowledge of *paideia* rather than for their expertise in any specific kind of scholarship. The category consequently comprises well-known authors of different types such as Plato, Juvenal and Aristarchus of Samothrace as well as rank and file *grammatikoi*.

1. ILLIBERAL SCHOLARS

Scholarly patronage is a subcategory of personal patronage, which can be defined as a personal relation of some duration involving the reciprocal exchange of goods and services between two persons of unequal status.[4] Among several examples of client scholars who produced authoritative literature under the Roman Empire, Martial, Plutarch and Juvenal are particularly informative about scholarly patronage, and they will be briefly discussed here.[5] These authors—a selection out of a large group of scholars—can help us understand why scholarly patronage was given only one extensive and explicit description, Lucian of Samosata's *On Hired Companions*.

The fact that descriptions of client scholars were usually allusive or abusive can be partly explained by a fact observed by Richard Saller: *patronus* and *cliens* being terms implying a difference in status, it could be degrading to use them to describe one's patron or one's client. As a rule, patrons and clients referred to each other as friends.[6] To this observation, we can also add that the aristocratic nature of *paideia* made client scholars even more likely to be represented either as friends or as venal and mercenary. Unease with the idea that one could buy access to truth had a long history.[7] The association of scholarship and financial independence might have produced some of the skewed representations of professional scholars of literature, the *grammatici/grammatikoi*. In Gellius' *Attic Nights*, the distinction between the aristocratic dilettante and the *grammaticus* splits scholarly groups in two. The aristocratic dilettante, who did not make a living out of his learning, was

---

[4]Saller 1982: 1.

[5]On Archias (client of Cicero), Theophanes of Mytilene (client of Pompey), Horace and Propertius, see Gold 1987. On Horace, Juvenal and Martial, see Damon 1995. On Martial and Statius, see Nauta 2002. On Plutarch, see Stadter 2014: 21–44. For a perceptive survey of "Hausphilosophen" during the first two centuries CE, see Hahn 1989: 148–155. For examples of earlier client scholars and philosophers, see Glucker 1978: 21–27.

[6]Saller 1982: 7–15. A succinct picture of Latin literary patronage c. 100 CE can be found in a letter of Pliny the Younger about Martial's death (3.21). See Nauta 2002: 1–90. For earlier discussion and debates, see White 1978, Saller 1983, 1989.

[7]See Henaff 2002: 9–82.

generally represented as authoritative. In contrast, Gellius usually represented the *grammaticus* as arrogant and uneducated.[8]

Remunerated work was not appropriate for what Gellius called "free and liberally educated men" (*hominibus liberis liberaliterque institutis*: 18.10.8).[9] This might be related to the fact that of the forty-odd teaching contracts and the hundred working contracts extant, none mentions an agreement to teach letters, grammar, rhetoric or philosophy.[10] In an edict regarding tax-breaks awarded to philosophers, Antoninus Pius made clear that philosophers should be unconcerned by wealth. "I feel sure," he wrote, "that those who are wealthy will voluntarily provide financial assistance to their cities. And if they quibble about the size of their estate, they will thereby make it quite clear that they are not really philosophers."[11] In *On Hired Companions*, Lucian described the patron capitalizing on the same scholarly disposition when negotiating the client scholar's wage (19). Simple scorn for private Greek education might have turned for the worse when client scholars cheapened the distinction of *paideia* by selling it to nouveaux riches. Anxiety over the loss of markers of aristocratic status was realistic in as much as the multiplication of teachers and schools of rhetoric in Rome could have disrupted traditional channels of influence or raised the minimal level of *paideia* expected from aristocrats.[12] Be that as it may, considering that the status of client scholar was relatively degrading, we should expect that ancient writers—and client scholars more especially—avoided mentioning scholarly patronage.

If many of Lucian's readers agreed that scholarly patronage was tantamount to slavery, this would explain why client scholars were rarely represented. Juvenal and Lucian are the exceptions that confirm the rule since their descriptions of scholarly patronage were meant to mock client scholars. The existence of scholarly patronage and competition between scholars is also suggested by the use of two stereotypes: the parasite, studied in this chapter, and the learned sorcerer, studied in chapters three and four.

---

[8] *Attic Nights*, 11.1.5, 17.2.15 and 16.7.13. Some grammarians were in Gellius' graces (e.g. 5.4), but they also kept their place. See Kaster 1988: 50–70, Vardi 2001, Keulen 2009: 28–31 and Johnson 2010, 101, 110–113. For a different perspective highlighting the formation of inclusive communities of scholars, see Jacob 2005.

[9] On the negative assessment of wage-labor and manual work in the period under study, see Plutarch, *Pericles*, 1.4–5, Lucian, *The Dream* (*Somnium*), 9, Philostratus, *Lives of the Sophists*, 506.

[10] Freu 2017: 24–26. Of disciplines related to *paideia*, Christel Freu notes two contracts for the teaching of stenography, one for music and one letter mentioning the acceptance of a student in a medicine course.

[11] *Digest*, 27.1.6.7. See also Epictetus, *Discourses*, 2.9.13.

[12] On the banning of philosophers and teachers of rhetoric from Rome, see Suetonius, *Teachers of Letters and Grammarians* (*De grammaticis et rhetoribus*), 25.1 and Gellius, 15.11 with Kaster (1988: 29–30, 52), who argued that rhetorical education was perceived as a threat to the traditional, hands-on education of aristocratic youths in the forum. See also Vardi 2001: 46–50 and Corbeill 2001.

Devouring Ambitions

According to Athenaeus, the name of *parasitos* was formerly used as the honorary title of officials who participated in meals following public sacrifices. Comedy parasites were originally called *kolakes* rather than *parasitoi* but both terms were later used interchangeably. In some cases, however, *parasitos* appears to have characterized the parasite by his hunger while *kolax* would have characterized him by his intrigues and his demagoguery.[13]

The comic Eupolis appears to have made the same association in *The Flatterers* (*Kolakes*) when he portrayed Protagoras "feasting on earthly food" while "speaking pretentiously about celestial matters" in the house of the rich Callias.[14] Not much is known from this lost comedy but the humor of the passage appears to have depended on the contradiction between Protagoras' abstract discourses and the basic nature of his appetite.[15] A scene from Xenophon's *Memorabilia* implies that orators who engaged in repeated court cases could be called *kolakes*. Archedemos, he wrote, was "poor, but an excellent speaker and man of affairs" who prevented litigations by threatening those planning lawsuits against Criton with preemptive lawsuits. In exchange for his services, Archedemos received oil, produce and invitations to Criton's sacrifices. His activities led some to say that he acted like a *kolax*.[16]

As Cynthia Damon showed in *The Mask of the Parasite*, the figure of the parasite as it appears in Greek and Latin authors of the first and second centuries CE corresponds to aspects of patronage that were taboo to mention. Martial's *Epigrams* are particularly rich in that regard. One of the epigrams addressed to a certain Lupus (11.18) can serve to exemplify the interpretive method used in this chapter. Lupus had not given an estate (*praedium*), the poet claims, but "lunch" (*prandium*). The occasion for the epigram is not entirely unrealistic. Martial's work suggests that a literary patron could be expected to provide a scholar with a property.[17] A literal reading of the epigram shows Martial taking the role of an ungrateful and disgruntled friend. While the stereotypical figure of the parasite was

---

[13] See Athenaeus, *Learned Banqueters*, 6.234c–235e and Nesselrath 1990: 309–317. Athenaeus' banqueters assumed that this distinction no longer existed (6.236e). Plutarch marked the difference but also noted that most people did not (*How to Tell a Flatterer from a Friend*, 50c-d). For the treatment of κόλακες/κολακεία and παράσιτοι from the fourth century BCE to the first century CE outside of comedy, see Nesselrath 1985: 111–121. On the demagoguery of the κόλαξ, see Aristophanes, *Knights*, 48 and Plato, *Gorgias*, 463 and 527.

[14] Eupolis, *Flatterers*, fr. 157: ἔνδον μέν ἐστι Πρωταγόρας ὁ Τήιος ... ὃς ἀλαζονεύεται μὲν ἀλιτήριος περὶ τῶν μετεώρων, τὰ δὲ χαμᾶθεν ἐσθίει.

[15] Remaining fragments from Eupolis' *Flatterers* do not prove that the play explicitly cast the κολάκες found in Callias' household as σοφισταί but contemporary evidence about Callias implies that Eupolis' audience must easily have perceived the link between Protagoras, mercenary philosophers and Callias' entourage. See Plato, *Protagoras*, 314d–315b, Xenophon, *Symposium*, 1.

[16] Xenophon, *Memorabilia*, 2.9.

[17] See Martial, *Epigrams*, 2.19, 12.31, 12.4 and Saller 1983. On Lupus, see Nauta 2002: 46.

that of the hungry and opportunistic symposiast, greed and concern for the property's agricultural yield would also have likened the persona of the poet to that of a parasite. The epigram could also be read as Martial's persona depicting an act of munificence in an ironic and roundabout way, i.e. taking the role of the ungrateful parasite to deflect attention away from the importance of the gift by belittling it. Such a reading makes more sense when we assume that scholarly patronage was a well-known aspect of aristocratic life. Since it was part of the game of scholarly patronage to conceal the relative dependence of the scholar in regard to his patron,[18] simply acknowledging a gift of land would have revealed the unequal nature of a poet's relation with his patron. Donning the mask of the parasite and telling the rich that they have failed in standing up to their responsibilities,[19] poets also revealed the differences in status hidden behind the etiquette of patronage. Martial's calculated insolence could also be read in this way when, for example, he writes that he sent his work as a substitute for the morning *salutatio* or when he excuses his absence at dinner by evoking his literary duties (1.108, 10.58, 11.24). The same could be said of the concern with food, the characteristic obsession of the parasite. It was well known that some patrons marked the lower status of some of their clients by offering food of inferior quality.[20] Juvenal summarized his warning to clients with a pithy sentence: "know the color of your bread." It is consequently not surprising that clients fixated on food.[21]

Emphasizing the opportunism, insatiable appetite and ungratefulness of a guest—a common theme in Martial's poems[22]—exaggerated the dependency of the client in a comical way, thus hiding his subordinate status in plain sight. While of course not all representations of parasites were meant to describe client scholars, Martial's epigram 11.18 makes this reading possible. As the readings above illustrate, the existence of client scholars can be seen not in spite of but thanks to the satirical genre.

Lucian's *Lexiphanes* lends itself to a similar reading by bringing concern for food and misplaced scholarly pretensions into close connection. The largest part of this text consists in a reading of the *Symposium* of Lexiphanes, one of the protagonists of the dialogue. Despite what Lexiphanes claimed when introducing his *Symposium*, his dialogue concerned food rather than philosophy. Adding to the non-philosophical nature of the discussions, Lexiphanes also gave an important place to three latecomers of non-aristocratic backgrounds. Among them was a goldsmith with a "colorful" (*poikilos*) back (most probably a reference to whip

---

[18] See, e.g., White 1978: 78–82 and Gold 1987: 1, 5–6.
[19] See, e.g., Martial, *Epigrams* 2.19, Juvenal, *Satires*, 1.132–136, 5.14–23.
[20] See Pliny the Younger, *Letters*, 2.6.2, 7.3.2, Lucian, *On Hired Companions*, 26.
[21] See Juvenal, *Satires*, 5.74–75, 145, 156–173.
[22] Damon 1995: 146–191.

lashes he would have received as a slave).²³ The second newcomer was a corrupt and lazy "trial-seeker" (*dikodiphēs*), in whom one can recognize the litigant Archedemos from Xenophon's *Memorabilia*. The third was a boxer (*ōtokataxis*). As was fitting for Lexiphanes' unphilosophical symposium, his banqueters were not Greek-educated but unaristocratic and immoral. They cared more about food than about *paideia*. In other words, they were described as parasites. There could hardly be a character more opposed to the Greek ideal of the autarchic philosopher than the one who lived to eat.²⁴ Here and elsewhere in Lucian's work, parasites appears as the perfect foil for philosophers.

Plutarch, by contrast, never left the impression that he might have been dependent on his Roman friends and patrons. Plutarch could even use a professorial tone with Q. Sosius Senecio, his patron,²⁵ and, as a matter of fact, to educate a patron was how he claimed one could avoid being seen as a *kolax*. The *kolax* demonstrated his opportunism by his use of flattery. A real friend, however, would dare to criticize a friend.²⁶ The examples of frankness Plutarch chose in *How to Tell a Flatterer from a Friend* (e.g. Timagenes and Augustus, Plato and Dion, Solon and Croesus, Socrates and Alcibiades) confirm that he was concerned with the kind of friendship that took place between rulers and client scholars of the philosophical type.²⁷ Plutarch's exhortation to cultivate frankness was also written out of concern for intriguers who would accuse a magnate's close friend and advisor of flattery. Fear of slander appears in Plutarch's *That a Philosopher Should Converse Especially with Rulers*²⁸ and in the conclusion of *To an Uneducated Ruler* (*Ad principem ineruditum*). Plutarch's collection of sympotic dialogues, the *Symposiacs* (*Quaestiones convivales*), also displayed dinner conversations with relatively powerful Roman notables. All these treatises speak to the importance that the life of the client scholar had in Plutarch's writings and underline the important role that friendship played as mask and marker of scholarly patronage.

---

²³Several sympotic works described banqueters refusing to engage with the discussion topic proposed by their host and mocking him by referring to the scars on his back (which, like his naive question, signaled his origins). See Plutarch, *Symposiacs*, 2.1 (634c), Athenaeus, *Learned Banqueters*, 2.12 and Macrobius, *Saturnalia*, 7.3.

²⁴For a thorough study of the moral implications of this opposition in the sympotic works of Plutarch, Lucian and Athenaeus, see Romeri 2002.

²⁵See *Symposiacs*, 1.1, addressed (with the *Parallel Lives* and *Progress in Virtue*) to Senecio, a successful general whom Trajan rewarded with two consulates and who most probably helped Plutarch receive similar honors. See Jones 1971: 54–57.

²⁶*How to Tell a Flatterer from a Friend* (*Quomodo adulator ab amico internoscatur*), 49b–50e and 66e–74e.

²⁷On this, see also *Precepts of Statecraft* (*Praecepta gerendae reipublicae*), 806e–807a.

²⁸*Maxime cum principibus philosopho esse disserendum*, 778b–d.

2. THE SCHOLAR AND THE *MAGOS*

In several treatises, Lucian mocked the kind of irenic friendship Plutarch imagined taking place between *pepaideumenoi* and rulers. Together with the evidence presented above, Lucian's work *On Hired Companions* shows that scholarly patronage was a fairly well-known institution even if it did not receive a name. By examining Lucian and Juvenal's description of this institution, we can also see how it could help bring eastern lore and science into the ambit of *paideia*.

The Scholar

On Hired Companions, Lucian claimed, was written for "those who professed to do philosophy," for "men of letters" (*grammatistai*), "orators" (*rhētores*) and "poets" (*mousikoi*). "In a word," he wrote, for "all those who think fit to enter families and serve for hire as educators."[29] Lucian showed the patron addressing the scholar, in discussing his wage/compensation (*misthos*), as if his main role was to teach his children (19). He also appears to have portrayed highly educated men who continued the Roman tradition of hiring or acquiring Greek-educated tutors to teach members of their household.[30]

The socio-economic status of these tutors is difficult to determine. Several elements in the text suggest that Lucian was thinking that their work was remunerated. In a suggestive passage—the only one that could refer to scholars who were not independently rich—Lucian mentioned that the client scholar would receive his *misthos* "in time of need."[31] We could assume from this that he needed his wage to survive but we are not told what the *misthos* or the need consisted in.[32]

---

[29] Lucian, *On Hired Companions*, 4: ὅλως τῶν ἐπὶ παιδείαις συνεῖναι καὶ μισθοφορεῖν ἀξιουμένων (trans. A. M. Harmon). On γραμματικοί and ῥήτορες (as well as σοφισταί) as names for teachers, see Cribiore 2005: 53–57.

[30] On teachers of Greek literature and rhetoric in Rome from Livius Andronicus to the first century CE, see Suetonius, *Teachers of Letters and of Rhetoric*. These were famous teachers who worked in Rome, sometimes for the Imperial house (17). Aemilius Paulus hired many different Greek specialists to teach his children (Plutarch, *Aemilius Paulus*, 6.8–9). We have little evidence for in-house professors but Quintilian took the practice of hiring private teachers for granted (*Institutio oratoria*, 1.2). For a similar assumption, see Pliny the Younger, *Letters*, 3.3. Besides the well-known examples of Seneca and Fronto as imperial tutors, Tacitus mentions the remuneration of the tutor of Britannicus (*Annals*, 11.4.3). For in-house philosophers and teachers in Rome in the first two centuries CE, see Hahn 1989 and Bonner 1977: 20–33. Ilsetraut Hadot (2005) argued that the complete cycle of liberal arts never constituted the core of ancient education. Rather, the higher levels of education were dispensed by specialists, who included philosophers. These could also have been hired as private teachers. If schools in the western part of the Roman Empire were relatively rare (Harris 1989: 233–244) and if home schooling was popular among Latin-speakers (Marrou 1965: 390), private teachers might have also been more in demand there.

[31] Lucian, *On Hired Companions*, 13: καὶ τόν τε μισθὸν ... ἐν καιρῷ τῆς χρείας ἀπραγμόνως ἀποδίδοσθαι.

[32] Thomas Schmitz 1997: 57-58 argues that Lucian was describing socially mobile scholars.

Client scholars, Lucian reported, claimed that they worked for a patron to "avoid poverty" (5). Others would have claimed that they were too old for manual labor (6) or that they craved the honor of being seen with aristocrats (9). The true reason, he rather argued, was "desire for what is unnecessary and envy for what is abundant and costly" (7). Lucian's claims and those of his purported sources are not unanimous and they need to be distinguished. First, it should be mentioned that *misthos* does not necessarily refer to a recurrent remuneration. Besides the mention that the client would receive the *misthos* in time of need, Lucian did not otherwise give the impression that he needed wages to survive. In fact, the text gives the impression that he had relatively famous scholars in mind (25).

On the other hand, the claims reported by Lucian are incompatible with the conclusion that client scholars came from relatively wealthy families. Since a wealthy scholar was unlikely to hide his desire for "what is unnecessary" by pretending that he had to work for a living, it is likely that Lucian reported the claims of Greek-educated scholars who were not independently rich. Suetonius mentioned that enthusiasm for rhetoric in Rome under the Julio-Claudians enabled some teachers with the lowest of origins (*ex infima fortuna*) to rise into the senatorial order.[33] Lucian's ideal reader, however, was the kind of aristocratic scholar (25) one can read about in Philostratus' *Lives of the Sophists*. Most of them had an aristocratic background.[34] That being said, there is no reason to rule out the hypothesis that scholars of different status and background considered the position of client scholar profitable.

Besides Lucian's *On hired Companions*, Juvenal's third *Satire* (c. 100 CE) is the only other extensive description of client scholars. In this text, Juvenal describes the vexations of a friend called Umbricius, an unsuccessful and relatively rich *cliens* (188). About to leave Rome for Cumae, Umbricius complained about Roman nouveaux riches, a decrease in literary standards and the stiff competition of those he called "Greeklings" (*graeculi*).[35] As such, it complemented Juvenal's seventh *Satire*, which decried the life of patron-less scholars and praised the aristocrats who supported them.

Explaining why he could not stay in Rome, Umbricius described the expectations of the average Roman patron for their client scholars: praising (bad) books (41–42),[36] predicting the future (42–45), bringing a secret message to an adulterous lover (45–46) and traveling with him as he plundered the provinces (46–48).

---

[33] *On Teachers of Letters and of Rhetoric*, 25.3.

[34] See Bowersock 1969: 21–23, Bowie 1982: 29–59 and Eshleman 2012: 125–148.

[35] On Umbricius, see Armstrong 2012: 68–77. The description of being denied seats reserved to *equites* (3.152–159) and the *topos* of being shoved off these seats for lack of the proper status (see Martial, *Epigrams*, 3.95.10, 6.9 and 5.23) should be read in parallel with Plutarch, who described a flattering maneuver consisting in occupying front seats to offer them to the rich later (*How to Tell a Flatterer from a Friend*, 58c).

[36] See Juvenal, *Satires*, 7.36–39, Lucian, *On Hired Companions*, 35.

"Greeklings" (*graeculi*), he complained, were particularly good at playing this game:

> The race that's now most popular with wealthy Romans—the people I want especially to get away from—I'll name them right away, without any embarrassment. My fellow-citizens, I cannot stand a Greekified Rome. Yet how few of our dregs are Achaeans? The Syrian Orontes has for a long time now been polluting the Tiber, bringing with it its language and customs, its slanting strings along with pipers, its native *tympana* too, and the girls who are told to offer themselves for sale at the circus. Off you go, if your taste is a foreign whore with a painted *mitra*. Ah, Quirinus, that supposed rustic of yours is putting on his *trechedipna* and wearing his *niceteria* on his oiled neck (*ceromatico*).[37] They come—this one leaving the heights of Sicyon, this other from Amydon, this one from Andros, that one from Samos, this one from Tralles or Alabanda—heading for the Esquiline and the hill named from the willow, to become the innards and the masters of our great houses. They have quick wit, shameless presumption, words at the ready, more gushing than Isaeus. Say what you want him to be. In his own person he has brought anyone you like: school teacher, rhetorician, geometrician, painter, masseur, prophet, funambulist, physician, *magus*—your hungry Greekling has every talent. Tell him to go to heaven and he will. In short, it wasn't a *Maurus* or a Sarmatian or a Thracian who sprouted wings, but a man born in the centre of Athens.[38]

Rather than a critique of Greeks and *paideia* in general, Umbricius attacked the "little Greeks," who are also described as half-Greeks: men, none of whom came from *Achaea*—"the real Greece" according to Pliny the Younger[39]—and who overburdened *paideia* with Syrian ways.[40] Even though Umbricius attacked men he called Greeks, it is evident that he did not despise their mastery of authentic *paideia*. On the contrary, Umbricius objected that these men smuggled non-Greek elements into *paideia*.[41] Changes in the tastes of Roman patrons are described in ways calling to mind eastern ways: "foreign prostitutes with painted *mitra*" (*picta lupa barbara mitra*)—the *mitra* being a headdress Herodotus attributed to the Assyrians.[42] If the man who could actually fly to heaven was neither a *Maurus*, a Sarmatian or Thracian, it is because he was Daedalus, known as an Athenian

---

[37] The three terms used here, *trechedipna*, *niceteria* and *ceromatico* (adjective of *collo*) come from Greek expressions, the first one appearing in a sense not attested in extant Greek. *Trechedipna* appears as a form of footwear. The term appears related to τρεχέδειπνος, an adjective used of a parasite running (τρέχω) to dinner (δεῖπνον). *Niceteria* refers to prizes and *ceromatico collo* to a neck smeared with the oil used at the gymnasium (κήρωμα). See Courtney 2013: 138–139.

[38] Juvenal, *Satire* 3.58–78 (trans. Braund modified).

[39] *Letters*, 8.24.2.

[40] For a similar accusation, see Dionysius of Halicarnassus, *On the Ancient Orators*, 1 with Whitmarsh 2005: 49–52.

[41] *Chordas obliquas*, said of non-Greek lyres; *tympana*, associated by Juvenal with the cult of Cybele. See Courtney 2013: 138.

[42] *Histories*, 1.195.

of royal stock.[43] The alleged versatility of the *graeculus*, Umbricius suggests, has nothing to do with their thorough knowledge of *paideia*. In fact, we could assume the contrary, as Lucian claimed in *On Hired Companions* (40). Biographical details concerning Lucian's authorial voice or the character of Lycinus, his main alter ego, suggest a background similar to the one Juvenal attributed to the generic *graeculus*. According to this evidence, Lucian was a native speaker of Syriac who studied in Greece, taught in Gaul and worked as public officer in Egypt.[44] In other words, he was a Greek-educated scholar of eastern origins and was probably not independently wealthy.

In *On Hired Companions*, Lucian describes a situation similar to that of Juvenal's third *Satire* while taking the point of view of the Greek-educated scholar. Its leitmotiv is that scholarly patronage masqueraded slavery as friendship. Scholarly patronage, Lucian wrote, served the interests of rich Romans who wished to appear cultivated by befriending philosophers and men of letters. After introducing the topic and likening the scholar entering an aristocratic house to an initiation into mysteries (1–4), Lucian dealt with the reasons why educated men usually decided to sell their services as client scholars. His source of information, he asserted, was not his own experience but that of others. Their tales, he claimed, formed the basis for the biographical narrative of the stereotypical client scholar he constructed. The first task of the prospective client scholar was to make himself known to a rich man (*plousios*), most probably a Latin-speaking Roman aristocrat (3, 17, 24; if not the emperor himself, 20) until he managed to attract his attention (10–14). If all went well, the scholar would be given an invitation to dinner where the new friendship could be formalized. During dinner, the client scholar would be given a brief glimpse of his future life (15–18). First tricked into accepting a low *misthos* (19–20), he would slowly realize the wretchedness of his new condition (21–24). Unused to the life of a "slave" (*doulos*), the new client scholar would be unable to act in ways appropriate to his new position (23). He would soon realize that he had not been hired to share his *paideia* with his patron:

> To be sure, the purpose for which he engaged you, that he wanted knowledge, matters little to him [....] Truly, he does not want you for that purpose at all, but as you have a long beard, present a distinguished appearance, are neatly dressed in a Greek mantle, and everybody knows you for a grammarian or a rhetorician or a philosopher, it seems to him the proper thing to have a man of that sort among those who go before him and form his escort; it will make people think him a devoted student

---

[43] Frontisi-Ducroux 1975: 89–94.

[44] See *Double Indictment* (*Bis accusatus*), 27, *Apology* (*Apologia*), 15. His *Portraits* (*Imagines*) and *In Defense of Portraits* (*Pro imaginibus*) were most probably praises intended for Pantheia, a woman in the entourage of the Emperor Lucius Verus (130–169 CE). Compare *Imagines*, 10, where the name of the lady who is being addressed is said to be the same as Abradatas' wife (i.e. Pantheia; see Xenophon, *Cyropaedia*, 6.4), with Marcus Aurelius, *Meditations* 8.37, where a Pantheia is said to mourn the death of Verus.

of Greek learning and in general a person of taste in literary matters. So the chances are, my worthy friend, that instead of your marvelous lectures it is your beard and mantle that you have let for hire. You must therefore be seen with him always and never be missing; you must get up early to let yourself be noted in attendance, and you must not desert your post. Putting his hand upon your shoulder now and then, he talks nonsense at random, showing those who meet him that even when he takes a walk he is not inattentive to the Muses but makes good use of his leisure during the stroll.[45]

After a while, the patron's interest in the new client scholar would gradually decrease (26). This would push the scholar to agree to his patron's interests even if these compelled him to write erotic poetry or to act like a *kinaidos*,[46] a *magos* or a *mantis* to keep his standing (27). Suffering different forms of humiliation (28–38), the scholar would also be suspected of attempting to seduce the master's wife or children (29). Realizing that the client scholar's knowledge of the patron's family might become burdensome, the patron would finally expel him from his household (39–41). News of the disgrace would help propagate rumors that the scholar was a poisoner/sorcerer (*pharmakeus*) and an adulterer (*moichos*). Capitalizing on their higher standing, patrons made sure that their former client would not use their insider's knowledge to blackmail them. By saying that patrons plotted (*epibouleuousin*) against abandoned scholars for fear that they might blackmail them, Lucian suggested that the rumors of drug-making, cursing and adultery were spread by the patrons themselves (41). Through an interpretation of the *Picture of Cebes*, Lucian finally sketched the rejected client scholar at the end of his career (and of his life) as poor, hopeless and suicidal (42).

The fact that Juvenal's third *Satire* presented a Greek-educated hireling in a similar situation suggested to Jacques Bompaire that Lucian simply rehashed tropes. One need not take such an extreme stance nor question the usefulness of Lucian's *On Hired Companions* for social history.[47] Assuming that satire is only effective if it can produce some semblance of reality, it would be relatively well suited for a study of the representations of ancient social roles. I consequently see no reason to deny Lucian's claim to have drawn on the reports of men who were client scholars—or, at least, to have created false reports that could pass for real ones.[48] The imagined biography he presented was not meant to represent any single experience. It rather appears as the summation of a multitude of viewpoints in one single narrative.

---

[45] Lucian, *On Hired Companions*, 25 (trans. Harmon).

[46] The Greek κίναιδος (Latin: *cinaedus*) could be used of a type of dancer. The term was also used of men who were perceived as womanly, e.g. of men who were penetrated by other men, of the castrated priests of Cybele (pseudo-Lucian, *Lucius, or the Ass*, 35–36, Petronius, *Satyricon*, 23.3) and of unmanly philosophers (Juvenal, *Satires* 2.9–10). See Williams 2010: 193–197, 230–239.

[47] See Bompaire 1958: 499–513. On Lucian and on reading *On Hired Companions*, see Jones 1986, Swain 1996: 298–329, Whitmarsh 2001: 247–294, Goldhill 2002: 60–107 and Cribiore 2007a: 71–86.

[48] Lucian, *On Hired Companions*, 3.

More importantly, similarities between Lucian's and Juvenal's texts are superficial. Less harsh on the client scholar, Lucian argued that the fault also lay on the side of the patrons since their immorality and lack of education forced client scholars to debase themselves. Rather than demonstrating that the figure of the client scholar was fictional, the differences in the uses of this character type suggest that Lucian and Juvenal perceived a similar social reality from two different points of view. If we can expect that Lucian invented or exaggerated details in his account, we can also assume that its outline cohered with some shared representation of scholarly patronage. Taken together, the coexistence of similarities and differences in these representations shows that scholarly patronage could be classified as a subcategory of "euergetism." We could treat both phenomena as institutions even though ancient Greek and Latin writers had no name to describe them.

The commonplaces of the client as the necessary ornament of the rich and of the patron looking to acquire a veneer of Greek education appear in several of Lucian's works. In *Timon, or the Misanthrope*, a rich man dreams of torturing professional litigants (*sycophantai*) doubling as flatterers (*kolakes*) by refusing to share his fortune with them.[49] Like *On Hired Companions*, *Timon* mocked those who were overly dependent on the fortune of rich men. Lucian's *Nigrinus* presents a philosopher voicing similar ideas about the entourage of the Roman elite.[50] In the *Uneducated Book-Collector*, a Syrian aristocrat is mocked for buying books that he could not understand (4). Accusing the unnamed book-collector of wishing to curry favor with the emperor Marcus Aurelius (22–23), Lucian again emphasized the pretentions of uneducated aristocrats. Such pretentions could be lucrative since aristocrats of the second century had fiscal incentive to present themselves as philosophers. Cassius Dio (71.52.2) claims that Marcus Aurelius' decision to exonerate philosophers from some taxes created many false philosophers. The law of Antoninus Pius cited above was most likely enacted to resolve this situation.[51] Such regulations could also have pushed many aristocrats to patronize Greek-educated scholars even if they were relatively uninterested in or ignorant of *paideia*.[52] All this contributes to considering Lucian's *On Hired Companions* not as the repetition of literary tropes but as the representation of a certain point of view on scholarly patronage in the second century CE.

As in his other works, Lucian kept most of his venom for flatterers of the philosophical type. The longest and most vivid picture of the client scholar in Lucian's work can be found in *On Hired Companions*. Lucian relates an anecdote concerning the travel of a certain Thesmopolis, described as a venerable Stoic, to

---

[49] *Timon*, 45–46.
[50] *Nigrinus*, 23.
[51] *Digest*, 27.1.6. See Bowersock 1969: 32–34.
[52] A passage from Philostratus' *Lives of the Sophists* (488) portraying the friendly relationship between Trajan and Dio Chrysostom also appears to echo Lucian's critique.

the country estate of a rich lady. On the way to his patroness' estate, Thesmopolis was seated beside a man called Chelidonion and described as a *kinaidos* (33). Adding to the apparent ridiculousness of this juxtaposition, the patroness also asked Thesmopolis to take care of her Maltese dog, which peed and gave birth in his lap. Chelidonion later described the event in public, adding that the Stoic had finally "turned cynical" (*kunikos*, i.e. dog-like/a cynic, 34). The philosopher's journey from Stoicism to Cynicism was a cautionary tale warning well-meaning scholars of the problems linked with uneducated patrons. Through an unequal power balance, an aristocrat's ignorance of *paideia* could force client scholars to compete in domains of expertise that were more or less alien to *paideia*. By agreeing to compete and to dispute on topics that were unrelated to *paideia*, scholars also unwittingly consented to legitimize these topics.

That Lucian understood this social mechanism is indicated by the way he compared philosophers to prostitutes and parasites. One of his *Dialogues of the Courtesans* stages a courtesan, perhaps not incidentally called Chelidonion, complaining to a friend that her lover had developed a new relationship with a philosopher who forbade him to associate (*suneinai*) with her (10).[53] The philosopher, she claimed, was a *paiderastēs* who "associated" (*suneinai*) with young men for his pleasure rather than for the sake of education (10.4). By the end of the dialogue, the philosopher stole the courtesan's "client." In the very act of competing with a courtesan, the philosopher was compared to the courtesan and put on the same level with her. The anecdote that juxtaposed the Stoic Thesmopolis and a *kinaidos* suggests a similar conclusion. The double-entendre on *suneinai* found in the *Dialogues of the Courtesans* is also suggested in the title of *On Hired Companions*—Περὶ τῶν ἐπὶ μισθῷ συνόντων, literally "on those who are paid to be with." *On Hired Companions* also likened scholarly patronage to a perverted form of erotic attachment when comparing the relationship between the client scholar and his patron with pederasty (7).

On the Parasite is an alternate version of the opposition of the philosopher and the *kinaidos*. Imitating the philosophical dialogue, this text brings dialectic to an absurd end by trying to prove the superiority of the parasite over rhetoricians and philosophers (58). Simon, the parasite of the dialogue, likened the philosopher to the parasite by claiming that philosophy was a subcategory of the parasitic art.[54] Bringing the parasite closer to the client scholar as described in *On Hired Companions*, Simon defended the role of the parasite as the necessary ornament of the rich: "Just as a soldier without weapons is more contemptible, or a garment with no purple dye, or a horse without trappings, in the same way a rich man without

---

[53]This was undoubtedly a commonplace. The famous fourth-century BCE courtesan Glycera made the assimilation herself when a philosopher accused her of corrupting young men during a banquet (Athenaeus, *Learned Banqueters*, 13.584a).

[54]Lucian, *On the Parasite*, 36–38.

a parasite looks like a humble pauper."⁵⁵ By the end of the dialogue, Simon managed to transform the philosopher into a student (*mathētēs*, 61). In other words, the parasite had become the philosopher's teacher, and the philosopher a kind of parasite.

Playing One's Part

As Lucian wrote in *On Hired Companions*, the average client scholar sensed the necessity of performing several acts unrelated to the normative definition of *paideia* while keeping to his role of scholar:

> You would be glad, I think, to become a composer of erotic ditties, or at all events to be able to sing them properly when somebody else had composed them; for you see where precedence and favour go! You would put up with it if you had to act the part of a magician (*magos*) or a soothsayer (*mantis*), one of these fellows who promise legacies amounting to many thousands, governorships, and tremendous riches.⁵⁶

In Lucian's vision of scholarly patronage, patrons expected client scholars to act as writers of pornographic poems, as *magoi* and as diviners (*manteis*). According to Lucian's succinct history of scholarly patronage, former client scholars were responsible for the last two of these expectations. This history also explained the bad reputation of client scholars:

> Nobody else would take you in, now that you have passed your prime and are like an old horse whose hide, even, is not as serviceable as it was. Besides, the scandal of your dismissal, exaggerated by conjecture, makes people think you an adulterer or poisoner/sorcerer (*pharmakeus*) or something of the kind. Your accuser is trustworthy even when he holds his tongue, while you are a Greek, and easy-going in your ways and prone to all sorts of wrong-doing. That is what they think of us all, very naturally. For I believe I have detected the reason for that opinion which they have of us. Many who have entered households, to make up for not knowing anything else that was useful, have professed to supply predictions, *pharmakeiai*, charms for lovers, and incantations against enemies;⁵⁷ yet they assert they are educated, wrap themselves in the philosopher's mantle, and wear beards that cannot lightly be sneered at. Naturally, therefore, they entertain the same suspicion about all of us on seeing that men whom they considered excellent are that sort, and above all observing their obsequiousness at dinners and in their other social relations, and their servile attitude toward gain.⁵⁸

---

⁵⁵*Id.* 58 (trans. Sidwell). The passage is a likely reference to a saying of Diogenes the Cynic: "education is wisdom for the young, consolation for the old, wealth for the needy and an ornament for the rich" (Diogenes Laertius, 6.68).

⁵⁶Lucian, *On Hired Companions*, 27 (trans. Harmon).

⁵⁷πολλοὶ γὰρ εἰς τὰς οἰκίας παρελθόντες ὑπὲρ τοῦ μηδὲν ἄλλο χρήσιμον εἰδέναι μαντείας καὶ φαρμακείας ὑπέσχοντο καὶ χάριτας ἐπὶ τοῖς ἐρωτικοῖς καὶ ἐπαγωγὰς τοῖς ἐχθροῖς.

⁵⁸Lucian, *On Hired Companions*, 40 (trans. Harmon, slightly modified).

If we limit ourselves to the implications of this reading of *On Hired Companions*, Lucian's judgment on the bad taste of patrons and the servility of clients can be re-described more neutrally as a situation in which the interests of patrons affected the work of scholars, and through them, the limits of *paideia*. Assuming, as Lucian suggested, that client scholars had to go along with their patron's vision of their role to keep their place, it follows that they were likely to produce cultural goods that corresponded to their patron's expectations. Lucian's description also suggests that this type of relationship produced substandard products of *paideia* such as erotic poetry and pantomime plays—scenic displays involving music, dance, chant as well as erotic themes (27). These were maligned by some scholars but popular among the elite.[59]

One could also assume from Lucian's *On Hired Companions* that scholars working for Roman aristocrats might have worked in some sense as "religious professionals" providing their patrons with "predictions, drugs, charms for lovers, and incantations against enemies." Whether scholarly patronage actually involved the trade of curses and divination or not, the important detail here is that Lucian stated that patrons routinely expected scholars to play the role of a *magos*. The next chapter will detail the connotations of this term. It is sufficient to point out here that this could have referred to the art and science of the Persians, to witchcraft or to both at the same time (i.e. to the art and science of the Persians considered as witchcraft).

3. CLIENT SCHOLARS IN LATE ANTIQUITY

Later mentions of resident teachers indicate that scholarly patronage persisted in late antiquity. Again, direct evidence is difficult to come by.[60] Theodosius and Valentinian's law regulating teaching, delivered in Constantinople in 425 CE protected those who dispensed their teaching in private houses from competing with public teachers.[61] The existence of these laws implies that the practice of hiring private teachers was relatively widespread in Constantinople. We can expect a similar situation in other wealthy cities of the Empire.

Besides the novels and literary sources studied in chapters three and four, several texts from the third and fourth century attest to the presence of client scholars working at Rome or at the residence of emperors. Robert Kaster's prosopographical study of late antique specialists of Latin literature (*grammatici*) shows that

---

[59] See, e.g., Seneca the Elder, *Suasoriae*, 2.19, Plutarch, *Symposiacs*, 7.8 and Lucian, *On the Dance*, 83.

[60] One of the few relevant anecdotal pieces of evidence can be read in Paulinus of Pella, *Eucharistikos*, 72–80. When Henri-Irénée Marrou (1965: 390, 440) discussed "private education," he did not seem to have made a distinction between teachers using their home as a school (e.g. Augustine, *Confessions*, 5.12) and aristocrats hiring tutors for their children (e.g. Pliny the Younger, *Letters*, 3.3).

[61] See *Theodosian Code*, 14.9.3.

they only exceptionally served as tutors for the imperial family in the fourth and fifth century CE. He nonetheless remarked that many of them benefited from patronage.[62]

Ammianus Marcellinus' descriptions of Rome and of its patrons also imply the presence of scholarly patronage. In the first of two mentions of the customs of the rich and poor Romans under the prefecture of Orfitus (14.6.1–26), Ammianus described the meeting of a client with a busy patron. Stylistically and thematically, the short description is close to Lucian's *On Hired Companions*. The first part of the description is addressed to the reader in the second person singular, as in Lucian's text, and shows the patron affecting interest in his clients. It ends with Ammianus announcing, still in the second person, that the scholars wasted their time "paying court to the blockhead."[63] Foreigners invited to dinner by patrons, Ammianus complained, were usually fans of horse races, professional dice-players or people pretending to be privy to some secret. Roman patrons, Ammianus wrote, "avoid learned and serious people as unlucky and useless" (14.6.13–15). In the second description, attendants are compared to parasites, caring more about food than literary discussions. The only thing lacking was a primary school teacher (*magister ludi literarii*), but this was normal, Ammianus added sarcastically, since the typical Roman aristocrat was simply not interested in (real) literature.

Ammianus never mentioned client scholars but his misgivings about the scholarly disposition of the average patron imply that other patrons made friends with learned men. Similarities between Ammianus' descriptions and some passages from Juvenal's *Satires* have suggested to some that Ammianus borrowed from Juvenal. As in the comparison of Juvenal and Lucian, differences in the way the commonplace was reproduced inform us about the different points of view of authors. Ammianus presented the scene from that of a Roman. Unlike Juvenal, who complained about the deviousness of foreign clients, he (more than Lucian) focused on the immorality and ignorance of patrons. The fault, according to Ammianus, was entirely on the side of the ignorant patron who, as it appears, was barely interested in literature (the proof being that he read Juvenal and Marius Maximus, 28.4.12–14). The combination of similarities and differences in all three accounts suggests that Juvenal, Lucian and Ammianus were describing the same institution from different perspectives.[64]

---

[62] See Kaster 1988: 130–132, 206–215. One late antique example of a Greek-educated client scholar is Maximus, a pupil of the philosopher Aedesius who was invited by Julian to be his adviser in 361–362 CE. See Ammianus, *Histories*, 25.3.23. Aedesius was pupil of Iamblichus, whom Julian admired (see Julian, *Letters*, 12 Bidez).

[63] 14.6.12–13 (trans. Rolfe).

[64] Thematic and textual similarities between Ammianus' descriptions of rich and poor Romans (14.6 and 28.4) and Juvenal's satires have been conveniently collected by Rees 1999: 125–137. I see no reason to oppose the indignant tone of the satirist to the sincere tone of the historian/autobiographer as strongly as Alan J. Ross (2015: 366–367) does. It seems less complicated to read Ammianus' so-called

CONCLUSION

The main objective of this chapter was to demonstrate the existence and nature of scholarly patronage from the late first century to the fourth century CE. As argued, the almost complete absence of explicit evidence on scholarly patronage can be partly explained by the fact that client scholars were unlikely to represent their ties with patrons as anything else but friendship. However, several literary figures (e.g. the parasite) share certain characteristics with client scholars and appear to have represented them implicitly. Chapters 3 and 4 will provide more evidence of that sort by looking at the figure of *magoi* who doubled as scholars.

These figures of scholars-*magoi* or "learned sorcerers," as I will call them here, were foreshadowed by Lucian and Juvenal, who both mentioned that client scholars could play the role of *magoi/magi*. For the purpose of the present argument, the important point to retain from this is not that client scholars might have acted as religious professionals but rather that describing scholars as *magoi* was one way to describe "miseducated" scholars, i.e. scholars who were known for their knowledge of non-classical scholarship and who introduced it into the house of aristocrats. Taking a step back to analyze the use of the term *mageia* and cognates, the next chapter will show the inherent ambiguity of these terms and how they sustained a connection with *paideia* as well as political power from the fifth century BCE to the fourth century CE. This also suggests that, like the parasite and the "flatterer" (*kolax*), the figure of the *magos* could also be used to misrepresent the kind of scholar who catered to the interests of the powerful.

---

digressions for what he meant them to be: truthful accounts (see 14.6.2) of the vices of a few Romans (14.6.7). In the second satirical passage, Ammianus wrote that he would "make an account" (*digeremus*) of similar vices, which he described as the result of the lack of restraint imposed by the urban prefect Ampelius (28.3–5).

CHAPTER 2

Mageia and *Paideia*

What irritated Lucian and Juvenal most was probably not the idea that patrons hired client scholars to provide them with erotic poems, "predictions, *pharmakeiai*, charms for lovers and incantations for enemies,"[1] but rather that they suspected patrons to be more interested in these services than in *paideia*. Considering the satirical nature of Juvenal's and Lucian's texts, I suspect that most modern readers would assume that Lucian's mention of *pharmakeiai* was a reference to witchcraft and interpret the passages as rhetorical inventions. A survey of the uses of the term *mageia* and cognates suggests a simpler interpretation. In manifesting interest for *mageia*, patrons may simply have followed the scholarly tendency to demonstrate serious interest in the philosophy of the Persians. Tracing the uses of *mageia* and cognates will demonstrate how the interest in this and other "eastern philosophies" was prevalent among Greek-educated scholars in 100–400 CE.

In part 1, I revisit the literature on the term *mageia* and cognates and propose to date the first extensive discussion of the *magoi* to Herodotus rather than to Heraclitus. Tracing the history of the terms shows how the two main denotations of *mageia* (witchcraft or trickery/Persian lore and science) and *magos* (Persian priest or officer/sorcerer or religious professional) were not mutually exclusive. Demonstrating the existence of a third semantic group combining the first two will help understand how *mageia* came to be associated with scholarly patronage. In part 2, special attention is given to the association of *mageia* and philosophy in the literature of the Roman Empire. Looking at well-known passages, such as Pliny's discussion of the "magical art" (*ars magica*), Apuleius' *Apology* and less well-known ones such as Eusebius' polemical representation of Porphyry as purveyor of witchcraft, I show how different scholars of the second to the early fourth century CE pulled the definition of the term *mageia* in opposite directions without ever coming to terms with its polysemy.

---

[1] Lucian, *On Hired Companions*, 40.

1. THE TERM *MAGOS* AND COGNATES IN EARLY GREEK TEXTS

One simple but fundamental step of the last forty years of research on the topic of ancient magic has been to recognize that ancient authors disagreed as to what should be called *mageia* and to accept the methodological limitations that this realization imposes on research. Contextualizing the uses of terms that had been formerly thought to refer to ancient magic as a unified and unambiguous concept has advanced our understanding of ancient discourses on the power of rituals.[2] Assuming that translating *magos* by "sorcerer" or the like glosses over complex social realities, it has been argued that the uses of such translations masked the existence and activities of different types of religious professionals.[3] Several scholars have also studied how the names of *magos*, *pharmakis* ("witch") and *goēs* ("sorcerer") functioned as labels that accompanied processes of social exclusion and group definition.[4]

Few scholars have tried to find out what resulted from the accretion of meanings given to *magos* and *mageia* and whether the two main sets of denotations were as clear cut as is commonly assumed.[5] In fact, studies dealing with the meanings of *magos* and cognates could be said to have bifurcated into two separated branches. For those who looked at the meaning of the terms in their Greek-speaking context, the question of understanding how these terms kept their reference to Persia (whether real or imagined) usually receded into the background. Conversely, scholars who concentrated on uses of the term *magos* and cognates for their Persian referents have not usually studied the terms for their reference to witchcraft and to sorcerers.[6]

This is problematic since some ancient scholars made no distinction between the two semantic groups, namely what I call here "witchcraft" and "Persian" or "eastern philosophy." The following survey draws attention to the relatively clear manifestation of the third denotation starting with Pliny in the first century CE.

---

[2] See, e.g., Gordon 1999.
[3] See, e.g., Burkert 1983: 115–119. For the Roman Empire, see Frankfurter 1998: 198–237 and 2000. For a wide-ranging argument dealing with the first and second century CE, see Wendt 2016.
[4] See, e.g., Stratton 2007.
[5] Such studies include, e.g., Bremmer 2002, Carastro 2007, esp. 17–36 and 189–214, Calvo Martínez 2007: 301–314, Busch 2006: 85–92 and Horky 2009: 47–103. See also Kingsley 1995b: 217–232, for a reading of Empedocles' fragment B111 DK associating the figure of Empedocles with that of the μάγος.
[6] See, e.g., Bidez and Cumont 1938: 1.117, 1.130 and 1.143–150, West 1971, de Jong 1997, Burkert 2007: 99–124, Panaino 2006: 19–53 and 2010: 49–76.

Clement of Alexandria's Paraphrase of Heraclitus Concerning Mystery Cults

A study of the first alleged use of the term *magos* will exemplify how the two main denotations of the term were not mutually exclusive. The term, it is often claimed, first appeared in a work by Heraclitus that was excerpted by Clement of Alexandria in the following passage from of the *Protrepticus*.

> The rites [of the Eleusinian mysteries] are then worthy of the night, of the flame, of the "great-hearted," or rather, "idle-minded" people of the Erechtheid tribe [i.e. the Athenians] as well as of the other Hellenes, for whom lie in store after death things that they do not even hope for. For whom does Heraclitus of Ephesus prophesy then? He threatens night-goers, *magoi*, bacchants, maenads and initiates with what (comes) after death; for these he prophesies the fire. For they are initiated in an unholy fashion in the mysteries customary among humans.[7]

Fritz Graf and others have argued from the combined appearance of *magoi* and of celebrants of Dionysian mystery cults that the term *magos* must have referred to a group of "itinerant experts in private cults" who were involved in apotropaic rituals and who were described in several texts from the fifth and fourth century CE: *Magoi* removing *daimones* with sacrifices appear in column 6 of the Derveni papyrus; individuals with a similar role are found in Plato's *Republic* (364b–365a), where they are called *agurtai* and *manteis*; *magoi*, "begging-priests" (*agurtai*), "purifiers" (*kathartai*) and "charlatans" (*alazones*) are mentioned performing purificatory rituals in the Hippocratic treatise *On the Sacred Disease*. While the use of different titles suggests that the activities performed were probably not the preserve of a distinct group of professionals, it remains true that the term *magos* was associated with experts in purificatory rituals.[8] Graf moreover assumed that *magos* would have ceased to be used with this specific meaning by the second

---

[7] 2.22.1–2 (= B14 DK): Ἄξια μὲν οὖν νυκτὸς τὰ τελέσματα καὶ πυρὸς καὶ τοῦ μεγαλήτορος, μᾶλλον δὲ ματαιόφρονος Ἐρεχθειδῶν δήμου, πρὸς δὲ καὶ τῶν ἄλλων Ἑλλήνων, οὕστινας μένει τελευτήσαντας ἅσσα οὐδὲ ἔλπονται. τίσι δὴ μαντεύεται Ἡράκλειτος ὁ Ἐφέσιος; νυκτιπόλοις, μάγοις, βάκχοις, λήναις, μύσταις· τούτοις ἀπειλεῖ τὰ μετὰ θάνατον, τούτοις μαντεύεται τὸ πῦρ· τὰ γὰρ νομιζόμενα κατ' ἀνθρώπους μυστήρια ἀνιερωστὶ μυεῦνται (all translations are mine except where otherwise noted). See the arguments and references for and against the attributions in Bremmer 2014: 70.

[8] See Betegh 2004: 14, 76–78, *On the Sacred Disease*, 1.7, 18 and 1.12 with Carastro 2007: 43–49, Plato, *Republic* 364b–365a with Graf and Johnston 2007: 144–148 and Euripides, *Iphigenia in Tauris*, 1336–1338: ἀνωλόλυξε καὶ κατῇδε βάρβαρα μέλη μαγεύουσ', ὡς φόνον νίζουσα δή. In Euripides' *Suppliants* (1110), Iphis refers to μαγεύματα as tools used by those who try to stop aging. The reference is probably to the techniques used by Medea to rejuvenate Jason's father, as told in the *Nostoi* epic (fr. 7 Bernabé) and in Euripides' lost *Peliades*. See Kingsley 1995b: 223 n. 20. The mention of a "magical [technique] concerning evil-warding devices (ἀλεξιφάρμακα)" in Plato's *Statesman* (280e) and of the use of the μῶλυ plant by Theophrastus' informants was perhaps made with a similar association in mind (*Historia Plantarum*, 9.5.17: χρῆσθαι δὲ αὐτῷ [i.e. μῶλυ] πρός τε τὰ ἀλεξιφάρμακα καὶ τὰς μαγείας). On the term ἀγύρτης, see Eidinow 2017: 255–275.

century CE and concluded that the mention of the list of "night-goers" could not have been written by Clement.⁹

There are good reasons not to read the sentence concerning the "night-goers" as a citation or even as a paraphrase of a work by Heraclitus. First, its language does not clearly indicate a citation. "Τίσι δὴ μαντεύεται Ἡράκλειτος ὁ Ἐφέσιος;" would be a rather oblique way for Clement to introduce a quotation of Heraclitus.¹⁰ The passage, however, could reflect Heraclitus' views on initiatory cults. The last sentence forms a thematic unit with a Heraclitean fragment that criticized the ritual procession of Dionysian *phalloi*. Since Heraclitus probably considered these to be initiatory,¹¹ it is probable that the last sentence of the passage was a paraphrase or a citation of Heraclitus.¹²

Be that as it may, Clement's approach to philosophy and revelation strongly suggests that the passage as a whole does not convey Heraclitus' ideas but rather how Clement interpreted them. A first clue can be found in the combination of the images of night, light, fire and punishment, which mirrors the images used by Clement in the same section of the *Protrepticus*. The presence of initiates and the tone of the passage also correspond to Clement's purpose, which was to refute the practice of initiatory cults. Moreover, the use of a definite article to mention the fire (*to pur*: "the fire") rather than simply *pur* (i.e. "fire") is better suited to Clement's eschatology. Of course, this interpretation depends on how one interprets the Heraclitean notion of fire. It is however problematic that our understanding of Heraclitus on this point is almost entirely dependent on that of Clement.

⁹See Graf 1997: 21–27. See also Johnston 1999: 102–123, who identifies the religious experts of Plato (*Republic* 364b–365a) with γόητες and their art with γοητεία, described as an art meant to control the souls of the dead. See also Burkert 1983 and 1992: 41–87, Graf and Johnston 2007: 144–146 and Bremmer 2002, who rather see the mention of μάγοι of the Derveni papyrus as a reference to contemporary Persian or Hellenized μάγοι. On μάντις as a generic term for religious experts in Athens, see Parker 2005: 116–135.

¹⁰Clement usually introduces ideas or passages from Heraclitus explicitly. "Hear!" (ἄκουσον), *Protrepticus*, 4.5.4 (= B5 DK) is perhaps the only expression not clearly signaling the beginning of a quotation. Elsewhere, Clement writes "he says, said, reveals, saying, etc." (φημί, εἴρηκεν, μηνύει, λέγων…): *Protrepticus*, 2.34.5 (= B15 DK), 10.92.4 (= B13 DK), *Paedagogus*, 2.10.99 (= B16 DK), *Stromata*, 2.4.17 (= B18 DK), etc. The other phrases or terms are "according to" (κατά): *Stromata*, 2.2.8, 4.7.49.3; "as can be taken from Heraclitus" (ὅπερ ἐστὶ παρὰ Ἡρακλείτου λαβεῖν): *Stromata*, 4.22.141.2 (= B26 DK); "Heraclitus writes" (Ἡρακλείτῳ γράφοντι, γράφει): *Stromata*, 5.14.115 (= B32 DK), etc.; and "you will find (reading) the Ephesian…" (εὕροις πρὸς τοῦ Ἐφεσίου): *Stromata*, 5.14.115 (= B34 DK).

¹¹See B5 DK and B15 DK (also from Clement). The use of Ionic forms in the second fragment also suggests that Clement was effectively quoting a text rather than paraphrasing: ὡὐτός and ἑωυτός occur only three times in Clement and always in citations of Heraclitus (*Paedagogus*, 3.1.2, *Protrepticus*, 2.34.5 and *Stromata*, 2.2.8.1). The argument, however, is complicated by the obvious fact that the Ionic dialect can be imitated (see, e.g., Lucian, *On the Syrian Goddess*). There is also an anecdote, found in an Arabic translation of Galen, which tells that Lucian wrote several pastiches of Heraclitus and that he brought them to a famous philosopher to confuse him with obscure but meaningless formulations of his own making. See Strohmaier 1976: 118–119.

¹²See Marcovich 2001: 465–467 and Kahn 1979: 80, 262–263.

Scholars have sometimes assumed or argued that, taken together with fragments B28 and B66 DK,[13] the passage in question here (B14 DK) confirmed that Heraclitus did not simply hold a theory of universal conflagration but that he also spoke about an eschatological judgment in fire. The argument hinges on the readings of two words from a fragment of Heraclitus found in the *Refutation of All Heresies* (B66 DK):

> he [i.e. Heraclitus] says that a division/judgment (*krisin*) of the cosmos and of everything that is in it will occur through fire; for, he says, the advancing fire will divide/judge (*krinei*) and seize/condemn (*katalēpsetai*) everything.[14]

The quotation suggests a final conflagration of the universe but does not imply an eschatological judgment in fire since *krisis*, *krinō* and *katalambano* do not necessarily refer to a moral judgment. To support a moral reading of this fragment, scholars usually refer to another Heraclitean fragment, this time from Clement's *Stromata* (B28 DK):

> and indeed, said the Ephesian, justice will overtake (*katalēpsetai*) those who fabricate and testify to lies.[15]

While the use of *katalambanō* in this context implies a moral judgment, the fragment is too brief to be ascribed to an eschatological theory. Moreover, there is no explicit indication that the action of "Justice" was to take place at the end of times. Finally, the fact that Diogenes Laertius attributed a conflagration theory to Heraclitus but made no mention of an eschatological judgment reinforces the hypothesis that Clement read his own doctrine back into his interpretation of Heraclitus.[16]

Looking at Clement's rhetoric provides more evidence suggesting that we should not take the language of the passage as a verbatim citation of Heraclitus. First, the formulation of Heraclitus' alleged prophecy played on the double role given by Clement to fire. From the presence of "wild men of fiery aspect" in the afterworld journey of Er in Plato's *Republic*, Clement concluded that Plato and the other philosophers believed in an eschatological judgment in fire and that they borrowed this doctrine from the *magoi*.[17] This reading can be explained by the fact that Clement assumed that this Er was the same as Zoroaster, considered to be the source of Plato's myth, and that Zoroaster had acquired this knowledge from the

---

[13] Scholars before the 1960s tended to see B66 DK—the key fragment in this argument—as inauthentic. See, e.g., Guthrie 1962: 456, West 1971: 144 n. 1. The new tendency has been to reverse this trend. See Conche 1986: 299–301, Robinson 1987: 127, Kahn 1979: 271–276 and Marcovich 2001: 436–437, among others. For a recent commentator reading B66 DK in a physical sense, see Fronterotta 2013: 153–154.

[14] *Refutation of All Heresies*, 9.10.7: λέγει δὲ καὶ <τὴν> τοῦ κόσμου κρίσιν καὶ πάντων τῶν ἐν αὐτῷ διὰ πυρὸς γίνεσθαι· πάντα γάρ, φησί, τὸ πῦρ ἐπελθὸν κρινεῖ καὶ καταλήψεται.

[15] 5.1.9: καὶ μέντοι καὶ δίκη καταλήψεται ψευδῶν τέκτονας καὶ μάρτυρας, ὁ Ἐφέσιός φησιν.

[16] Diogenes Laertius, 9.7–8.

[17] *Stromata*, 5.14.90–5.14.91.1, citing Plato, *Republic*, 615e–616a: ἄνδρες ... ἄγριοι, διάπυροι.

Hebrew prophets.[18] Clement believed that ancient philosophers and "barbarians" all had access to an ancient wisdom originally revealed to the Hebrew prophets but that they had cut down the ancient truth into pieces, each erroneously taking his single piece of the truth for the whole. In the *Stromata*, he explained that Greek philosophy was borrowed from "barbarian philosophy" and that, in their error, Greek philosophers worshipped the elements.[19] Clement also mentioned in the *Protrepticus* that "the Heracliteans" (or perhaps, "Heraclitus": *hoi amphi Herakleiton*) learned to worship fire from the *magoi*.[20] It would have consequently made sense for Clement that the prophecy announced to fire-worshipers and initiates came from Heraclitus—whom he saw as one of the most enlightened philosophers[21] and whom he also believed to have written about an eschatological judgment in fire.

"For whom does Heraclitus of Ephesus prophesy" then? That is, for whom does he prophesy the eschatological judgment in fire? To initiates (those criticized by Clement in the passage) who celebrate their impious rites by torchlight. The eschatological fire that Heraclitus allegedly promised to the *magoi* and to the other night-goers offers a striking parallel to Clement's use of fire as an image for enlightenment or eschatological punishment. In the introduction to the *Protrepticus*, Clement interpreted the pillar of smoke and fire that led the Jews out of Egypt as Christ the *logos* who struck "terror into men by fire, kindling the flame out of a cloudy pillar, as a token at the same time of grace and fear." This token, Clement added, meant different things to different people: "to the obedient light, to the disobedient fire."[22] More importantly, obscurity, light and fire are repeated

---

[18] *Stromata*, 5.14.103. On the identification of Er with Zoroaster, see the concise account of Momigliano 1971: 142–143 and Horky 2009.

[19] *Stromata*, 1.13–15. Plato's myth of Er was the only Greek source that Clement could muster to argue that the writings of Plato and the Greek philosophers—through those of Zoroaster—referred to the Christian doctrine of an eschatological judgment in fire. His other arguments were more suggestive. Mentions of a universal conflagration (ἐκπύρωσις) among the Stoics or among other philosophers, Clement argued, were also references to this doctrine (see *Stromata*, 5.1.9). Clement perhaps borrowed from a contemporary cosmology involving universal conflagration and which Dio Chrysostom (*Orations*, 36.51–54) attributed to the μάγοι. Nigidius Figulus (fr. 67 Swoboda) doubted that the *magi* proclaimed an ἐκπύρωσις-like doctrine. According to Dio, this myth did not involve an eschatological judgment. This would be unlikely considering that Avestan, Persian and Pahlavi texts do not mention an eschatological judgment in fire. There is an eschatological purification in molten metal in the Middle Persian *Bundahišn* (9th century CE), 34.18–19, and allusions to this can be found in the older *Yasna* 32.7 and 51.9. See Boyce 1975: 242 and Stausberg 2009: 233. There is punishment by fire in the underworld of the *Ardā Wirāz Nāmag* (among other forms of punishment) but this text, also written in Middle Persian and dated around the 9th century CE, was probably influenced by the descriptions of Hell found in the *Revelations of Peter* and the *Revelations of Paul*. See Tardieu 1985: 17–26.

[20] See Clement, *Protrepticus*, 5.64.6–65.4. See also de Jong 1997: 343–350.

[21] See Osborn 2005: 16–18, 145–146.

[22] 1.8.3 (trans. Butterworth). In *Stromata*, 5.5.29.5–6, Clement repeated the same image by com-

throughout Clement's critique of initiatory cults and appear to culminate in the passage in question: *Magoi*—i.e. fire-worshipers—going through the night with initiates in a shameful cult that gave an important role to fire. Clement finished the section of the *Protrepticus* dealing with initiatory cults by expanding on this image, rephrasing the words he put earlier in the mouth of Heraclitus and using the Eleusinian mysteries as a paradigm for all Hellenic mysteries:

> Douse the fire, hierophant! Fear the torches, torchbearer! The light convicts your Iacchus. Let the mysteries be hidden in the night! May the orgies be honored in darkness! The fire is not acting a part; it is rather ordered to convict and to punish.[23]

A torchbearer had brought fire but neither he nor the hierophant was able to profit from the fire's light. To put *magoi* among the unenlightened idolaters at Eleusis was obviously not out of place since Clement believed that they had taught the worship of fire to Greek philosophers.

To come back to the main argumentative line, this is not to say that Clement referred exclusively to *magoi* as Persian philosophers. While he often used the term *magos* in reference to Persia, he also mentioned *magoi* controlling *daimones* to achieve "impious deeds."[24] By the second century CE, non-Christian authors associated the *magoi* with *nekuomanteia*, which involved some control over the souls of the dead.[25] Clement must also have been aware of similar cults through his reading of the Greek poets.[26]

---

paring Greek philosophy to the light of a lamp. Greek philosophy, he wrote, could shine the "sun's intelligible light" into the night only if it was accompanied by the *logos* (i.e. Christ). On the divine fire as a force of enlightenment, see *Stromata*, 1.17.87: ἔστιν οὖν κἄν φιλοσοφίᾳ, τῇ κλαπείσῃ καθάπερ ὑπὸ Προμηθέως, πῦρ ὀλίγον εἰς φῶς ἐπιτήδειον χρησίμως ζωπυρούμενον, ἴχνος τι σοφίας καὶ κίνησις περὶ θεοῦ ("There is then in philosophy, which was stolen as if by Prometheus, a bit of fire serviceably kindled into useful light, some trace of wisdom and an impulse concerning God").

[23]Clement, *Protrepticus*, 2.22.7: Ἀπόσβεσον, ὦ ἱεροφάντα, τὸ πῦρ· αἰδέσθητι, δᾳδοῦχε, τὰς λαμπάδας· ἐλέγχει σου τὸν Ἴακχον τὸ φῶς· ἐπίτρεψον ἀποκρύψαι τῇ νυκτὶ τὰ μυστήρια· σκότει τετιμήσθω τὰ ὄργια· τὸ πῦρ οὐχ ὑποκρίνεται, ἐλέγχειν καὶ κολάζειν κελεύεται.

[24]*Protrepticus*, 4.58.3: Μάγοι δὲ ἤδη ἀσεβείας τῆς σφῶν αὐτῶν ὑπηρέτας δαίμονας αὐχοῦσιν, οἰκέτας αὐτοὺς ἑαυτοῖς καταγράψαντες, τοὺς κατηναγκασμένους δούλους ταῖς ἐπαοιδαῖς πεποιηκότες ("*Magoi* boast of their own *daimones* helping them in their impious deeds, whom they have enrolled as their servants and whom they have enslaved with the help of incantations"). At *Stromata*, 6.3.31, the μάγοι appear to be contemporaries. Exemplifying the notion that freak weather is caused by certain δαίμονες and ἄγγελοι οὐκ ἀγαθοί, Clement wrote that μάγοι from Κλεωναί diverted the threat of anger from hail with sacrifices and incantations. Note that the power to control weather was also attributed to the μάγοι by Herodotus (see n. 29 below). The other mentions of μάγοι are found in *Protrepticus*, 5.65.1–4, *Paedagogus*, 2.8.63, *Stromata*, 1.4.25.3–4, 1.15.66–71, 1.21.127, 3.2.11, 3.6.48, 6.3.33, 6.7.57 and *Excerpts from Theodotus*, 4.75. All appear to refer to the Persian wise men.

[25]See Strabo, 16.2.39 and Lucian, *Menippus*, 6.

[26]Clement, *Protrepticus*, 2.22: ἄλλοι τὰς ἀμοιβὰς τῆς κακίας ἐπισκοπήσαντες θεοποιοῦσι τὰς ἀντιδόσεις προσκυνοῦντες καὶ τὰς συμφοράς. ἐντεῦθεν τὰς Ἐρινύας καὶ τὰς Εὐμενίδας Παλαμναίους τε καὶ Προστροπαίους, ἔτι δὲ Ἀλάστορας ἀναπεπλάκασιν οἱ ἀμφὶ τὴν σκηνὴν ποιηταί ("Others, re-

To sum up, considering that 1) Clement did not present any term introducing a citation of Heraclitus, 2) that he imbedded his reading of Heraclitus in apologetic rhetoric concerning the metaphorical role of fire, 3) that this rhetoric was better suited to his own eschatology, and 4) that he was convinced that the *magoi* and Heraclitus transmitted Christian teachings, there are sufficient reasons to conclude that Clement combined the image of *magoi* and of "night-goers" because he saw an irony in the fact that their rites required the use of the same fire with which they would be ultimately punished. Finally—and more importantly—the passage shows that it would not have been incongruous for Clement to recognize that the *magoi* played a useful role in the transmission of Hebrew prophecy while also admitting that some of their rituals involved the invocation and control of *daimones*.

The Political and Philosophical Connotations of Magos and Mageia in Early Greek Texts

As Marcello Carastro showed in *La cité des mages*, the political role of the *magoi* was recurrently evoked in Greek texts from the fifth and fourth century BCE. Later scholars, as I will show here, did not forget this implication. In the first known descriptions, Herodotus emphasized the *magoi*'s role as diviners at the courts of Persian and Median kings.[27] Almost all of the rites they performed in Herodotus' *Histories* presented them in a pejorative way or associated them with *goētes*, a term which normally had a pejorative connotation.[28] The only passage of the *Histories* that did not include pejorative elements was a non-narrative one which described a Persian sacrifice (1.131–132). The fact that the *magoi* relied on *goētes* to stop the winds that had destroyed the Persian fleet (7.191), or that they "used *pharmaka*" (*pharmakeusantes*) before crossing the river Strymon (7.113–114), made the *magoi* very close to *goētes* themselves.[29] Herodotus also claimed that the Medes had been

---

flecting upon the punishments of evil-doing, make gods out of their experiences of retribution, worshipping the very calamities. This is the source from which the Erinyes and Eumenides, goddesses of expiation and vengeance, as well as the Alastors, have been fashioned by the poets of the stage." trans. Butterworth).

[27] See Carastro 2007: 17–36. On the *magoi* as seers, see 1.107–108, 1.120, 1.128, 7.19, 7.37–38. We know little about the representation of the *magoi* made by Xanthus of Lydia in his lost *Lydiaka* (mid-fifth century BCE). See Kingsley 1995a: 173–209.

[28] 1.140, 7.43, 7.113–114, 7.191.

[29] Discussing a storm that devastated the Persian fleet (and which was said to have been invoked—ἐπεκαλέσαντο—by the Athenians, 7.189), Herodotus wrote that "the μάγοι stopped the wind on the fourth day by making trenches (i.e. by making offerings to the dead), by 'chanting down' with the help of *goētes*/loud cries and by offering sacrifices to Thetis and the Nereids. It might have also stopped of its own accord." (7.191: τέλος δὲ ἔντομά τε ποιεῦντες καὶ καταείδοντες γόησι [or, as sometimes proposed, βοῇσι] οἱ Μάγοι τῷ ἀνέμῳ, πρός τε τούτοισι καὶ τῇ Θέτι καὶ τῇσι Νηρηίσι θύοντες, ἔπαυσαν τετάρτῃ ἡμέρῃ, ἢ ἄλλως κως αὐτὸς ἐθέλων ἐκόπασε). Whether one decides to retain the γόησι or not, other aspects of the passage suggests that the μάγοι were involved in rites readers would have associated with γοητεία. As Collins (2008: 57) noted, Herodotus used the term ἔντομα elsewhere to refer to the sacrifice of children. This sacrifice was also done to control the weather (2.119). The stopping of winds and

previously called *Arioi* and that they would have changed their name to the *Mēdoi* after Medea came to their country.³⁰ The implication of this history was that the *magoi*, whom Herodotus considered to be a Median tribe (1.101), learned their art from Medea.

A reader of Herodotus' *Histories* could have expected *magoi* to be liars and traitors considering the misleading nature of their prophecies and the fact that a *magos* had usurped the Achaemenid throne.³¹ Later texts also sometimes mentioned *magoi* in connection with politics. Plato's use of the word *magos* to describe tyrant-makers (*turannopoioi*) in the *Republic* was related to the subversion of political bodies.³² Sophocles had Oedipus call the *mantis* Tiresias a "*magos* hatcher of plots" (*magon mēchanorrhaphon*) and a "crafty *agurtēs* who has sight only when it comes to profit, but who in his art is blind." Without implying that the term was necessarily meant or read as referring to either one of the two usual modern definitions, it seems likely that the *magos mēchanorrhaphos* of *Oedipus Rex* would have been understood chiefly as a reference to the treacherous *magoi* described by Herodotus.³³ Aeschines' calling Demosthenes a *magos* comes closest to the early use of the term as political libel.³⁴ The point was presumably to reiterate the comparison Aeschines had just made between Demosthenes and "dishonest leaders of the people," thus following the old association made earlier by Gorgias between rhetoric and *mageia*.

It is possible that the political connotations of the word *magos* were derived from Greeks having direct contacts with the Persian Empire. Inscriptions from the Achaemenid period show that *magoi* were present in various cities of the Empire

---

the "chanting down" is also reminiscent of activities that would later by associated with γόητες (see Johnston 1999: 100–116). According to Diogenes Laertius, a fragment of Empedocles dealing with techniques to defend against old age was allegedly demonstrated by Empedocles to Gorgias (the ultimate source of the story) as he was "bewitching" (Ἐμπεδοκλεῖ γοητεύοντι, 31 B 111 DK = Diogenes Laertius, *Lives of the Philosophers*, 8.2.59). This matches another characteristic of μαγεία/γοητεία perhaps hinted at by Herodotus in the story of the human offerings of Amestris (7.114). It was certainly suggested by Euripides in the *Suppliants*, 1110.

³⁰ Herodotus, *Histories*, 7.62. See also Strabo, 11.526c.

³¹ 3.61–88, 3.118, 3.136, 3.140, 3.153 and 4.132.

³² *Republic*, 572d-e: ἀγόμενόν τε εἰς πᾶσαν παρανομίαν, ὀνομαζομένην δ' ὑπὸ τῶν ἀγόντων ἐλευθερίαν ἅπασαν ("he is brought to complete lawlessness, which his guides call complete freedom"). The "magic of deception" is also connected by Plato to the act of bewitching (γοητεύω). See *Sophist*, 235a, *Laws*, 11.909b and 933a. On the use of the terms μάγος and γόης and their cognates to describe the manipulation of language for political purposes in fifth- and fourth-century BCE Athens, see Carastro 2007: 53–61, 190–192, 198–200.

³³ *Oedipus Rex*, 387–389 (trans. Lloyd-Jones). The ἀγύρτης would have probably been understood as a reference to a wide range of social roles generally tied to religious activities and profit. See Eidinow: 256–260. On reading the two words as denoting a practitioner of private cults, see Graf 1997: 22 and Bremmer 2002: 3.

³⁴ Gorgias, *Praise of Helen*, 10, 14 and Aeschines, *Against Ctesiphon*, 134, comparing Demosthenes to τοὺς πονηροὺς τῶν δημαγωγῶν and 137 where he calls him a μάγος and a γόης.

and its colonies (Persepolis, Nippur and Elephantine) and that they occupied different functions, some religious, some administrative.³⁵ Greek sources also show that the *magoi* were officers of the Persian Empire and not simply "priests." Xenophon did not describe the *magoi* as a tribe or as a caste but as a group of officials.³⁶ He also never described them sacrificing³⁷ and described Cyrus' father warning him not to employ diviners.³⁸ The contrast with Herodotus' stories about *magoi* giving disastrous advice to a Persian monarch seems almost deliberate.

The second important role of the *magoi* was that of seer and theologian. Most of what we know about this tradition comes from a report given by Diogenes Laertius concerning those who argued that philosophy did not originate among the Greeks.³⁹ Diogenes dismissed the idea but nonetheless listed several writers who wrote about the *magoi* and their doctrines. Greek philosophers remembered them for their discussions of the first principles, which they often quoted approvingly.⁴⁰

Authors tending toward philosophy were obviously aware that the *magoi* had a bad reputation. According to Diogenes Laertius, a work called the *Magikos* (attributed to Aristotle) and Dinon of Colophon (fourth century BCE) claimed that the *magoi* "did not know the *goētikē mageia*" (= *goēteia*).⁴¹ The attempt at distinguishing an illegitimate form of *mageia* from a legitimate one is clear in this and other texts dated from the early first century CE to the fourth century CE.⁴² The fact that some scholars repeatedly felt the need to assert this distinction implies that others ignored it.

The author of the *First Alcibiades* (121e–122a) mentioned that *mageia* dealt with the "worship of the gods" (*theōn therapeia*) and with "kingship" (*ta basilika*). The political aspect of *mageia* can also be found in Philo of Alexandria, where it is

---

³⁵ See Dandamayev 2012 and Panaino 2010: 50–51.

³⁶ *Cyropaedia*, 8.1.23.

³⁷ All mentions of μάγοι in the *Cyropaedia* describe them selecting the offerings that the king should make to the gods: 4.5.14, 4.5.51, 4.6.11, 5.3.4, 7.3.1, 7.5.35, 7.5.57, 8.1.23, 8.3.11, 8.3.24. Similarly, Herodotus' non-narrative segment describing the Persian's cult presented the *magoi* overseeing the ritual, not performing it.

³⁸ *Id.*, 1.6.2.

³⁹ *Lives of the Philosophers*, 1.1–9.

⁴⁰ See Aristotle, *Metaphysics*, 14.1091b, *On Philosophy* fr. 6 Rose (= Diogenes Laertius, 1.8), Eudemus of Rhodes, Fr. 150 Wehrli (= Damascius, *Treatise on the First Principle*, 125). On this, see Horky 2009: 74–77. This tradition is paralleled by Herodotus, who mentioned that μάγοι sang a theogony during Persian rituals (*Histories*, 1.131–132). Heraclides of Pontus, a student of Plato and head of the academy, also wrote a work entitled *Zoroaster* (Plutarch, *Against Colotes*, 1115a).

⁴¹ See Diogenes Laertius, 1.8: τὴν δὲ γοητικὴν μαγείαν οὐδ' ἔγνωσαν [i.e. οἱ μάγοι], φησὶν Ἀριστοτέλης ἐν τῷ Μαγικῷ καὶ Δείνων ἐν τῇ πέμπτῃ τῶν Ἱστοριῶν. See Rives 2004: 35–54.

⁴² Philo of Alexandria, *On Special Laws* (*De specialibus legibus*), 3.100–101, Dio Chrysostom, *Orations*, 36.40, Apuleius, *Apology*, 25–26 (who gives one of the most extensive definitions of the non-Persian type of *magia*/μαγεία), *Letters of Apollonius of Tyana*, 16–17 (of various provenance and of difficult dating but already quoted and mentioned in the third century CE; see, e.g., Philostratus, *Life of Apollonius of Tyana*, 8.20), Heliodorus, *Ethiopica*, 3.16.

combined with its divinatory aspect. In a short section of his commentaries on the laws of Moses dealing with poisoning and untraceable forms of aggression, Philo established a distinction between an "evil art" (*kakotechnia*) and the "true magical (art)" (*alēthēs magikē*), describing the former as the counterfeit (*parakomma*) version of the latter. This corresponds to the normal use of the term, which described the perverted version of a noble art.[43] In this case, the evil art in question is the corruption of the true magical art, described as a dignified and sought-out "visionary science (*optikēn epistēmēn*)[44] through which the works of nature appear in the clearest of representations." Philo's description was similar to that of the *First Alcibiades*, which described *mageia* as ancillary to kingship: "Not only do ordinary people practice it but also kings and even the greatest of kings, and particularly those of the Persians—so much so that it is said that no one among them can be brought to the throne if he was not introduced first within the tribe of the *magoi*."[45] Speaking of the tribe of the *magoi* in another treatise, Philo approved of the prophetic powers of the *magoi* with language particularly close to what he used to define the "true magical art."[46]

Philo also explained that the perverted form of the magical art was practiced by *mēnagurtai*, *bōmolochoi* and "the worst of women and slaves" and that it was

---

[43]Κακοτεχνία does not only refer to an "evil art" but more specifically to the perversion of a noble art (see Philo, *On the Changfes of Names* (*De mutatione nominum*), 150: ἐπεὶ καὶ ὑπὸ τῆς ἐναντίας ἕξεως πέφυκε γίνεσθαι τἀναντία, πόλεμος, ἀνομία, κακοπολιτεῖαι, συγχύσεις, δύσπλοιαι, περιτροπαί, ἡ ἐν ταῖς ἐπιστήμαις ἀργαλεωτάτη νόσος, πανουργία, ἀφ' ἧς ἀντὶ τεχνῶν κακοτεχνίαι προσερρήθησαν ("since, from the contrary habit, things of a contrary character do naturally arise—war, lawlessness, bad constitutions, confusion, unnecessary voyages, overthrows, that which, in science, is the most grievous of all diseases, namely, cunning, from which, instead of arts, they were given the name of κακοτεχνίαι." trans. Yonge modified), Quintilian, *Institutio oratoria*, 2.15.2: *prauitatem quandam artis, id est* κακοτεχνίαν). For the complete section on hidden forms of aggression, see Philo, *On the Special Laws*, 3.93–104.

[44]Considering that μαγεία was connected to divination, and that this is often the role played by Persian μάγοι in ancient representations (notably in Herodotus and in the gospels), it is likely that ὀπτικὴν was meant in the general sense of "related to vision" (as evidenced in later Greek; see Lampe, s.v. ὀπτικός, where cognates of the word can refer to the visionary powers of prophets) rather than in the sense of "optics."

[45]*On the Special Laws*, 3.100: τὴν μὲν οὖν ἀληθῆ μαγικήν, ὀπτικὴν ἐπιστήμην οὖσαν, ᾗ τὰ τῆς φύσεως ἔργα τρανοτέραις φαντασίαις αὐγάζεται, σεμνὴν καὶ περιμάχητον δοκοῦσαν εἶναι. οὐκ ἰδιῶται μόνον ἀλλὰ καὶ βασιλεῖς καὶ βασιλέων οἱ μέγιστοι καὶ μάλιστα οἱ Περσῶν διαπονοῦσιν οὕτως, ὥστ' οὐδένα φασὶν ἐπὶ βασιλείαν δύνασθαι παραπεμφθῆναι παρ' αὐτοῖς, εἰ μὴ πρότερον τοῦ μάγων γένους κεκοινωμηκὼς τυγχάνοι. This is similar to the definition given by Cicero, *De divinatione*, 1.90–91. For a translation of this passage and a discussion of the use of the category of magic in modern scholarship, see Aune 2007.

[46]*That Every Good Man is Free* (*Quod omnis probus liber sit*), 74: ἐν Πέρσαις μὲν τὸ μάγων, οἵ τὰ φύσεως ἔργα διερευνώμενοι πρὸς ἐπίγνωσιν τῆς ἀληθείας καθ' ἡσυχίαν τὰς θείας ἀρετὰς τρανοτέραις ἐμφάσεσιν ἱεροφαντοῦνταί τε καὶ ἱεροφαντοῦσιν. Many passages in Philo's work emphasize the metaphor of vision when describing prophecy. See *Quod deus immutabilis sit*, 139, *De migratione Abrahami*, 38 and the other references cited in Petit 1974: 195 n. 5

given the power to purge and to reverse the feelings of love and hatred through certain philters and incantations.⁴⁷ This *kakotechnia* could also "deceive and entice" virtuous men, make them "meet with great misfortunes" and thereby destroy large communities.⁴⁸

It is difficult to tell whom Philo had in mind and if the "*mēnagurtai, bōmolochoi* and the worst of women and slaves" represented a coherent group. Matthew Dickie suggested translating *bōmolochos* literally by "those who frequent altars" and to understand in this expression the same as *mēnagurtēs* (a term he understands as a form of *agurtēs*).⁴⁹ *Bōmolochos* has other denotations and could serve to characterize the "flatterer" (*kolax*).⁵⁰ Since the *kakotechnia* in question appears to have been, as Philo wrote, the "false coin" (*parakomma*) of a science used by individuals and especially rulers to discern physical realities, it should follow that its *kakotechnia* was mainly deceptive and offered to rulers. It would consequently be possible that the *kakotechnia* that perverted the "magical art" also included the techniques used by flatterers (*kolax*) deceiving and enticing rulers.

The survey up to the second half of the first century CE has shown that the term *magos* and its cognates could be used to denote different domains of expertise (divination, philosophy, medicine, knowledge of rituals, rhetoric) with positive or negative connotations. The positive ones were mainly made about a philosophical form of *mageia* and concerned theology or divination while the negative connotations referred to different techniques, mostly apotropaic rites, curses, sophistry and divination. While a neat subdivision such as this one probably had currency among some philosophers, the insistence with which philosophical *mageia* was repeatedly distinguished from technical *mageia* under the Roman Empire implies that the distinction was not shared by all.

2. THE LATER HISTORY OF *MAGEIA*

Definitions, discussions and reflections on *mageia* started to accumulate in the second century CE. This complex intellectual and cultural development, the same that led the jurist Paulus to delegitimize *mageia* itself as well as the simple possession of "books of the magical art" (*libros magicae artis*), can be detected three

---

⁴⁷Philo, *On the Special Laws*, 3.101: ἔστι δέ τι παράκομμα ταύτης, κυριώτατα φάναι κακοτεχνία, ἣν μηναγύρται καὶ βωμολόχοι μετίασι καὶ γυναίων καὶ ἀνδραπόδων τὰ φαυλότατα, περιμάττειν καὶ καθαίρειν κατεπαγγελλόμενα καὶ στέργοντας μὲν εἰς ἀνήκεστον ἔχθραν μισοῦντας δὲ εἰς ὑπερβάλλουσαν εὔνοιαν ἄξειν ὑπισχνούμενα φίλτροις καὶ ἐπῳδαῖς τισιν.

⁴⁸Philo, *On the Special Laws*, 3.101: εἶτα τοὺς ἀπλάστοις καὶ ἀκακωτάτοις ἤθεσι κεχρημένους ἀπατᾷ τε καὶ ἀγκιστρεύεται, μέχρις ἂν τὰς μεγίστας προσλάβωσι συμφοράς, δι' ἃς οἰκείων καὶ συγγενῶν ὅμιλοι μεγάλοι καὶ πολυάνθρωποι κατὰ μικρὸν ὑπορρέοντες ἀψοφητὶ ταχέως ἐξεφθάρησαν.

⁴⁹Dickie 2001: 226–227.

⁵⁰See the online *Diccionario Griego-Español*, s.v. βωμολόχος, I.2 (http://dge.cchs.csic.es).

centuries prior to the publication of his *Opiniones* c. 400 CE.[51] This kind of legal opinion made it possible to forbid curses, "impious or nocturnal rites" (*sacra impia nocturnaue*), as well as a large and heteroclite body of literature that had built upon the name of a few *magoi*.[52] The development of this literature implies the existence of literates who were able to use it.

From the first century CE on, references to books written by *magoi* start to multiply.[53] This literature might have grown relatively fast during the Hellenistic period. Pliny wrote that Hermippus of Alexandria (c. 200 BCE) commented on two million lines attributed to Zoroaster,[54] and the bibliographical notice to Book 30 of the *Natural History* shows that Pliny's understanding of the magical arts was derived from his readings of several books dealing with magian lore.[55] His short history of *magice*—i.e. "the magical (art)"[56]—beginning with Book 30 describes this art as the invention of a specific *magus*. It must be said, however, that Pliny rarely quoted legendary *magi* when listing techniques. Bibliographical references to *Oros*, "a king of the Assyrians" (30.145), *Osthanes* (1.30c) and *Zoroaster* (1.18c, 1.37c) demonstrate that recipes attributed to these individuals were taken from

---

[51] See Paulus, *Opinions*, 5.23 with Rives 2003: 313–339 and esp. 332–333. On this process, see Fögen 1993 with the comments of Gordon 1999: 264–266.

[52] For a concise history of the figure of Zoroaster in Greek texts up to the first century BCE, see Momigliano 1971: 141–150.

[53] Origen, *Against Celsus*, 1.16, Clement of Alexandria, *Stromata*, 15.69, Pseudo-Clementine *Recognitions*, 4.27, Zacharia of Mytilene, *Life of Severus of Antioch*, 16 Kugener (= Bidez and Cumont 1938: 2.306–307). The scholion 60 Cufalo to the *First Alcibiades*, 122a also mentions that Zoroaster left various writings (*sungrammata diaphora katalipein*). Dioscorides, *Materia Medica* (1st century CE) listed the names given by "Osthanes" (1.10, 2.164, 176, 178, 3.11, 35, 65, 102, 4.33, 68, 78, 127) and by Zoroaster (2.118, 136, 164, 4.68, 75, 176) to several plants, which suggests that he used some textual source attributed to them. Philo of Alexandria (1st century CE) mentioned that the *magoi* studied nature (*That Every Good Man is Free*, 11.74, *On Special Laws*, 3.100). The *Suda* Z 159 attributed books on nature (Περὶ φύσεως), on precious stones (Περὶ λίθων τιμίων), on astronomy (Ἀστεροσκοπικά) and on astrology (Ἀποτελεσματικά) to Zoroaster. Clement (*Stromata*, 5.14.103) and Proclus (*Commentary on the Republic of Plato*, 2.109–110) quoted the same passage of a book attributed to Zoroaster. Philo of Byblos, 790 F4 FGrH, 815.30–31 (= Eusebius, *Preparation for the Gospel*, 1.10.52), cited Zoroaster as he read him in the *Holy Collections of Writings on Persian Matters* (Ἱερὰ Συναγωγὴ τῶν Περσικῶν). An Ὀκτατεύχος is attributed to Ostanes in the same fragment (816.6–7). Porphyry (*Life of Plotinus*, 16) mentioned that Plotinus asked his pupils to write refutations of the revelations attributed to legendary sages, among whom he listed Zoroaster and Zostrianos. See Poirier et al. 2000: 480–481 and 661–662. See also Bidez and Cumont 1938: 1.85–163, 167–207.

[54] Pliny, *Natural History*, 30.2.4.

[55] See, e.g., 1.30a.3–4, 30.8.1. For the bibliographical notice, see 1.30b-c: *Ex autore: M. Varrone. Nigidio. M. Cicerone. Sextio Nigro qui Graece scripsit. Licinio Macro. Externis: Eudoxo. Aristotele. Hermippo. Homero. Apione. Orpheo. Democrito. Anaxilao. Medicis: Botrye. Apollodoro. Menandro. Archedemo. Aristogene. Xenocrate. Diodoro. Chrysippo philosopho. Philippo. Oro. Nicandro. Apollonio Pitanaeo.*

[56] *Magice* is the Latin transliteration of the expression already seen in Philo's *On the Special Laws* 3.100. See also Rives 2010: 59.

books. Pliny read in one of his sources that Zoroaster had written on the *magicae artes* derived from stones, on the virtues of plants and on the astronomical alignments most propitious for harvests.⁵⁷ For other references to the recipes of the *magi*, it is more difficult to tell. Many of them might well have been taken from traditional lore and identified by Pliny as the inventions of *magi*.⁵⁸

Despite the fact that Pliny derived some of his knowledge of "the magical art" (*magice*) from books directly attributed to *magi*, he did not make any distinction between a specifically Persian tradition and a much wider realm of practices.⁵⁹ Pliny's definition of the *magicae artes* lumped different techniques relating to medicine (*medicina*), astrology (*artes mathematicas*), cultic practices (*vires religionis*) together with the power of self-transformation and verbal charms.⁶⁰ This does not mean, however, that he considered the category of *magice* to cover all forms of extraordinary power. While remarkably vague and capacious, Pliny's notion of the "the magical arts" was also informed by the Greek tradition that saw *mageia* as the lore and craft of Persian philosophers. The Greeks, he wrote, were zealous followers of Ostanes, who he thought to have been the first to write about *magice*. The Jews, Celts, Greeks and Romans, he claimed, had also adopted the "magical arts" (see 25.13 and 30.1–13). One can hardly escape the impression that Pliny's narrative about the origin and spread of *magice* was an attempt to attach a host of practices found throughout the Empire to historical narratives (those of Zoroaster and Ostanes) as well to the magian pseudepigrapha he had access to.

Mageia *as a Domain of Greek Philosophy*

Pliny was one of many scholars who thought that the *magi*, the Egyptians or other foreign philosophers were at the origin of Greek philosophical doctrines.⁶¹ Apu-

---

⁵⁷Zoroaster is reported to have celebrated in verses the use of the stone *astrion* for the *magicae artes* (37.133). Pliny also quoted him as an authority on stones (37.150, 157, 159; see also 1.37c). See also 11.242 and 18.200.

⁵⁸See, e.g., 30.16, 54, 64, 82, 84, 91, 100, 110, 141. All other mentions of *magi* can be found at 20.74, 21.166, 22.50, 61, 24.72, 164 25.106, 130, 28.47, 69 (citing Ostanes), 85–86, 92, 188, 198, 201, 215, 226, 228, 229, 232, 249, 256 (citing Ostanes), 259, 260, 261 (citing Ostanes), 29.59, 66, 76, 117, 138, 32.34, 49, 55, 73, 115, 36.142, 37.144, 156.

⁵⁹See 25.13 and 30.3–11 and the comments of Gordon 1987: 74–78.

⁶⁰30.2, 14. See also 30.5–6, where Pliny shows his understanding of *magice* as covering the metamorphosis of Proteus, the charm of the Sirens and the necromantic incantations of Circe as told in the *Odyssey*. Pliny also claim that Ostanes invented cannibalism (28.6).

⁶¹Pliny, *Natural History* 25.13 and 30.3–11. Aristotle quoted μάγοι as credible sources in *On Philosophy*, fr. 6 Rose (= Diogenes Laertius, 1.8) and *Metaphysics* 14.1091b. Diodorus of Sicily claimed that Egyptian priests (οἱ ἱερεῖς τῶν Ἀιγυπτίων) brought their sacred books forward to prove that the most famous Greek poets and philosophers visited Egypt and borrowed their doctrines from them, thus closing his section on Egypt by mentioning that he recorded what was "worthy of memory" (*Historical Library*, 1.96–98). See also Numenius, fr. 1a Bidez (= Eusebius, *Preparation for the Gospel*, 9.7), Clement of Alexandria, *Protrepticus*, 5, The *Refutations of All Heresies* (attributed to Hippolytus), 1.2.5, 1.2.12, 1.13, Philostratus, *Lives of the Sophists*, 494, *Life of Apollonius of Tyana*, 3.19–26, Porphyry,

leius' *Apology* suggests that Pliny's understanding of the *magicae artes* was current among Latin-speaking aristocrats from Oea (province of Africa) in the second century CE. We can deduce from Apuleius' defense that he was accused of having used a love-charm and that his accusers pointed to his enthusiasm for *paideia* and natural philosophy to support their claim. Their circumstantial evidence included, e.g., that he had been looking for species of fish with obscene names (29–36) and that he had sent a poem including a recipe for toothpaste mentioning foreign ingredients (6). Apuleius also argued that simply behaving like a philosopher could be grounds for an accusation of witchcraft:

> If, on the other hand, they [i.e. the accusers] follow common practice and use the term *magus* for one who, through immediate communication with the immortal gods, commands incredibly powerful charms to achieve anything he wants, then I am really astonished.... These are all reproaches commonly made against philosophers through the errors of the ignorant. They suppose that those who investigate the absolute and basic principles of bodies are "irreligious" and so they claim such men deny the gods. This has happened to Anaxagoras, Leucippus, Democritus, and Epicurus, and other advocates of the nature of things. Others, who inquire into providence in the world with greater care and honor the gods more intensely are called *magoi* by the people, as if they knew how to achieve whatever they know to occur. Long ago this happened to Epimenides, Orpheus, Pythagoras, and Ostanes; later on the *Purificatory Rites* by Empedocles, the *daemonion* of Socrates, and the Absolute Good of Plato came to be regarded with mistrust. I congratulate myself for being rated among so many famous men![62]

This description corresponds in part to Pliny's association of *magice* with the work of some, if not all, Greek philosophers (30.8–9). This undoubtedly came from the fact that many scholars repeatedly pointed to the Persian or Egyptian sources of philosophy while others forged these alleged sources. Whether his accusers purposefully confused *paideia* with *magia* solely to support their case—and whether Apuleius' case was real or not—the logic of the defense implies that some conflated philosophy of the *magoi* and witchcraft. After Pliny's *Natural History*, this is the second Latin text exemplifying what Lucian claimed in *On Hired Companions*, namely, that Latin-speaking aristocrats would expect a specialist of *paideia* of the philosophical type to know something about *mageia*.

Later sources confirm the literary and philosophical basis of the technical expertise attributed to the *magoi*. Recipes and axioms for the production or counterfeiting of gold, silver, gems and textile dyes—the basis of what we now call ancient Greek alchemy—was thought by some to have been revealed by Ostanes

---

Life of Pythagoras, 12, Iamblichus, *Life of Pythagoras*, 4, Diogenes Laertius, 1.1–9, 8.3 and 9.34. On discerning between those scholars who accepted "barbarian philosophy" in as much as it confirmed Greek philosophy (like Numenius) and those who considered it as superior to Greek philosophy, see Burns 2014: 20–31.

[62] Apuleius, *Apology*, 26–27 (trans. Harrison, Hilton and Hunink with slight modifications).

to Democritus.⁶³ The redactor of the introduction to the Orphic *Lithica* preempted readings that would have identified those revealing the powers of stones with *magoi*.⁶⁴ This precaution implies that the author assumed that some could have indeed perceived him as a *magos*.

The notion that eastern sages knew *mageia* is exemplified by the introduction to the *De virtutibus herbarum*, an herbal originally attributed to Thessalus of Tralles.⁶⁵ This short text introduces a list of cures with the story of a Greek physician who went to Upper Egypt and befriended learned high priests (*archiiereis philologoi*) to ask one "whether he kept some magical power for himself."⁶⁶ This *magikē energeia* was not simply attributed to an unspecified ritual professional but to an Egyptian high priest described as literate and learned (*philologos*).⁶⁷

The fact that Plotinus (c. 205–270 CE) would enjoin his students to refute treatises attributed to Zoroaster also suggests that magian pseudepigrapha had gathered enough credibility by the beginning of late antiquity to be worth arguing about.⁶⁸

Plotinus and Origen also discussed *mageia* in a similar way and both responded to criticism leveled at contemporary ritual practices. Plotinus saw "great difficulties" in knowing whether prayers could be considered to have an automatic or delayed effect on celestial bodies, i.e. divine beings. He also remarked that they were "much talked about by those who dislike the idea that gods should be culpable accomplices in improper behavior, especially in love-affairs and wanton couplings." Those who held these views, he claimed, did not simply bring charges against "the gods in the sky" but against the universe itself.⁶⁹

Plotinus's solution to the problem posed by the seemingly evil power of the gods/celestial bodies was to turn to natural philosophy and argue that the power of prayers on these beings functioned through the principle of universal sympa-

---

⁶³ Martelli 2013: 69–73.

⁶⁴ See the Orphic *Lithica*, 71–72 in Halleux and Schamp 1985: 85. The text is difficult to date but the attribution of the wisdom of the stones to Hermes, as well as the presence of an apocalypse very similar to that found in Hermetic texts, suggests that the text is post-classical.

⁶⁵ The text can only be given a *terminus post quem* of the late 1st century CE since it was attributed in some manuscripts to the methodist physician Thessalus of Tralles. See Friedrich 1968 and Moyer 2011: 208–273.

⁶⁶ Thessalus, *De virtutibus herbarum*, prol., 13: εἴ τι τῆς μαγικῆς ἐνεργείας σῴζεται. The text is usually translated by "if some magical power is preserved" or the like. This raises the question why Thessalos would have assumed that almost all "magical power" had disappeared from Egypt. Reading σῴζεται as "he keeps for himself" or "secretly" (LSJ, s.v. σῴζω I.2) would make more sense considering the normal use of secrecy in Egyptian priestly circles and the fact that the prologue of the *De virtutibus herbarum* shows awareness of the conventions of Egyptian literature (see Moyer 2011: 254–264).

⁶⁷ For a similar story, where the νεκυομαντεία attributed to Egyptian μάγοι is sought after to provide proof for the eternity of the soul, see the Pseudo-Clementine *Homilies*, 1.5 and *Recognitions*, 1.5.

⁶⁸ Porphyry, *Life of Plotinus*, 16. See Burns 2014: 21–30.

⁶⁹ Plotinus, *Enneads*, 4.4.30 (trans. Armstrong here and for all subsequent citations of Plotinus).

thy, "a sort of linking and a particular disposition of things fitted into the whole."[70] In what must have passed for healthy provocation, Plotinus described nature as the "first *goēs* and *pharmakon*-maker" from which humans learned to use *pharmaka* and *goēteumata*.[71] In other words, the extraordinary feats ascribed to certain humans were nothing in comparison to the power of cosmic sympathy, "the true *mageia*."[72] The point of Plotinus' comparison was obviously not to discredit nature but rather to suggest that the apparent powers of *goēteia* and of the *magoi* were nothing more than the expression of fate (*heimarmenē*).[73] For Plotinus, only the inward gaze—that is, the turning of a soul toward itself—was "without *goēteia*," i.e. truly self-willed and liberated from fate.[74] Similarly, speaking about love-charms, he naturalized "the techniques of the *magoi*" (*magōn technais*) by reducing them to the work of universal sympathy.[75] Normal desires and compulsions were also said to follow an irresistible power comparable to the "art of the *magoi*."[76]

One of the remarkable features of Plotinus' treatment of *mageia* and *goēteia* was that it conceded efficacy to the activity of *goēteumata* ("witchcraft") explicitly, contrary to Plato's treatment of *pharmaka* in the *Laws*. A second is that it dealt with witchcraft in a morally neutral way throughout the treatise. Plotinus, however, could also use *mageia* and *goēteia* in a derogatory way.[77] It is, however, clear that, in comparison with earlier treatment of topic, Plotinus demonstrates an exceptional interest in broaching the topic of *mageia* and ritual efficacy publicly.

In defending the use of the name of Jesus in rituals, Origen responded to a different criticism but provided a similar answer. Celsus accused Christians of obtaining powers by pronouncing the names of *daimones* and claimed that Jesus had accomplished miracles thanks to *goēteia*.[78] Origen's answer was that Christians

---

[70] *Id.*, 4.4.26.1–4.

[71] *Id.*, 4.4.40.1–9: Τὰς δὲ γοητείας πῶς; "Ἢ τῇ συμπαθείᾳ [...] καὶ ἡ ἀληθινὴ μαγεία ἡ ἐν τῷ παντὶ φιλία καὶ τὸ νεῖκος αὖ. Καὶ ὁ γόης ὁ πρῶτος καὶ φαρμακεὺς οὗτός ἐστιν, ὃν κατανοήσαντες ἄνθρωποι ἐπ' ἀλλήλοις χρῶνται αὐτοῦ τοῖς φαρμάκοις καὶ τοῖς γοητεύμασι.

[72] *Id.*, 4.4.40.6–7.

[73] See also *Enneads*, 3.1.

[74] *Id.*, 4.4.43.17–20: μόνον δὲ τὸ πρὸς αὐτὸ ἀγοήτευτον. See also *Enneads*, 1.6.8.

[75] *Id.*, 4.4.26.1–4.

[76] *Id.*, 4.4.43.23–25: "Why does a man direct himself to something else? He is drawn not by the arts of *magoi* but of nature, which brings illusion and links one thing to another not spatially but by the philters which it gives" (trans. Armstrong modified). This image was not new. See Plutarch, *To an Uneducated Ruler* (*Ad principem ineruditum*), 780e.

[77] When refuting the Christian scholars whom Porphyry called the γνωστικοί (Porphyry, *Life of Plotinus*, 16), Plotinus used both terms when describing their use of incantations (ἐπαοιδάς) to assuage divinities (Plotinus, *Enneads*, 2.9.14.1–11).

[78] Origen, *Against Celsus*, 1.6.1–3: Κέλσος φησὶ δαιμόνων τινῶν ὀνόμασι καὶ κατακλήσει δοκεῖν ἰσχύειν Χριστιανούς; 1.6.16–18: κατηγορεῖ ... τοῦ σωτῆρος, ὡς γοητείᾳ δυνηθέντος ἃ ἔδοξε παράδοξα πεποιηκέναι.

pronounced the name of Jesus together with the recitation of stories about him.[79] He also preempted the kind of criticism against which Plotinus wrote by arguing that Jesus had warned that his name could be used by evil men. In the second objection, which concerned the use of names in Christian rituals, Celsus argued that the names used to invoke God were human conventions. This led him to develop a universal theory of "powerful names,"[80] which he had already sketched when he discussed the powers of the name of Jesus:

> Now if by a special study we could show the nature of powerful names some of which are used by the Egyptian wise men, or the learned men among the Persian *magi*, or the Brahmans or the Samanaeans among the Indian philosophers, and so on according to each nation, and if we could establish that so-called magic is not, as the followers of Epicurus and Aristotle think, utterly incoherent, but as the experts in these things prove, is a consistent system, which has principles known to very few; then we would say that the names Sabaoth, and Adonai, and all the other names that have been handed down by the Hebrews with great reverence, are not concerned with ordinary created things, but with a certain mysterious divine science, that is related to the creator of the universe.[81]

Theoretically speaking, Origen's focus on certain names seems to be a specific application of Plotinus' notion of a "natural *goēteia*." Both Plotinus' and Origen's theories also appear to have been based on the notion of universal sympathy—or at least, of a theory of sympathy that would put words on the same level as natural substances. Their theory could also explain the mysterious power of *mageia/goēteia* while at the same time ruling out attempts to ascribe the origin of these powers to a divine being. In both cases, the two scholars took particular care in explaining activities and disentangling their association with illegitimate rites. Both also predate the only other substantial theories of *mageia/magia* in antiquity by almost two centuries.[82]

Summing up the second part of the survey: c. 50–150 CE, Pliny and Apuleius showed that the distinction between a "true" or philosophical *mageia* and an "evil" or technical *mageia* was not necessarily acknowledged by all. About the same time, literature attributed to *magoi* appears to have become more popular. Finally, Plotinus' and Origen's discussions of *mageia* show that the topic had acquired some salience among Greek-educated scholars by the third century CE. They both responded to criticisms by disposing of the moral baggage of *mageia* (and *goēteia*, in Plotinus' case) and replacing it with a physical theory.[83] Their ef-

---

[79] Origen, *Against Celsus*, 1.6.

[80] For a similar theory, see Iamblichus, *De Mysteriis*, 7.5. On these, see Dillon 1985: 203–216 and Graf 1997: 218–220. On "barbarian names," see the *Corpus des énoncés des noms barbares*, http://www.cenob.org/.

[81] Origen, *Against Celsus*, 1.24 (trans. Chadwick).

[82] See Markus 1994, Graf 2001.

[83] Incidentally, the similarity of this original thesis can reinforce the claim that Origen "the philos-

fort to naturalize the exceptional powers attributed to *mageia* is the first of its kind and the first to reach that level of reflection and originality. Their polemical nature suggests that the definition of *mageia* could now be an issue among scholars with a philosophical bent. As the final section of this chapter will show, the ambiguity of the term *mageia* already observed in Pliny and Apuleius could be exploited to undermine the authority of an opposing scholar.

Eusebius of Caesarea's Rhetorical Use of the Term Mageia

The role played by *mageia* in Eusebius' polemics against traditional cults and theology can be explained by looking at the larger context of his apologetic work, the *Preparation for the Gospel*. Presenting a critique of ancient myths and of their allegorical readings in the first three books, Eusebius turned in Book 4 to the refutation of "political theology," i.e. the cults that had been established in each city and region and which were protected by customs. Continuing through Book 5, this critique centered on oracles and turned in Book 6 to a criticism of the divinatory capacities of the oracular gods and to a refutation of the concept of fate (*heimarmenē*). In the rest of the *Preparation for the Gospel* (7–15), Eusebius attempted to demonstrate the superiority of "the oracles (*logia*) of the Hebrews" over philosophy.[84] Divination and its corollary, fate, thus played a central role in Eusebius' charge against non-Christian "theologies."

The main thrust of the argument in Books 4 through 6 was to demonstrate through his interpretation of oracles that the entities to which civic sacrifices were made were not gods but evil *daimones*. To do so, Eusebius cited large parts of Porphyry's *Philosophy from Oracles*.[85] In Books 4 through 6, Eusebius argued his case by picking oracles from Porphyry's work and from Oenomaeus of Gadara's *The Exposure of the Goētes* (*Goētōn phōra*). Most of the time, he pointed to inconsistencies or inadequacies in the oracles themselves and ignored Porphyry's commentaries.

Noting in Book 6 that Apollo explained that his temple was destroyed because Zeus let the Moirai decide on the temple's fate, Eusebius argued that, following the logic of the oracle, Porphyry should have accepted that "the all-ruling god" controlled fate and that there was no reason to question it or to try to change it. Citing another oracle from Porphyry's book, Eusebius argued that Porphyry himself had ignored this lesson:

4. THAT THEY SAY THAT WHAT WAS FATED IS UNDONE THROUGH *MAGEIA*

When a man had prayed to receive a visit from a god, the god said that he was unfit because he was bound by nature. This is why he prescribed apotropaic rites and added:

A daimonic force agitated by rushing motion has fallen

---

opher" was the same as Origen "the Christian." On this hypothesis, see DePalma Digeser 2012: 23–48.
[84] *Id.*, 15.62.16–17.
[85] On Eusebius' reading of Porphyry's *Philosophy from Oracles*, see Busine 2005: 322–360.

upon your generation; it is necessary that you escape it through these magic rites (mageiais).

It is clearly meant by this that *mageia* was given by the gods to undo what was fated so that it may be averted as much as it is possible. Porphyry told you these things, not I. So how is it that he who urges us to undo the bounds of fate with magic rites (*mageiais*), himself being a god, did not undo that his own temple was fated to be burnt down by lightning? How could it not be clear what kind of person is the one who urges us to practice *mageia* (*mageuein*) rather than philosophy?[86]

The citation from Porphyry's work appears to end with the mention that the gods gave *mageia* to humans to avert fate, i.e. the "daimonic forces" that can attack generations. It is likely that Porphyry understood the oracle to mean that the rites of the Persian *magoi* were useful in purifying oneself before engaging in divination. The fact that their rituals could have coerced *daimones* is not a priori strange for Porphyry since he agreed that certain rites were necessary to avert *daimones* even if he conceded that philosophers such as himself should not participate in them.[87] When he referred to the subjection of the embodied soul to the forces of nature as the result of the "*mageia* of the world," this was not a critique of *mageia* as a whole but rather an echo of the theory of cosmic sympathy found in Plotinus' *Enneads*.[88] Porphyry's discussion of *magoi* and Persia found elsewhere in his work also suggests that he took (valid) oracular mentions of *mageia* as positive references to the lore and science of the Persian *magoi*. We know that Porphyry wrote approvingly of the cultic and theological tradition attributed to Zoroaster.[89] In contrast, Porphyry always used the term *goēs* to describe those who practiced *goēteia*, i.e. the "making of philtres, love-charms and other reprehensible activities done with the help of evil *daimones*."[90] Porphyry was part of a larger intellectual movement of

---

[86] Porphyry, *Philosophy from Oracles*, fr. 339F Smith (= Eusebius, *Preparation for the Gospel*, 6.4): ΟΤΙ ΔΙΑ ΜΑΓΕΙΑΣ ΦΑΣΙ ΤΑ ΤΗΣ ΕΙΜΑΡΜΕΝΗΣ ΛΥΕΣΘΑΙ. Δεηθέντος γάρ τινος καταδέξασθαι θεόν, εἰπὼν ὁ θεὸς ὅτι ἀνεπιτήδειός ἐστι διὰ τὸ ὑπὸ φύσεως καταδεδέσθαι, καὶ διὰ τοῦτο ἀποτροπιασμοὺς ὑπαγορεύσας ἐπάγει·

ῥιπῇ δαιμονίῃ γὰρ ἀλεῖσ' ἐπιδέδρομεν ἀλκὴ
σαῖσι γοναῖς, ἃς χρή σε φυγεῖν τοίαισι μαγείαις.

δι' ὧν καὶ σαφῶς δεδήλωται ὅτι ἡ μαγεία ἐν τῷ λύειν τὰ τῆς εἱμαρμένης παρὰ θεῶν ἐδόθη εἰς τὸ ὁπωσοῦν ταύτην παρατρέπειν. ταῦτά σοι ὁ Πορφύριος, οὐκ ἐγώ. ὁ τοίνυν μαγείαις παραινῶν λύειν τὰ τῆς εἱμαρμένης πῶς αὐτὸς θεὸς ὢν τὰ πεπρωμένα κατὰ τοῦ ἰδίου ναοῦ κεραυνῷ πιμπραμένου μὴ ἔλυσεν; ὁ δὲ δὴ μαγεύειν, ἀλλὰ μὴ φιλοσοφεῖν παρορμῶν, πῶς οὐκ ἂν εἴη δῆλος ὁποῖος ὢν τυγχάνει τὸν τρόπον;

[87] Porphyry, *On Abstinence*, 2.43 and Eusebius, *Preparation for the Gospel*, 4.23.1-5 (= 326F Smith).

[88] *On Abstinence*, 1.28, 1.43. All other uses of *mageia* and cognates refer either neutrally or positively to the rites of Persian priests. The only exception is in Porphyry's *Life of Plotinus*, 10.3-5: ὃς καὶ οὕτως αὐτῷ ἐπέθετο, ὥστε καὶ ἀστροβολῆσαι αὐτὸν μαγεύσας ἐπεχείρησεν.

[89] *On Abstinence*, 4.16, *Commentary on the Timaeus*, 16 Diehl and 28.12-22 Sodano (= Proclus, *In Timaeum* 1.208), *Life of Pythagoras*, 6, 33, 41.

[90] *On Abstinence*, 2.41-42 (cited by Eusebius, *Preparation for the Gospel*, 4.22.10-12). See also Por-

the imperial age that took a critical stance regarding the practice of blood-sacrifice, the pollution it involved and the importance of recognizing the existence of evil *daimones* and the usefulness of blood-sacrifices in averting them.[91] He was concerned with traditional cult and criticized it but he did not entirely reject the practice of sacrifices or of divination.[92] We also know from Augustine that he believed that certain rites could purify part of the soul so as to permit it to contact divine beings.[93] Since this appears to be what the oracle referred to by the name of *mageiai*, it is likely that Porphyry would have approved of the oracle, as Eusebius' comments imply.

On the other hand, Eusebius saw any reference to *mageia* as a reference to the work of *daimones* and these beings, in his mind, could only be evil. The fact that Porphyry, "the friend of *daimones*," as Eusebius wrote,[94] could welcome the teachings of the oracle on the practice of *mageia* coincided with the picture of the philosopher Eusebius wanted to paint. However, Porphyry's position on the status of *daimones* was complex. He recognized that certain oracles could be misleading,[95] and that oracular cults dealing with petty questions could not relate divine wisdom. Extant fragments from Porphyry's *Letter to Anebo* cited by Eusebius show that Porphyry believed that these oracles came not from gods or from good *daimones* but from somebody else he called "the impostor."[96] Porphyry thus considered different possible explanations for the existence of misleading oracles, and he appears to have derived them from his demonology.

That Porphyry did not criticize the use of *mageiai* in the oracle cited above is

---

phyry, *Letter to Anebo*, fr. 78 Saffrey-Segonds (for its context, see fr. 64) and fr. 13 Saffrey-Segonds (= Eusebius, *Preparation for the Gospel*, 5.10.10).

[91] On this question, see Camplani and Zambon 2002: 59–99 and Marx-Wolf 2016: 13–37.

[92] E.g. *On Abstinence*, 2.33: θύσωμεν τοίνυν καὶ ἡμεῖς· ἀλλὰ θύσωμεν, ὡς προσήκει, διαφόρους τὰς θυσίας ὡς ἂν διαφόροις δυνάμεσι προσάγοντες, following Plato, *Republic* (433a). See Camplani and Zambon 2002: 62–74.

[93] See the fragments of Porphyry's *De regressu animae* in Augustine, *De civitate dei*, 10.9–10, 21, 27–28 (= fr. 286–296F Smith).

[94] Eusebius, *Preparation for the Gospel*, 4.6.

[95] See *Id.* 5.10.11, 6.1.1, 6.5 (= fr. 316F, 331F, 340F Smith). False oracles were also a concern for Iamblichus, *De Mysteriis*, 3.28–31. Responding to Porphyry's question about problematic oracles being produced by evil *daimones*, Iamblichus replied that this was a false problem produced by *atheoi* (by which he was very likely to mean Christians, in view of the efforts devoted to this question in Eusebius' *Preparation for the Gospel*, 4–6).

[96] Porphyry, *Letter to Anebo*, fr. 13 and 100 Saffrey-Segonds (= Eusebius, *Preparation for the Gospel*, 5.10.10–11): οὐκ ἦσαν ἄρα οὔτε θεοὶ οὔτε ἀγαθοὶ δαίμονες, ἀλλ᾽ ἢ ἐκεῖνος ὁ λεγόμενος πλάνος. The expression "the one who is called πλάνος" is not used anywhere else in the work attributed to Porphyry. He did however write of a chief of the δαίμονες in *On Abstinence*, 2.42, and this might be the so-called πλάνος. Eusebius also wrote that πλανός was the name given to Christ by most unbelievers (Eusebius, *Demonstration of the Gospel*, 3.2.78.10–14), and this could be what Porphyry meant by "the one called the imposter." The term is also found earlier in Justin Martyr's *Dialogue with Trypho* (108.2) in an example of slander attributed to Trypho and the Jews in general.

almost certain. It is also clear that Eusebius presented Porphyry as encouraging the practice of witchcraft. His polemic was also simplified by the fact that *mageia* could refer to very different things at the same time. As Eusebius' comments on the second citation of Porphyry show, he indeed appears to have played on the ambiguity of *mageia* to portray the divinities behind the oracles as evil *daimones*:

> The gods often make clear that even what they tell of the future is made in cognizance of one's horoscope. This made them, if we can say so, excellent *magoi* and excellent casters of nativities. And again, he says that Apollo spoke this oracle:
>
>> *Summon Hermes and Helios according to the same (rites) / on the day of Helios, the Moon Goddess when her day is present, / and Kronos, Rhea and then Aphrodite / with silent names. They were found by the best of the Magoi, / the king of the seven-stringed lyre, whom everybody knows.*
>
> When they [i.e. those consulting him] said "you speak of Ostanes," he added:
>
>> *Exactly, and always call the gods seven times each.*[97]

Commenting on this oracle, Eusebius accused Porphyry of having unwittingly helped the evil *daimones* set their traps. The fact that oracles enjoined the use of *mageiai* or that they cited the authority of Ostanes fulfilled the same argumentative goal. This is made clear in Eusebius' concluding critique:

> With these (oracles) and other similar ones, the noble philosopher of the Hellenes, the wonderful theologian, the initiate in the mysteries, indicates that the *Philosophy from Oracles* contains secret oracles of the gods while at the same time revealing the traps that a truly demonic and evil power set up for humans. For what could this deceptive *goēteia* produce that is profitable to humans? What could be pleasing to God in the impious curiosity of inanimate statues? Of what kind of divine power could be the representation produced by the formation of such figures? Should he not have advised us to examine ourselves rather than to engage in *mageia* and to seek after

---

[97] Porphyry, *Philosophy from Oracles*, fr. 330F Smith (= Eusebius, *Preparation for the Gospel*, 5.14.1): Ἐμφαίνουσι δὲ πολλαχοῦ οἱ θεοὶ καὶ ἃ προλέγουσιν προσημαίνοντες τῷ ἑκάστου γινώσκειν τὴν τῆς γενέσεως σύστασιν, ὥστ' εἶναι αὐτούς, εἰ χρὴ οὕτω φάναι, ἄκρους τε μάγους καὶ ἄκρους γενεθλιαλόγους. Καὶ πάλιν ἐν χρησμοῖς ἔφη τὸν Ἀπόλλωνα εἰπεῖν·

κλῄζειν Ἑρμείην ἠδ' Ἥλιον κατὰ ταὐτὰ
ἡμέρῃ Ἡελίου, Μήνην δ' ὅτε τῇσδε παρείη,
ἠδὲ Κρόνον καὶ Ῥέαν ἠδ' ἐξείης Ἀφροδίτην
κλήσεσιν ἀφθέγκτοις, ἃς εὗρε μάγων ὄχ' ἄριστος,
τῆς ἑπταφθόγγου βασιλεύς, ὃν πάντες ἴσασιν·

Ὀστάνην λέγεις· εἰπόντων ἐπήγαγε·

καὶ σφόδρα· καὶ καθ' ἕκαστον ἀεὶ θεὸν ἑπτάκι φωνεῖν.

There is nothing indicating without any doubt that the first paragraph is a citation. Philoponus, who introduced the same passage of Porphyry's *On the Philosophy from Oracles*, simply mentioned that Porphyry declared the gods to be ἄκροι γενεθλιαλόγοι. See Philoponus, *De opificio mundi*, 200.2–7 (= fr. 330aF Smith).

what is forbidden since the self-sufficient way to reach a happy and blessed life is to follow virtue and philosophy?[98]

Since *mageia* for Eusebius could only be evil, oracles prescribing its practice could have only been produced by *daimones*, i.e. by evil *daimones*. Through this form of reasoning, Eusebius concluded that "the theology of every nation was dedicated to evil *daimones*."[99] After citing some of Porphyry's critical questions concerning traditional civic sacrifices and the presumed power that certain rites had on divinities, Eusebius concluded that the rites of the *daimones* amounted to *mageia/goēteia*:

> Truly, the first teachers of this treacherous (*kakotechnou*) *goēteia* were the noble gods. How indeed could humans be aware of it if the *daimones* themselves had not revealed what concerns themselves and if they had not indicated the bindings that (they use) against each other?[100]

For Eusebius, the problem of cultic orthodoxy had been radically simplified. His argument ignored the complexities of Porphyry's position, who admitted that purification and propitiation could be necessary for some individuals and cities. Since this was just what the *mageiai* were supposed to provide, he was likely to have approved of them. Eusebius, however, did not acknowledge that his adversary made a distinction between the *mageia* of the Persian *magoi* and *goēteia*. This rhetorical technique is similar to the one seen earlier with Apuleius' opponents: interest in eastern philosophy and wisdom, whether manifest or implied, could be taken as an interest in witchcraft.

CONCLUSION

Eusebius' rhetorical strategy, the charges of Apuleius' accusers, Pliny's disregard of the different attempts at distinguishing a *goētikē magikē* from a *magikē* (*technē*), all show that the double definition of *mageia* found in most dictionaries—e.g. the

---

[98] Eusebius, *Preparation for the Gospel*, 5.14.3-4: διὰ τούτων καὶ τῶν τούτοις ὁμοίων ὁ γενναῖος Ἑλλήνων φιλόσοφος, ὁ θαυμαστὸς θεολόγος, ὁ τῶν ἀπορρήτων μύστης, τὴν ἐκ λογίων φιλοσοφίαν ὡς ἀπόρρητα θεῶν περιέχουσαν λόγια παραφαίνει, ἄντικρυς τῆς πονηρᾶς καὶ δαιμονικῆς ἀληθῶς δυνάμεως ἐξαγορεύων τὰς κατ' ἀνθρώπων ἐνέδρας. τί γὰρ ἂν γένοιτο βιωφελὲς ἀνθρώποις ἐκ τῆς κακοτέκνου γοητείας; τί δ' ἂν ἔχοι θεοφιλὲς ἢ τῶν ἀψύχων ξοάνων περιεργία; ποίας δ' εἰκὼν γένοιτ' ἂν ἐνθέου δυνάμεως ἢ τῶν τοιῶνδε σχημάτων μόρφωσις; τί δ' οὐ μᾶλλον φιλοσοφεῖν περὶ ἡμᾶς ἢ μαγεύειν καὶ τὰ ἀπειρημένα διώκειν συμβουλεύειν ἐχρῆν, τοῦ κατ' ἀρετὴν καὶ φιλοσοφίαν τρόπου πρὸς εὐδαίμονα καὶ μακάριον αὐτάρκους τυγχάνοντος βίον;

[99] Eusebius, *Preparation for the Gospel*, 4.17. See also 4.5.1-3.

[100] Eusebius, *Preparation for the Gospel*, 5.10.12-13: καὶ μὴν καὶ διδάσκαλοί γε τῆς κακοτέχνου γοητείας αὐτοὶ δὴ πρῶτοι οἱ γενναῖοι θεοὶ κατέστησαν. πόθεν γὰρ ἀνθρώποις ταῦτα παρῆν εἰδέναι ἢ τῶν δαιμόνων αὐτῶν τά τε περὶ ἑαυτῶν ἐξειπόντων καὶ τοὺς καταδέσμους τοὺς κατ' ἀλλήλων ἐξηγορευκότων;

"Theology of the Magians" and a so-called derived sense more or less equivalent to the modern "magic" or "witchcraft"—glosses over a third interpretation, that which considered that the lore and science of the Persian *magoi* included the practice of witchcraft. This third interpretation was most clearly expressed by Pliny, who claimed that the "magical arts" had been invented in Persia while at the same time observing that almost all people of the world practiced it. Pliny moreover noted that the Greek philosophers had been deeply influenced by these arts. This, however, should not be read as a criticism of *paideia* in general. As with Umbricius' critique of the *graeculi* in Juvenal's third *Satire*, the critique was aimed at a kind of philosophy practiced by a certain kind of scholar. It reflected the tendency for post-Hellenistic scholars to emphasize the learned aspect of *mageia* and to claim that Greek philosophy had its roots in a foreign country, usually Persia or Egypt. As Apuleius' *Apology* demonstrates, it was possible in the second century CE to imagine that interest in natural philosophy indicated an interest in witchcraft. The fact that *mageia* was already associated with natural philosophy can explain why Apuleius' versified toothpaste recipe could be brought as evidence of his practice of *magia*.[101] The same can be assumed from the distinction made between "true" and "false" *mageia* (or *goēteia*) by Philo of Alexandria and several authors writing under the Roman Empire. It also implies that this distinction was of special concern to scholars interested in natural sciences and theology.

That this conflation had potential for polemics can be seen in the way Origen and Plotinus discussed or justified certain ritual practices. We can also witness an exploitation of the conflation in Eusebius' arguments against Porphyry's *Philosophy from Oracles*. *Mageia*, for Eusebius, was a *kakotechnos goēteia* (a choice of words recalling that used by Philo of Alexandria to designate the counterfeit form of the "true magical art").

Applying the perspective gained here to the interpretation of Lucian and Juvenal suggests that both authors described a kind of patronage that attracted scholars thought to have some knowledge of *mageia* or of other eastern philosophies. In other words, understanding the popularity of these philosophies—rather than the popularity of providers of divination and various rituals among Roman aristocrats—can change the way we read the kind of polemical account representing learned sorcerers, i.e. clients of Roman aristocrats like Atomos, who, Josephus tells us, pretended to be a *magos*, or like Thrasyllus, who was not (or much more than) a court astrologer.[102] The character-type of the learned sorcerer, such as Bar-Jesus/Elymas already mentioned in the introduction, was often presented as the loser in a conflict opposing the sorcerer to a learned man. As shown in the two

---

[101] See Apuleius, *Apology*, 6.1. On this detail and the association of *paignia* with *magia*, see Pliny, *Natural History*, 30.27, which attribute a toothpaste recipe to the *magi* and Barbara 2014: 133–170.

[102] On Atomos, see Josephus, *Jewish Antiquities*, 20.142. On Thrasyllus, see Tarrant 1993, who argues that Thrasyllus may have had an important influence on later Platonism and early Christian thought.

following chapters, the *Acts of the Apostles* was not the only text of the second, third and fourth centuries CE that represented a Roman aristocrat and "sensible man" (*anēr sunetos*) entertaining friendships with Greek-educated scholars who were associated with *mageia* or with an eastern philosophy.

CHAPTER 3

Representations of Scholars as Learned Sorcerers

The following chapter gathers evidence concerning the literary figure of the learned sorcerer and shows how it combined characteristics attributed to client scholars. These representations always contain two of four elements: a man is represented as a *magos*, he is shown to possess *paideia* to some degree, he is the companion of an aristocrat and he might also be concerned or involved with banquets or meals. Stereotypical representations of learned sorcerers can be found in polemical texts dating from the second to the fourth century CE. Except Anaxilaus—about whom we know next to nothing—Simon, Apion and Pancrates/Pachrates were represented as Greek-educated scholars and *magoi* of Egyptian, Jewish or Samaritan origin. Their representations, I argue, correspond in many ways to the figure of the *graeculus* found in Juvenal: they are Greek-educated scholars bringing Syrian/"eastern" customs to Rome and playing the role of *magus*. They also correspond to some aspects of the figure presented by Lucian in *On Hired Companions* in that they are Greek-educated scholars who agreed to play the role of *magos* and/or to produce substandard forms of scholarly work (e.g. erotic poetry). Starting first with Anaxilaus will introduce a special use of the term *paignion* and its relation to scholarship and aristocratic entertainment.[1]

---

[1] For an interpretation of the same material as testifying to the collection of "occult" material by ancient "magicians," see Dickie 1999: 163–194 and 2001: 211–216. See also Wendt 2016: 114–145, who argues that evidence about *mageia* and what modern scholars call magic from the two first centuries CE testifies to the emergence of a "religion of freelance experts." These religious experts would have offered various "practices—initiations, purifications, divination, textual exegesis, myth-making, and so forth—that bear continuities with other religious and intellectual activities but are best classified as subsets of freelance *religious* expertise" (116). In contrast to Dickie, who framed the evidence according to an implicit definition of the category of magic, Wendt framed it in religious terms and focused on competition between religious professionals operating outside of institutional settings.

1. ANAXILAUS OF LARISSA

The purpose of Anaxilaus' work remains unknown but most extant recipes (No. 1–4) can be categorized as *paignia*. At its most general, the term *paignion* was used to describe games and toys as well as playful poetry. *Carmina figurata*—poems whose disposition created different figures according to the different meters chosen—could also be called *paignia*.[2] Commenting on a passage from Aristotle's *Metaphysics* dealing with automata, Alexander of Aphrodisias called self-moving contraptions *paignia* and described them as "wonders that are revealed by wonder-workers."[3] As the following will show, some *paignia* could be used in scholarly discussions and it is possible that they would have been considered as appropriate objects of philosophical inquiry.

According to Jerome's translation of the *Chronicle* of Eusebius, Anaxilaus was a "Pythagorean and *magus*" who was expelled from Rome by Augustus in the year 28 BCE. A letter addressed to Anaxilaus and mocking the idea of reincarnation confirms that Anaxilaus was associated with a Pythagorean idea at some point. Epiphanius also described him as an author of *paignia*.[4] Besides this, all we know about Anaxilaus are recipes cited in Pliny's *Natural History* and in *P.Holm*. By comparing Anaxilaus' recipes with similar ones, we can deduce that these were what Epiphanius referred to as *paignia*. As with other *paignia*, the setting imagined for most of Anaxilaus' *paignia* appears to have been the banquet.[5]

Recipe 1

Anaxilaus states that if this linen (*linum vivum*) is wrapped round a tree it can be felled without the blows being heard, as it deadens their sound.[6]

This recipe was used by Pliny to demonstrate one more surprising characteristic of

---

[2] See Hephaistion, *Introductio metrica*, 62.5–6.

[3] *Commentary on Aristotle's Metaphysics*, 18.17–18 (commenting on *Metaphysics* 983a): θαύματα δὲ εἶπε τὰ ὑπὸ τῶν θαυματοποιῶν δεικνύμενα παίγνια, ἃ ἐξ αὑτῶν δοκεῖ καὶ αὐτομάτως κινεῖσθαι.

[4] See Jerome, *Chronicle*, BCE 28, Epiphanius, *Panarion*, 2.5.13. For the letter attributed to Diogenes of Sinope (No. 19 Hercher), see Malherbe 1977: 112–113.

[5] Recipes attributed to Anaxilaus were collected by Wellmann 1928: 77–80. Fragments 7–10 are not citations or precise paraphrases of Anaxilaus' *paignia*. Fr. 7 comes from Psellus' summary of Africanus' *Kestoi*. Wellmann asserted that it came from Anaxilaus but did not explain why. In fr. 8, Irenaeus (*Against Heresies*, 1.13) and Epiphanius (*Panarion*, 2.5.13) described Marcus' Eucharist as "mixing the games (*paignia/ludicra*) of Anaxilaus with the misdeeds of those called *magi*" (see below). Fr. 9 (in the anonymous treatise *De Rebaptismate* ch. 16, *Corpus Scriptorum Ecclesiasticorum Latinorum* 3.3 *appendix*, 89) is a reference to Anaxilaus' techniques that was made to discredit the claim that a true baptism must produce flames as the catechumen enters the water. This suggests the existence of a similar *paignion*. Fr. 10 is the spurious letter of Diogenes of Sinope criticizing Anaxilaus for his belief in reincarnation as mentioned above.

[6] Pliny, *Natural History*, 19.19–20: *Anaxilaus auctor est linteo eo circumdatam arborem surdis ictibus et qui non exaudiantur caedi* (trans. Rackham).

this form of "linen," which appears to have been asbestos. Explaining the fireproof property of *linum vivum* by referring to its growth in the hot and dry deserts of India, Pliny provided the reader with a natural-philosophical explanation typical of those found in Plutarch's *Symposiacs* (*Quaestiones convivales*; see chapter 4). That Pliny claimed to have seen towels of *linum vivum* cleaned by being thrown into a fire at a banquet strengthens the suspicion that the discussion of this plant was related to banquet discussions.

Recipe 2

> The ink of the cuttle fish has so great power that Anaxilaus reports that poured into a lamp the former light utterly vanishes, and people appear as black as Ethiopians.[7]

Anaxilaus' recipe puns on *aithiopas* ("Ethiopians"/"burnt-faces"). In the eleventh century CE, Michael Psellus cited another trick to the same effect, adding that it was performed during banquets.[8] The parallel is admittedly late but it comes from a summary of Julius Africanus' *Kestoi* (c. 200 CE), which contains recipes similar to those seen in the fragments of Anaxilaus. As with the first recipe, it is difficult to understand what could have been the different purposes of this trick. Performed at a banquet, it could have been a performative reference to the "Sun's table" of Herodotus (3.17–26), at which the Ethiopians feasted together with the gods. In other words, besides its purported effect, performing the trick could have also compared the hosts of a dinner to the Ethiopians of the tale or to the gods themselves. Moreover, it would have also showcased the surprising powers of a natural product—again, the same topic found in many of the discussions recorded by Plutarch in his *Symposiacs*.

Recipe 3

> Anaxilaus has informed us that the fluid coming from mares when covered, if ignited on lamp wicks, shows weird appearances of horses' heads, and similarly with asses.[9]

The closest parallel to this recipe comes from a third-century sheet of papyrus, PGM XIb. The recipe describes how smearing the wick of a lamp with the blood of a donkey is supposed to make drinkers at a banquet look as if they have donkey snouts. A similar trick was imagined in the *Cyranides*, a collection of recipes deal-

---

[7] *Id.* 32.141: *sepiae atramento tanta vis est, ut in lucernam addito aethiopas videri ablato priore lumine anaxilaus tradat* (trans. Jones).

[8] Περὶ παραδόξων ἀκουσμάτων, 70–71 in Duffy 1992: Αἰθίοπα δὲ ποιήσεις ἐν συμποσίῳ φανῆναι σηπίας τὸ μέλαν ἐγχέας τῷ ἐλλυχνίῳ.

[9] Pliny, *Natural History*, 28.181: *equarum virus a coitu in ellychniis accensum Anaxilaus prodidit equinorum capitum visus repraesentare monstrifice, similiter ex asinis* (trans. Jones).

ing with the special properties of natural products. The recipe mentions how donkey tears mixed with oil and ignited in a lamp can make everybody at a banquet look as if they have donkey heads (2.31.21–23). The collection is difficult to date. It must have been started during late antiquity but the complete text most probably accrued over time.[10] The *Cyranides* also includes several other recipes that were intended to be used during banquets: how to make friends drinking together avoid contention (1.161–169), how to make banqueters drunk and cheerful (1.8.13–17), how to make them leave suddenly (2.40.19–21) and how to make them fall asleep (3.13.6). The similarity with the *Cyranides*' recipe and PGM XIb as well as with recipe No. 2 suggests that Anaxilaus intended it to be used during banquets as well.

Recipe 4

Anaxilaus even made a sport with it [i.e. sulfur] by putting some in a cup of wine and placing a hot coal underneath and handing it round at dinner-parties, when by its reflection it threw on their faces a dreadful pallor as though they were dead.[11]

The specific verb used by Pliny (*ludo*) shows that the trick was presented by Anaxilaus as a practical joke or *paignion* (the Latin for *paignion* being *ludicrum*).[12] The fact that many *paignia* were intended for the banquet (see below) reinforces the impression that this and the preceding recipes were *paignia* meant to be used or discussed during banquets.

Recipe 5

Anaxilaus is responsible for the statement that if the breasts are rubbed with hemlock from adult maidenhood onwards they will always remain firm.[13]

Recipe 6

... for incontinence of urine they [i.e. the *magi*] prescribe dog fat with split alum in doses the size of a bean, African snails burnt with their flesh and shell, the ash being taken in drink, three roasted geese tongues taken in food. Sponsor for this treatment is Anaxilaus.[14]

---

[10] On the *Cyranides*, see Kaimakis 1976 and Bain 2006: 224–232.
[11] Pliny, *Natural History*, 35.175: *lusit et Anaxilaus eo, addens in calicem vini prunaque subdita circumferens, exardescentis repercussu pallorem dirum velut defunctorum effundente in conviviis* (trans. Rackham).
[12] Compare Irenaeus, *Against Heresies*, 1.13 with Epiphanius, *Panarion*, 2.5.13.
[13] Pliny, *Natural History*, 25.154: *Anaxilaus auctor est mammas a virginitate inlitas semper staturas* (trans. Jones).
[14] *Id.*, 30.74: *ad urinae incontinentiam caninum adipem cum alumine schisto fabae magnitudine, cocleas Africanas cum sua carne et testa crematas poto cinere, anserum trium linguas inassatas in cibo. huius rei auctor est Anaxilaus* (trans. Jones).

Recipes similar to No. 5 and 6 were attributed to a certain Salpe, whom Pliny called a midwife (*obstetrix*). Pliny mentioned three medical recipes from her as well as an aphrodisiac recipe, a depilation recipe (or slave-maintenance recipe since it was specifically meant to remove the hair of slave boys) and a recipe to stop dogs from barking.[15] The last recipe comes from *P.Holm.*, a third century book of tinctorial (or alchemical) recipes found in Egypt.

Recipe 7

Another [recipe for "the creation of silver"].

Anaxilaus attributed this one to Democritus as well. Having thoroughly ground common salt and flaky alum together in vinegar and having formed pellets, he dried them for three days in a balan(e)ion. Then, after grinding the copper, he cast it with [the pellets] three times and cooled it by quenching it in seawater. Experience will determine the result.[16]

Such a recipe could be used to produce debased silver coinage or for silvering jewelry or other objects. Other recipes found on the same papyrus show that the recipe Anaxilaus attributed to Democritus belonged to the tradition of *baphai*, "tinctures," which would later be called *chēmeia*, i.e. alchemy.

Paignia, Banquets and Mageia

The term *paignion* was also applied to practical, entertaining or intriguing tricks that were sometimes performed during banquets. The best examples of the trick-kind of *paignia* were attributed to Democritus and written with a fourth- or fifth-century CE hand on a papyrus roll, PGM VII:

To make bronze ware look like it's made of gold: mix native sulfur with chalky soil and wipe it off.

To make an egg become like apples: boil the egg and smear it with a mixture of saffron and wine.[17]

To make the chef unable to light the burner: set a houseleek plant (*aei[zō]on*) on his stove.[18]

---

[15] See Pliny, *Natural History*, 28.38, 66, 82, 262, 32.135, 140. It is difficult to tell what the literary genre called *paignia* consisted in and if it included the kind of recipes attributed to Salpe. See Davidson 1995: 590–592 and Bain 1998: 262–268. Whether or not Salpe's recipes were also called *paignia*, they remain related to Anaxilaus' recipes in that they pointed to the powers of natural substances in a practical, facetious or surprising way.

[16] *P.Holm.*, 2.

[17] The application of saffron (κρόκος) would have made the egg yellow. For a courtesan making a joke about "expensive" or "bronze" (ἔγχαλκος) eggs at a banquet, see Athenaeus, *Learned Banqueters*, 13.584e. See Roy Kotansky's notes *ad loc.* in Betz 1986.

[18] The ἀείζωον plant was well known for its cooling property. See *Refutation of All Heresies*, 4.33.4 and Nepualius (or Neptunianos), *On Sympathies and Antipathies*, 58 (in Gemoll 1884: 1–3).

To be able to eat garlic and not stink: bake beetroots and eat them.

To keep an old woman from either chattering or drinking too much: mince some pine and put it in her mixed wine.

To make the gladiators painted [on the cups] "fight": smoke some "hare's-head" underneath them.

To make cold food burn the banqueter: soak a squill (*skilla*) in hot water and give it to him to wash with. To relieve him: [Apply] oil.

To let those who have difficulty intermingling perform well: give gum mixed with wine and honey to be smeared on the face.

To be able to drink a lot and not get drunk: eat a baked pig's lung.[19]

To be able to travel [a long way] home and not get thirsty: gulp down an egg beaten in wine.

To be able to copulate a lot: grind up fifty tiny pinecones with 2 ozs. of sweet wine and two pepper grains and drink it.

To get an erection when you want: grind up a pepper with some honey and coat your "thing."[20]

The topics found in this list include both drinking as seen in Anaxilaus' recipes and the aphrodisiacs and medical recipes as seen in Salpe's and Anaxilaus' recipes (nos. 5–6). Collections of recipes such as those attributed to Democritus, Salpe and Anaxilaus appear to have covered a wide range of concerns that clustered around eating, drinking, banquet entertainment, conversations, corporeal appearance and sex. The fact that most of Anaxilaus and Democritus' *paignia* mentioned food, cutlery, wine, cups or a cook suggests that they were connected with dining.

Recipes similar to those attributed to Anaxilaus and Democritus can be found on roughly contemporary papyri or compendia and these also often show links with banquets.[21] We can also find several *paignia* related to banquet entertainment

---

[19] Athenaeus, *Learned Banqueters*, 2.52d-e cites Plutarch (*Symposiacs*, 1.6.4) who wrote that almonds have the same effect.

[20] See PGM VII.167–186 (trans. Kotansky with modifications).

[21] These are PGM VII and XIb, already mentioned above, as well as PGM CXXVII and *Papyrus Yale* 2.134.7–8 (= *Suppl.Mag.* 2.76). The "dog-bitten stone," said to provoke quarreling when it is thrown in wine (and more specifically during a banquet in the version given by Aelian), stands out as likely to have been imagined to be performed or discussed during banquets and was relatively common. See *Suppl.Mag.* 2.76.7–8, Aelian, *On the Characteristics of Animals*, 1.38, Pliny, *Natural History*, 29.102. Besides the relevant recipes from PGM VII, other recipes showing how to produce illusions with cups or more specifically during banquets are Anaxilaus' *Recipes* 3 and 4, Sextus Empiricus, *Pyrrhonian Outlines*, 1.46, and *Cyranides*, 1.161–169, 1.8.13–17, 2.31.21–23, 2.40.19–21, 3.13.6.

in the eleventh-century CE summary of Julius Africanus' *Kestoi*.[22] The fact that some of the *paignia* preserved were meant to be used while drinking or eating and that they contained evidence about the natural world made them doubly appropriate as banquet entertainment.

Since the symposium was the quintessential venue for learned discussions, it is not surprising that some of the plants mentioned in the recipes can be found in similar recipes in Athenaeus' *Learned Banqueters*.[23] These suggest that the mention or performance of *paignia* could be used to initiate discussions. Pliny's mention of the cleaning of asbestos towels in fire during a banquet shows that *paignia*-like tricks also contained noteworthy information about the natural world. For instance, Sextus Empiricus quoted a similar recipe to prove how vision and senses in general were relative to the constitution of each species and of particular affections in individuals.[24] Following Sextus' argument, the effect of the *paignion* was real even though it was attributed to *goētes* ("sorcerers" or "tricksters"). It appears likely—as Pliny showed with the asbestos towels and Sextus with the lamp trick—that *paignia* could be used as "philosophical appetizers" during banquets. Most of Plutarch's *Symposiacs* revolved around minor questions of physics spurred by the mention of surprising observations, and his explanations almost inevitably followed the principles of natural philosophy (see ch. 4.1).

For some, *paignia* were also connected with *magoi*, *mageia* or *goēteia*. Besides the passage from Sextus Empiricus already mentioned, Irenaeus and the author of the *Refutation of All Heresies* (both writing c. 200 CE) argued that *magoi* used *paignia* to trick others. Irenaeus affirmed that a certain Marcus, a Christian from Asia Minor, persuaded rich women that they could perform the Eucharist by combining "the *paignia* of Anaxilaus and the trickery of those called *magi*." Marcus allegedly managed to change the color of the wine of the Eucharist and produce the illusion that women could fill up a large cup with a smaller one. The goal of "Marcus Magus" and of his followers, Irenaeus wrote, was to attract many people to their cult and embezzle from rich women. It is reported that he had a *daemon* as assistant, from whom he acquired powers of prophecy. While this last explanation shows that Irenaeus believed Marcus' prophetic powers to be real, he described the special Eucharist as an illusion. The corresponding passage of the *Refutation of All Heresies* explained the changing of the color of the wine by the fact that Marcus surreptitiously dropped a drug (*pharmakon*) into it.[25]

---

[22] Psellus, Περὶ παραδόξων ἀκουσμάτων, 65–90 in Duffy 1992.

[23] See nn. 17 and 19 above.

[24] Sextus Empiricus, *Pyrrhonian Outlines*, 1.46: καί γε οἱ γόητες χρίοντες τὰς θρυαλλίδας ἰῷ χαλκοῦ καὶ θολῷ σηπίας ποιοῦσιν ὁτὲ μὲν χαλκοῦς ὁτὲ δὲ μέλανας φαίνεσθαι τοὺς παρόντας διὰ τὴν βραχεῖαν τοῦ μιχθέντος παρασποράν ("*Goētes*, too, by means of smearing lamp-wicks with the rust of copper or with the juice of the cuttle-fish make the bystanders appear now copper-colored and now black—and that by just a small sprinkling of extra matter." trans. Bury modified).

[25] See Irenaeus, *Against Heresies*, 1.13.1–7 and 1.13.1: *Anaxilai enim ludicra cum nequitia eorum*

The *Refutation of All Heresies* attributed similar procedures to Simon of Gitta and also described how his practices combined two different techniques:

> Simon, a man expert in *mageia*—and who made fun of many in part according to the art of Thrasymedes (in the manner we exposed earlier) and in part through the evil works of demons—attempted to divinize himself.[26]

We do not know who this Thrasymedes was but it is almost certain that his art dealt with the different tricks mentioned in an excursus of the *Refutation* on the "art of the *magoi*" (4.42.1).[27] As Richard Ganschinietz (1913) showed, many of the practices described there are comparable to those found in various texts dealing with the properties of natural substances or with the machines described by Heron and others.[28] In some cases, the author of the *Refutation* quoted sources describing the surprising effects of natural substances and techniques that were not intended to be deceptive tricks. For instance, the *Refutation* described the confection of an invisible ink that could be used in a divinatory trick. In a complex scenario described by the author of the *Refutation*, a man presenting himself as intercessor between an oracular deity and an inquirer secretly learns the request of the inquirer through different methods, one consisting in the use of a fumigation of gallnut to reveal a request that had been previously written with a mixture of water and vitriol (4.28). The use of gallnut to darken vitriol was most probably not common knowledge in antiquity but it was known by Pliny.[29] Mixing gallnut with iron or copper sulfate (i.e. vitriol) and some form of binder would later become the standard recipe to produce ink in Europe. While it is not clear when iron (or copper) gall ink started to be used in the Mediterranean basin, a similar technique was described by Martianus Capella (fifth century CE). Some scholars could have recognized the invisible ink of the *Refutation* as a simple ink recipe.[30]

---

qui dicuntur magi commiscens (cf. Epiphanius, *Panarion*, 34.1: τὰ γὰρ Ἀναξιλάου παίγνια τῇ τῶν λεγομένων μάγων πανουργίᾳ συμμίξας), *Refutations of All Heresies*, 6.39.

[26] 6.7.1: οὗτος ὁ Σίμων, μαγείας ἔμπειρος ὢν καὶ τὰ μὲν παίξας πολλοὺς κατὰ τὴν Θρασυμήδους τέχνην—ᾧ τρόπῳ ἄνωθεν ἐξεθέμεθα—τὰ δὲ καὶ διὰ δαιμόνων κακουργήσας, θεοποιῆσαι ἑαυτὸν ἐπεχείρησεν. Thrasymedes might be the Pythagorean listed by Iamblichus, *Pythagorean Life*, 36.267.14. See also Plutarch, *On the Failure of the Oracles (De defectu oraculorum)*, 437f.

[27] I list here the headings of 4.28–42 in Litwa 2016: 1. A Request for an Oracle in Writing (28); 2. The Egg Trick (29); 3. Sheep Self-Decapitation (30–31.1); 4. Spontaneous Combustion (31.1–2); 5. Thunder (32.1–2); 6. Fireproofing and other Tricks (32.2–33); 7. Sealing and Resealing Letters (34); 8. Lecanomancy (35.1–2); 9. False Epiphanies (35.3–36); 10. Appearance of Heavenly Bodies (37–38); 11. Earthquake Simulation (39); 12. Divination from the Liver (40); 13. A Talking Skull (41).

[28] References to similar recipes in the PGM can be found in Kelhoffer 2008: 517–548.

[29] *Natural History*, 34.112.

[30] *On the Marriage of Philology and Mercury*, 3.225. When mixed with water, iron or copper sulfate and gallnut oxidize and form a black pigment. Ink was normally made this way from the late Middle Ages until the twentieth century (see https://irongallink.org/). It is unclear if this technique was widespread among Greek and Latin writers (see, e.g., Dioscorides, *Materia Medica*, 5.162, ignoring the use of gallnut. An ink recipe including gallnut, vitriol and gum arabic is found in PGM XII (397–400),

REPRESENTATIONS OF SCHOLARS AS LEARNED SORCERERS 59

That some said that a goat could be killed if one blocked its ear canals appears to be an elaboration on a theory of the Pythagorean Alcmaeon of Croton (4.31).[31]

The recipe for preventing textile from catching fire (4.33.3) is similar in its effect to the non-flammable napkins made of *linum vivum* mentioned by Pliny.[32] A parallel for the use of the juice of a species of clam to "light up" (*kaiesthai*) houses can be found in Pliny, who noted the bioluminescent property of the mollusk.[33] The same could be said of a trick for making thunder, which can also be found in Heron's *Automata*.[34] While potentially deceptive, some of the tricks mentioned by the author of the *Refutation* also appear at times to have been simply lifted from *paignia* or from books of mechanics or of natural philosophy.

Polemical texts that represented Apion, Simon of Gitta and Pancrates as *magoi* and *goētes* can help make sense of the strange similarities between ancient scholarship, *paignia* and the tricks attributed to sorcerers or quacks. Pointing to a scholar's knowledge of *mageia* could have been a possible reference to the treacherous advisors found in Herodotus' *Histories*. It could also have been read as a reference to the client scholars described by Lucian, i.e. to those who did not offer legitimate forms of learning. In this context, reference to the use of *paignia* or to witchcraft would have referred to their inadequate learning rather that to their use of *pharmaka*, love-charms, etc. As the representations of Apion, Simon and Pancrates show, representing learned men as client scholars doubling as *magoi*—i.e. as learned sorcerers—was a rhetorical technique that discredited certain types of scholars and the kind of learning that they embodied.

2. APION

According to the *Suda*, Apion was a specialist of Greek literature (*grammatikos*) who taught in Rome under Tiberius and Claudius. He was the author of histories and of literary commentaries, none of which were preserved in their entirety. Besides his so-called "Homeric glosses," Apion's best known work is his *Aiguptiaka*.[35]

---

dated to the fourth century CE.

[31] See *Refutation of All Heresies*, 4.31 with Aristotle, *On the Nature of Animals*, 492a13–16.

[32] Other recipes for heat-proofing mentioned by the *Refutation* involve a solution made with the ἀείζωον plant (4.33.4), which was known for its cooling property (see PGM VII.172–173), one with the salamander (a creature that extinguishes fire according to Pliny, *Natural History*, 10.188) and one with vinegar (on which see Gellius, *Attic Nights*, 17.8.14 and Pliny, *Natural History*, 23.54). The squill (σκίλλα) was used in the *Refutation* to trick a sheep into slaughtering itself by impelling it to scratch its neck on a blade (30.1). The caustic juice of the squill was well known by Pliny, who mentioned a book of Pythagoras specifically dedicated to that plant (*Natural History*, 19.93–94). It also appears in the *paignia* of Democritus (PGM VII.178–179) to make cold food seem to burn the one who eats it. The recipe for the coloring of eggs (4.29) has parallels in Lucian, *Alexander*, 14 and in PGM VII.170–171.

[33] See *Refutation of All Heresies*, 4.31 and Pliny, *Natural History*, 9.184.

[34] See *Refutation of All Heresies*, 4.32 and Hero of Alexandria, *On the Making of Automata*, 20.4.

[35] On Apion, see van der Horst 2002, Damon 2008 and Bremmer 2010b. For Apion's works, see

In texts transmitted through the literary tradition, Apion is usually depicted as an arrogant and uneducated Egyptian.[36] According to Pliny, the emperor Tiberius called Apion "cymbal of the world" (*cymbalum mundi*). This nickname was not necessarily ironic since Pliny thought it necessary to add that Apion should have rather been called "the drum of his own renown" (*propriae famae tympanum*).[37] He may have been associated with *mageia* or *goēteia* early on: Pliny, who mentioned meeting Apion during his youth (c. 40 CE), compared him to the "ancient lying *magi*" because he claimed to have used a plant in a necromantic rite to learn about Homer's homeland and parents.[38] It is perhaps for the same claim that Julius Africanus later called him "the most 'overly curious' (*periergotatos*) scholar of Greek literature"[39] since the adjective *periergos* may refer to the uselessness of Apion's learning.[40] By the second century CE, the same term as well as its Latin versions, *curiosus* and *curiositas*, started to be associated with the useless or illegitimate search for knowledge, with superstition and with *mageia/magia*.[41] It is likely that this connection already existed in the late first century CE when the *Natural History* was published. If this is correct, Pliny's short anecdote associated Apion with *mageia* and illegitimate scholarship on a double count.

A recently edited papyrus (c. 50–100 CE), which appears to be the copy of an inscription, shows that Apion was a respected scholar in many circles. According to the document, Apion received several prizes from cities, honorary positions at their museums (*sitēseis*) as well as statues.[42] We also know that he was well regarded by the members of the Alexandrian city council since they gave him citizenship and sent him to Rome to settle a dispute between Alexandrian Jews and Greeks.[43] Seneca also mentioned that Apion made a Pan-Hellenic tour under the reign of Caligula and that he had been "adopted in the name of Homer by all cities."[44] This clashes with the image of Apion found in the majority of the reports that were transmitted through the literary tradition.[45]

FGrH, No. 616, and "Apion's Γλῶσσαι Ὁμηρικαί" in Neitzel 1977: 185–300 with Bremmer 2010b: 85–86.

[36] Gellius, *Attic Nights* (5.14, 6.8, 7.8) praised him but also remarked on his arrogance. Tatian's praise was ironic. See *To the Hellenes*, 27 and 38. See also Aelian, *On the Characteristics of Animals*, 10.29, Seneca, *Letters to Lucilius*, 88.40, Josephus, *Against Apion*, 2.3, 12–14.

[37] Pliny, *Natural History*, pref. 26.

[38] *Id.*, 30.18.

[39] Eusebius, *Preparation for the Gospel*, 10.10.16.

[40] For a similar criticism, see Seneca, *Letters to Lucilius*, 88.40.

[41] See Lancel 1961, Walsh 1988, DeFilippo 1990: 480–83 and Martin 2004: 130–134.

[42] *P. Oxy.* 79.5202. This papyrus shows that the title of πλειστονίκης was entirely appropriate. See Ameling 2014: 5–7.

[43] Josephus, *Jewish Antiquities*, 18.257–260 and *Against Apion*, 2.28–32, 41.

[44] Seneca, *Letters to Lucilius*, 88.40: *Apion grammaticus, qui sub C. Caesare tota circulatus est Graecia et in nomen Homeri ab omnibus civitatibus adoptatus.*

[45] See Damon 2008.

Two or three centuries after his death, Apion was portrayed in the *Pseudo-Clementines* as a follower of Simon "Magus." Apion's image there is mostly negative and corresponds in many ways to the figure Pliny described. The *Homilies*, one of the two *Pseudo-Clementine Novels* and written at some point between 222 and 411 CE, is the pseudepigraphic and autobiographical account of the conversion of Clement of Rome to Christianity.[46] Clement is described as a young aristocrat "fully trained in Greek *paideia*" (4.7). He is also said to have been a relative of Tiberius Caesar (4.7.2) and to have studied philosophy (1.3). Having searched in vain for a proof of the immortality of the soul in the works of the philosophers, Clement found an answer in the Christian teachings of Barnabas and Peter. Framed narratively by Clement's voyage with the apostles and the re-discovery of his parents, most of the *Homilies* consist in the exposition of points of doctrine and in the refutation of the doctrines attributed to Simon and Apion.

The story begins with Clement's search for truth and his meeting with Barnabas. The first chapters of the novel also introduce the author's—i.e. Clement's—mastery of *paideia*.[47] Clement also shows the usefulness of his education by defending Barnabas, "a Hebrew" who "spoke the truth without dialectical art" (1.9), from the mockery and the rhetorical attacks of philosophers formed in "worldly *paideia*." Interrupting Barnabas' preaching, one the philosophers asked him "why [...] the gnat, which is so small, has six feet as well as wings while the elephant, the largest of animals, is not only deprived of wings but has only four legs" (1.10). In response, Clement criticized the scholars for ignoring the wisdom of Barnabas and for making a show of their literary art (*grammatikē technē*). These, he claimed, were "lovers of words" (*philologoi*) rather than "lovers of truth" (*philalētheis*) and "lovers of wisdom" (*philosophoi*, 1.11). The accusation was not simply a condemnation of rhetoric.[48] The author of the *Homilies* also emphasized the contrast between the frank speech of the true sage and the dishonest rhetoric of the philosophers, a trait usually attributed to *kolakes* and *parasitoi*.[49]

Clement's refutation of Apion in Books 4 to 6 repeats the same criticism while combining the accusation of rhetorical deceitfulness with the accusation of witchcraft. It is likely that the depiction of Apion and Simon served the goal of refuting the ideas or interpretive method that they embodied in the novel. Apion's narrative role in the *Homilies* was mainly that of a defender of the allegorical interpretation of myths. A similar argument could be made with Simon and his other acolytes, Annubion, an astrologer, and Athenodorus, an Epicurean. Each represented doctrines commonly fought in apologetics: the denial of free will (astrology) and the denial of providence (Epicureanism). The notion that the creator of the uni-

---

[46] Bremmer 2010a.
[47] See *Homilies*, 1.14.1.
[48] Peter later makes the same accusations. See *Homilies*, 2.8. On the condemnation of rhetoric, see also *Homilies*, 1.9.2, 1.20.7, 1.21.4–5 and 5.10–19, with Côté 2006: 189–210.
[49] See Plutarch, *How to Tell a Flatterer from a Friend*.

verse was a lower god (usually attributed to Gnostics) was attributed to Simon.[50]

Several details of the narrative show that Apion was presented as a sorcerer and a client scholar. This is suggested by an anecdote from Clement's youth. Pretending to be sick and incapacitated because of his love for a married woman, Clement had asked Apion to help him. Apion proposed that he could force demons to charm the woman and Clement asked if he could use his persuasion instead. In response, Apion wrote a letter to Clement's fictitious love in which he argued that adultery was justified.

The episode strikes several points against Apion. First, he is shown professing expertise in love-charms and willing to write a defense of adultery. Secondly, in both versions of the novel, Apion is described as a friend of Clement's father, a Roman aristocrat.[51] The name of "friend" (*philos*) being an ambiguous sign of the presence of patronage, it is worth paying attention to other details that could bring us to the conclusion that client scholars such as those described by Juvenal and Lucian inspired the depiction of Apion in the *Pseudo-Clementine*. As William Adler (1993) showed, Clement's story also rehashed an old Hellenistic tale about Antiochus' love for Stratonike, one of the wives of king Seleucus, his father. In this story, the physician Erasistratus discovered Antiochus' love and astutely convinced Seleucus to leave Stratonike to his son. The story presents Erasistratus as an honest and competent client scholar who proved to be an indispensable friend and counselor. Described as a friend (*philos*) of Clement's father and helping Clement in a (false) case of adulterous love, the author of the *Homilies* imagined Apion in a role similar to that of Erasistratus, i.e. that of a client scholar curing the lovesickness of his patron's son. Further suggesting his status of client scholar, Apion was also described in Tyre as the friend of a rich man who invited Clement, Apion and Apion's followers to continue a debate in his garden (4.10). Apion's portrayal also fulfills most of the characteristics of the client scholar found in Lucian's *On Hired Companions*. He is learned, devious, and pretends to know how to produce love-charms.

Apion's known biography also shares some similarities with Apuleius and Anaxilaus, whose interest in natural philosophy was associated by some with the practice of *mageia*. Some of the remaining fragments from Apion's work indicate interest in the kind of material that was typically discussed during Plutarch's banquets: surprising words, surprising observations about the natural world and notable customs.[52] Like Pliny, the real Apion was interested in recording observa-

---

[50] See Geoltrain 2005: 1178–1179, Cirillo and Schneider 2005: 1606–1613.

[51] *Homilies*, 5.2: πατρικὸς ὤν μοι φίλος. In the *Recognitions* (10.52), Clement's father calls Apion and Annubion *valde amici*.

[52] See Athenaeus, *Learned Banqueters*, 1.16e–17b (on the Homeric πεσσεία, a ball game) and Gellius, *Attic Nights*, 6.8 (Alexander refused to look at the Persian king's wife as a mark of respect for his opponent).

tions that supported the theory of sympathy and antipathy.⁵³ Athenaeus quoted his book *On the Luxury of Apicius* in his *Learned Banqueters*.⁵⁴ Aulus Gellius also recorded Apion's solution to a question typical of those found in Plutarch's *Symposiacs*.⁵⁵ Together with his alleged use of a necromantic rite, Apion's "curious" interest in the extraordinary properties of natural products probably fostered his later reputation as a *magos*.

Besides matching chronologies and his purported hatred of the Jews,⁵⁶ one reason why Apion was chosen by the author of the *Homilies* to personify the allegorical interpretation of myths was probably his reputation among contemporary and future scholars. It is, however, difficult to say why he was disliked. In boasting that those to whom he dedicated his work would acquire immortality, Apion had an illustrious predecessor in the person of Theocritus (also a client scholar).⁵⁷ Plants said to have extraordinary properties are relatively common in Pliny's work. Apion was cited as a source for six books of his *Natural History*.⁵⁸ Necromancy was not necessarily taboo even if it was often associated with *mageia*.⁵⁹ His etymologies might appear wild by modern standards but they were not out of the ordinary in antiquity.⁶⁰

3. SIMON

Early Christian writers remembered Simon "Magus" of Gitta as the archetypal heretic.⁶¹ Details in the staging of the *Acts of Peter* and the *Pseudo-Clementines* indicate that Simon was not simply represented in the guise of a sorcerer and heretic but also in that of a teacher and specialist of *paideia*.

Probably composed around 200 CE,⁶² the *Acts of Peter* depicts the conflict between Peter and Simon in Rome. After the arrival of Simon at Aricia near Rome and the departure of Paul, Barnabas and Timothy, the Christian community is said to have renounced Paul and to have considered him as a *magus* and a deceiv-

---

⁵³See Pliny, *Natural History*, 37.59 with Gaillard-Seux 2003: 113–128. Cases of universal sympathy/antipathy: Gellius, *Attic Nights*, 5.14, 6.8, Pliny, *Natural History*, 24.167, 31.22.
⁵⁴Athenaeus, *The Learned Banqueters*, 7.294, 14.642e, Pliny, *Natural History*, 32.19.
⁵⁵*Attic Nights*, 10.10. See Plutarch, *Symposiacs*, 4.8.
⁵⁶*Pseudo-Clementine Homilies*, 5.2.4. On the problem with verifying Josephus' claims, see Jones 2005: 278–315 and Gruen 2005: 31–51.
⁵⁷Pliny, *Natural History*, pref. 26. See Theocritus, *Idyll* 17, offered to Ptolemy II.
⁵⁸See 1.30–32 and 35–37.
⁵⁹See Ogden 2001: 264 and Dickie 2001: 29–31.
⁶⁰See van der Horst 2002: 215–220.
⁶¹See Edwards 1997: 69–91.
⁶²Bremmer 1998: 19. On the transmission history of the *Acts of Peter*, see Thomas 2003: 14–39. I am limiting the study of this tradition to the version from the Vercelli manuscript. Numbers in the text refer to the separation of the *Acts* into paragraphs; numbers in the footnotes to the page and lines of the edition of Lipsius.

er (4). Receiving a vision, Peter was told to sail to Rome to fight Simon, who was described in the vision as a *magus* (5). Introduced later in the text as a Jew who dispersed the Christian community with "a magical incantation and his wickedness" (*magico carmine adque sua nequitia*, 7), Simon is said to have stayed (*morantem*) at the house of Marcellus, a senator who helped Christians and the poor. Through his art, Simon forced Marcellus to stop almsgiving (8).[63] Once in Rome, Peter intervened and convinced the Christian community (8) as well as Marcellus (9–10) to repent of their sinful association with Simon. After several confrontations, Peter finally managed to convince Marcellus to reject Simon (14). Marcellus then purified his house and invited Peter to come in, thus effectively replacing Simon (19). The final contest between Peter and Simon (23–28) and the resolution of the story of the *Acts of Peter* do not need to be considered here.

The actions and the choice of venues for the first confrontation between Peter and Simon suggest the figures of two scholars competing for aristocratic patronage. Both men attracted crowds with their debate (11, 13) and stayed in the house of a rich patron (9, 17, 20, 28). Peter is also shown convincing rich or well-known Romans such as Nicostratus, a young man "honorable ... and much loved in the senate."[64] Most of the contests of the *Acts of Peter* took place in the house of Marcellus, which is described as a hub for the Christian community of Rome. The narrative framework of the *Acts of Peter* also suggests that Marcellus and his household were instrumental in attracting attention to the teachings of Peter and Simon.

The fact that most of the activity of these teachers took place in dining halls furthers the impression that the author of the *Acts of Peter* portrayed the interactions between Marcellus and the two competing teachers as scholarly patronage. As Lucian showed, banquets were an important venue for exchanges between scholars and patrons. In *On Hired Companions*, the banquet appears to have been the typical event at which a client scholar created or sustained his reputation (15–18, 29–31, 34–36).[65] Some of the illusions Simon is said to have created consisted in "making certain spirits enter dining rooms."[66] Many important events in the *Acts of Peter* also occurred in dining halls: Marcellus rejected Simon as he found him in his house sitting in a dining hall (14). The same is also true of Peter: just after Marcellus announced to Peter that he had cleaned his house of the presence of Simon—notably, in the dining rooms (19)—and welcomed him, Marcellus' household gathered in a dining room to listen to Peter (20).

In the *Pseudo-Clementines*, Simon was described as a *magos* and an accom-

---

[63] *Acts of Peter*, 54.31–33, 56.23–24.

[64] *Acts of Peter*, 75.14–15.

[65] The representation of the leisurely stroll also showed that the banquet was not the only venue for exchanges between the patron and his scholar (10). See also Gellius, *Attic Nights*, 4.1 with Jacob 2005: 513–519 and Johnson 2010: 98–136.

[66] *Acts of Peter*, 31 (= *Martyrium of the Saint Apostle Peter*, 2.23–25).

plished scholar. In the *Homilies*, Simon is said to have attached himself to John, called the "Hemerobaptist," and to have become one of the thirty leaders (*exarchoi*) of his group. His short biography depicts him making a scholarly trip. Studying "Greek *paideia*" (*hellēnikē paideia*) in Alexandria, he came back to his homeland as a powerful *magos* (2.22.3). It is important to note that Simon did not go to Egypt to study with Egyptian *magoi* or the like; he went to Alexandria to study *paideia* but returned as a *magos*. As Simon stayed in Alexandria, Dositheus became head of the faction (*hairesis*) of John. Upon his return to the school (*diatribē*), Simon pretended to enter the rank of the disciples (*summathētai*) of Dositheus but quickly started to undermine his authority. Slandered by Simon with a "cunning accusation," Dositheus attempted to punish Simon. As the rod he used to beat Simon disappeared through his body, Dositheus recognized his divinity and gave him his place as leader of the group.[67]

Simplified to its bare elements and read in the context of ancient Greek scholarship, the plot of the story of Simon's early career is that of a student overturning the hierarchy of a school through his use of dissimulation, rhetorical accusation and *mageia*. The failed thrashing of Simon reinforces the impression that *paideia* and its institutions served as a framework to represent Simon as a scholar.[68]

Simon is consistently represented using rhetoric, or verbal accusations together with witchcraft.[69] In the *Homilies*, Simon is accused of having sacrificed a bull, offering a public banquet to the Tyrians and consequently tying them to *daimones* and spreading diseases.[70] He is also described as achieving several feats such as those found in the *Refutation of All Heresies* or Heron's *Automata*: making statues move, invoking *daimones*, walking on fire, turning furniture into servants at dinner, etc.[71] All these techniques, so the short biography of Simon suggests, came from his study of Greek *paideia* in Alexandria. In this connection, his first use of *mageia* in the school of Dositheus offers a tantalizing parallel to what Raffaella Cribiore called the "short road to rhetoric": the idea that a novel type of school curriculum appearing in the second century CE could guarantee much better results than the old and painful method.[72] In the *Teacher of Rhetoric* (*Rhetorum praeceptor*), Lucian gave ironic praises to this "newly cut road" (10) and to its sly and feminine-looking teacher (11). He described the new teacher of rhetoric as the son of a former slave from Egypt (24) who enjoined pupils to use their tongue "appropriately," by which he meant that they should perform barbarisms and fellatio (23). Lucian compared this teacher to the Sidonian merchant who allegedly offered Alexander the Great to lead him through a shortcut. Alexander, the

---

[67] For Simon's biography in the *Pseudo-Clementines*, see *Homilies*, 2.18–32 and *Recognitions*, 2.7–15.
[68] On the use of corporeal punishment in ancient schools, see Cribiore 2005: 65–73.
[69] See Côté 2001: 34–35, 191–196.
[70] See 4.4, 6.29.3 and 7.3.1.
[71] *Pseudo-Clementine Homilies*, 2.32.2.
[72] See Cribiore 2007a: 71–86.

teacher claimed, turned the offer down because the merchant was a *goēs* (5). One cannot miss the reference to the classical association of rhetoric and *goēteia* with figures of flatterers and untrustworthy advisers. Details of the life of the teacher of rhetoric, e.g. that he first lived with a lover on account of his poverty (24), his comparison to the Sidonian merchant turned down by Alexander, his general lack of morals and the cavalier way with which he disregards the norms of *paideia*, all likened him to the client scholar of *On Hired Companions*.

Both the *Acts of Peter* and the *Pseudo-Clementine Novels* opposed Peter to Simon and represented the latter as a deceitful teacher and *magos*. The *Pseudo-Clementine Novels* portrayed their conflict as part of a struggle between the forces of good and the forces of evil,[73] which refracted itself in the clash between Peter's and Simon's followers, Clement and Apion. In contrast to what is seen in the *Acts of Peter*, their struggle revolved more around philosophical debates than miracles.[74] The opposition between Peter's "useful miracles" and Simon's "useless miracles" also mirrored the common opposition between useful philosophy and useless erudition.[75] From the point of view of Marcellus, Peter and Simon were interchangeable characters occupying the same position of friend and teacher.

4. PANCRATES

Comparing different representations of Pancrates provides another example of the kind of historical re-rewriting that cast scholars as sorcerers. Pancrates was known as an Egyptian poet who dedicated a poem to the emperor Hadrian. One fragment named the rose lotus after Antinous, two others described Hadrian's and Antinous' lion hunt.[76] Pleased by Pancrates' work, the emperor rewarded him "with maintenance (*sitēsin*) at the Museum." By *sitēsis*, Athenaeus most probably meant the "Egyptian table" of Alexandria, which rewarded scholars.[77] If not a friend of Hadrian, Pancrates had at least once received the emperor's favor.

In Lucian's *The Lover of Lies*, the figure of Pancrates the poet is recognizable in that of Pancrates the Egyptian sorcerer. Lucian described this second Pancrates as "a sacred scribe from Memphis of extraordinary wisdom" who had been "instructed about *mageia* by Isis." The powers Lucian attributed to Pancrates were

---

[73] *Homilies*, 2.15–18. On the radical opposition of Peter and Simon as a structural principle of the *Pseudo-Clementine Novels* and especially of the *Homilies* (where the opposition takes cosmic proportions), see Côté 2001.

[74] See Côté 2001: 206–218.

[75] *Homilies*, 2.33–34. Apion's work on Homer appears in Seneca's *Letters to Lucilius* 88.40 as an example of useless erudition. See Côté 2001: 95–134.

[76] The first fragment is preserved in Athenaeus, *Learned Banqueters*, 15.677e-f, the others comes from two papyri. See Bowie 1990: 81–83. Athenaeus (*Learned Banqueters*, 11.478a) also named a Pancrates author of books called the *Bokchoreis*.

[77] Athenaeus, *Learned Banqueters*, 15.677f. See also Philostratus, *Lives of the Sophists*, 533 and 524.

strangely off for a Greek *magos* story. No mention was made of bringing down the moon, of charming lovers or of cursing enemies. Like Simon in the *Pseudo-Clementine Homilies*, Lucian's Pancrates knew how to create a servant out of pieces of furniture. This servant, Pancrates' apprentice said, "fetched water, went to acquire the main course, prepared (food) for us, served and ministered to us skillfully in all things."[78] The Egyptian origins of Pancrates were evident by the fact that he "did not speak pure Greek" (*ou katharōs hellēnizonta*).[79]

An Egyptian high priest with a similar name, Pachrates (*Pachratēs*), is mentioned in a fourth-century CE Greco-Egyptian book of recipes.[80] The recipe is an *agōgē* (attraction ritual) introduced by a short story explaining how Pachrates, "the high priest (*prophētēs*) at Heliopolis," revealed the rite to Hadrian. The emperor is said to have "marveled at the high priest" and to have given him "double fees." The coincidences with the poet Pancrates suggest that the figure of the Heliopolitan high priest of the Greco-Egyptian recipe was based on that of Pancrates, the second-century Egyptian scholar.[81]

The feats Lucian attributed to Pancrates are not usually found in the list of powers attributed to *mageia* or *magoi*. As far as I can tell, figures of wonder-workers in Demotic tales are never attributed these powers.[82] We can nonetheless find similar tricks described in the work of two near contemporaries. In his *True Discourse*, Celsus described Jesus' miracles in a way recalling Pancrates' tricks. Besides exorcism and the invocation of "heroes" (*hēroes*), these also included the display of "expensive banquets, dining-tables, cakes and dishes that are nonexistent." He also made "things move as though they were alive although they are not really so."[83] Philostratus wrote in his *Life of Apollonius of Tyana* about similar "banquet magic." Menippus, a young cynic philosopher, student of Apollonius of Tyana and groom-to-be, had fallen for a beautiful and rich Phoenician woman whom his master revealed to be a dangerous *empousa*. *Empousai*, Apollonius claimed, were normally thought to crave sex but what they really wished for was to "feast" (*dainumi*) on the flesh of their lovers. This *empousa*, Philostratus wrote, was an "apparition" (*phasma*) and the same was true of her servants and of the precious materials that decorated the banquet she had set up to celebrate the wedding.[84] Unmasked by Apollonius, the apparition vanished together with her illusions. The story gestures at the common philosophical avoidance of sensual desires. This impression is strengthened by the fact that the opposition between pleasure

[78] Lucian, *Lover of Lies* (*Philopseudes*), 34–36.
[79] Lucian, *Lover of Lies*, 34.
[80] PGM IV.2443–2451.
[81] For a similar argument, see Ogden 2004: 101–126.
[82] See, e.g. the translations of the two tales of Setne and the tale of Merire in Hoffmann and Quack 2018.
[83] Origen, *Against Celsus*, 1.68 (trans. Chadwick).
[84] Philostratus, *Life of Apollonius of Tyana*, 4.25.

and rationality was often found connected to the opposition between feasting and philosophizing in first- and second-century symposiastic literature.[85]

Transposed to the context of scholarly patronage, the banquet magic of Celsus and Philostratus condensed two ideas seen earlier in Lucian and Juvenal. First, Lucian highlighted Pancrates' foreign origins and hinted at his defective Greek. This remark would have been particularly ironic if it had been applied to Pancrates the Alexandrian poet. Secondly, Pancrates was involved with tricks that could help with the preparation of dinners. Again, this would be ironic if applied to a Greek-educated scholar since it would have suggested a rapprochement with the figure of the parasite. The use of special techniques for the consumption of food appears as an inversion of the philosophical stance regarding bodily desires, the same stance that was put forward in the story of Menippus' infatuation with the *empousa*. Behind Lucian's representation of Pancrates, we can also make out the figure of the parasitic client scholar who "played the *magos*" and enlivened banquets instead of providing his patron with philosophical advice.

CONCLUSION

The representations of Apion, Simon and Pancrates that appeared in the *Acts of Peter*, the *Pseudo-Clementine Homilies* and Lucian's *Lover of Lies* described different individuals with similar characteristics: they were not recognized as Greek but as Egyptians, Jews and/or Samaritans, they had learned Greek but their full Hellenization was incomplete, they were involved in *mageia* or called *magoi*, and their activities were related to those found in aristocratic banquets.

These figures of the learned sorcerer are found in polemical texts and, as argued in the first chapter, it should not come as a surprise if these are some of the rare texts hinting at scholarly patronage under the Roman Empire. That a polemical intent existed, however, is not a sufficient reason to limit our analysis to the representations themselves. In each time and place, some stock figures are more common than others, and it is worth wondering what influenced choosing some figures over others. That late antique authors chose to depict client scholars with the stereotype of the learned *magos* rather than that of the parasite, the *agurtēs* or the *grammatikos* suggests a social imaginary in which client scholars specializing in eastern philosophies competed for scholarly patronage.

---

[85] See Romeri 2002. A last literary parallel to Pancrates' trick can be found in a recipe attributed to the sacred scribe Pnouthis in a fourth- or fifth-century CE recipe book from Egypt. It shows how to invoke a divine assistant who would be able to produce food and drinks for a banquet (including a golden ceiling and marble walls), to heat or cool things, to light up and extinguish lamps as well as to shake and ignite walls. See PGM I.42–195. The two last details of this recipe were noted by the author of the *Refutation* as some of the magical tricks imputed to heresiarchs (4.31.1–2, 4.35.3). For similar examples, see PGM VII.149–154 and XIa.1–40.

In this social imaginary, *mageia* appeared as an exotic, immoral, spurious and/or useless form of learning typical of the pseudo-scholars described by Lucian and Juvenal. While it can now be seen that the narratives studied here were inspired by situations similar to those behind the satirical works of Juvena and Lucian, it is obvious that their main goal was not to represent reality. It is also doubtful that most Roman patrons were not interested in learning in general. That eastern philosophies were appealing for Greek-educated scholars can certainly explain why Plotinus was interested in the philosophy of the Persians and why he asked students to refute books attributed to Zoroaster.[86] How scholars could exploit the interest of aristocrats in eastern philosophies will be discussed in the next chapter.

---

[86] Porphyry, *Life of Plotinus*, 3, 16.

CHAPTER 4

Patrons, Scholars and the Limits of *Paideia*

The three authors studied in this chapter confirm that the stereotype of the learned sorcerer was well established by the fourth century CE. In part 1, I look at Plutarch's *Symposiacs* for the way it represents Plutarch's position in regard to Roman aristocrats, for its depiction of the interests of patrons and for the way Plutarch navigated them. Discussing the *Symposiacs* can also give an idea of the scholarly venues and themes found in the Delphian episode of Heliodorus' *Ethiopica*, studied in part 2. In contrast with the stereotype of the learned sorcerer presented in chapter 3, the *Ethiopica* is exceptional for its description of an Egyptian priest and Greek-educated scholar representing himself as *playing* the role of *magos* (i.e. not being described as if he actually was a *magos*). Calasiris, the character in question and narrator of the episode, also explains how he tricked his patron, the priest in charge of the oracle of Delphi, and how he ultimately taught him a lesson on the interpretation of divine signs. In part 3, I conclude by studying how Julius Africanus catered to the expectations of patrons and readers by depicting himself as an easterner exhibiting knowledge of techniques that were associated with *mageia*.

I argue that the representational strategies of Calasiris and Africanus build upon the assumption that some patrons would be particularly curious about eastern forms of wisdom. Studying how these figures of scholars were constructed also supports the theory that scholarly patronage could lead scholars to discuss themes lying outside of the domain of classical *paideia*. I will turn to this hypothesis when studying the work of Zosimus in the last two chapters.

1. PLUTARCH

Plutarch's *Symposiacs* presents itself as the record of banquet discussions that took place between Plutarch, Quintus Sosius Senecio and some of their friends in the late first century CE. Plutarch's Roman entourage included Roman aristocrats, the two most important being Lucius Mestrius Florus and Sosius Senecio. Mestrius Florus was consul suffect under Vespasian (75 CE) and most probably adopted Plutarch since the latter bore his name.[1] Sosius Senecio was another influential aristocrat. He had a successful military career and received his two consulships from Trajan.[2] Plutarch dedicated three works to Sosius Senecio, including the *Symposiacs*, which he wrote at his request.[3] While the characters appear to be real, the discussions themselves read more like idealized dialogues between aristocrats and scholars. Those interested in avoiding some of the problems described by Lucian in *On Hired Companions* and reinforcing friendship with a patron could have read Plutarch's *Symposiacs* with profit.

That the *Symposiacs* were intended to be read as an example of the best possible banquet discussions is indicated by its opening dialogue, which deals with sympotic norms. The main protagonist argued that banquet discussions should suit the philosophical inclinations of the average participant so as to bring all those present to an appreciation of philosophy.[4] That philosophers should apply themselves to bring philosophy to rulers was precisely what Plutarch advocated in two other texts.[5] A study of the overall content of the *Symposiacs* gives an idea of the topics Plutarch considered suitable for that goal. Discussion topics can be separated into three categories:

1. Discussions about banquets. These deal with suitable topics of conversation and with finer points of decorum as well, as in *Whether Flute Girls Should Be Allowed at a Banquet* (7.7). These questions make up 15 percent of the discussion topics.
2. Questions on classical works or about traditions (e.g. 8.2, on the Etruscan origin of Pythagorean prohibitions). These represent 30 percent of the discussion topics.
3. Minor physical questions. These concern *paradoxa* or surprising observations about nature (e.g. 7.3: *Why the Middle of Wine, the Top of Oil, and the Bottom of Honey is Best*) and represent about 55 percent of the dialogues.

That Plutarch considered *paradoxa* as an appropriate means to introduce educated men to philosophy must have had something to do with the interests of his patrons. Mestrius Florus was fond of seemingly intractable questions such as

---

[1] See Jones 1971: 22.
[2] Cassius Dio, 68.16.2. On Q. Sosius Senecio, see Jones 1970: 101–104.
[3] *Symposiacs*, 1, *pref* (612c-e).
[4] *Symposiacs*, 1.1 (612e–615c).
[5] *That a Philosopher Should Converse Especially with Rulers*, 776b–779c, *To an Uneducated Ruler*, 780e-f.

those found in the Aristotelian *problemata* and insisted that his guests find solutions.[6]

Plutarch and the Evil Eye

The evil eye was one topic that Plutarch's banqueters would have refused to discuss if it had not been for Florus.[7] Prodding them to discuss the matter, Florus built on the Socratic saying that philosophy begins in amazement. Those who categorically refused to grant credibility to incredible assertions, he argued, destroyed puzzlement (*to aporein*) and philosophy itself (680c-d). Plutarch obliged and attempted an explanation of the evil eye in accordance with natural philosophy. This specific instance of cursing, he claimed, was due to emanations (*aporrhoiai*) exuded by animals (680f). Such emanations, he asserted, could detach themselves from the body as pneuma pulsated inside. The eyes, he argued, were a likely opening for these emanations since they were said to be "predisposed to movement" (*polukinetos*).[8] The example of lovers charming each other through vision was also adduced to support the claim that eyes functioned as channels for emanations.

Florus' son-in-law Gaius added to Plutarch's explanation that Democritus said that the evil eye was caused by *eidōla* possessing sensation (*aisthēsis*) and desire (*hormē*) that brought evil intentions to dwell inside people and injure bodies and mind. Understanding that Gaius referred to animated beings, Plutarch restated the reason for his avoidance of vocabulary hinting at the Democritean theory: the emanations were not *eidōla* possessing soul (*to empsuchon*) and will (*prohairetikon*) but simply "things that flow out" (*rheumata*). These, in other words, had nothing to do with the "ghosts" (*eidōla*) invoked by Gaius. Plutarch also cut the conversation short with an ambiguous joke: "so that you do not think that I invoked apparitions (*phasmata*) or living and thinking *eidōla* to frighten and confuse you far into the night, let us examine these questions tomorrow morning if you like."[9] Plutarch's response to Gaius—that he disagreed with him only where his solution implied the existence of living and thinking *eidōla*—appears somewhat curt. While Plutarch insinuated that one should not be afraid of apparitions,

---

[6] *Symposiacs*, 8.10.

[7] *Symposiacs*, 5.7 (680b–683b). The other dealt with "horn-fallen" (i.e. particularly tough) grain (7.2).

[8] *Id.*, 681a: πολὺ δὲ μᾶλλον εἰκός ἐστι τῶν ζῴων ἀποφέρεσθαι τὰ τοιαῦτα διὰ τὴν θερμότητα καὶ τὴν κίνησιν, οἱονεί τινα σφυγμὸν καὶ κλόνον ἔχοντος τοῦ πνεύματος, τὸ σῶμα κρουόμενον ἐνδελεχῶς ἐκπέμπει τινὰς ἀπορροίας. μάλιστα δὲ τοῦτο γίνεσθαι διὰ τῶν ὀφθαλμῶν εἰκός ἐστι· πολυκίνητος γὰρ ἡ ὄψις οὖσα μετὰ πνεύματος αὐγὴν ἀφιέντος πυρώδη θαυμαστήν τινα διασπείρει δύναμιν, ὥστε πολλὰ καὶ πάσχειν καὶ ποιεῖν δι' αὐτῆς τὸν ἄνθρωπον. As Dickie (1991: 26) argued, it seems that Plutarch borrowed from an Aristotelian *Problem* (887a22–27) that explained ophthalmia by claiming that the propensity of the eye to be moved (εὐκινητότατον) was directly connected to its becoming like what it saw. According to this theory, ophthalmia was produced when healthy eyes looked at ophthalmic eyes and became like them. On the underlying theory for this explanation, see Aristotle, *On the Soul* 2.5.

[9] *Id.*, 683a-b.

this was not because he denied their possibility. In his *Life of Dion and Brutus*—offered like the other *Parallel Lives* to Sosius Senecio—he accepted the ghost stories attributed to Dion and Brutus. However, he wrote that both men had not been visited by *eidōla* but by "evil and bewitching *daimones*" (*phaula daimonia kai baskana*).[10] Discussing *living* and *thinking eidōla* would then probably have forced Plutarch to address the complex issue of evil *daimones* during a banquet. There are reasons to believe that Plutarch was wise in avoiding this matter.

Topics dealing with theological problems—that is, those involving the existence and nature of divine beings directly—appear to have been too serious or too controversial.[11] Plutarch also made clear elsewhere that divine beings or events should not be interpreted from a purely natural perspective, which was the perspective he took in the *Symposiacs*.[12] Discussing the Jews' abstention from pork, one of the banqueters brought mythology (*ta muthika*) into the discussion as if it would have been somewhat out of place.[13] The discussion as to why dreams occurring in the Fall are given lesser credit (8.10)—also prompted by Florus—brought back the Democritean theory of the sentient *eidōla*. Dreams, the explanation implied, were caused by the presence of *eidōla* in the dreamers' bodies since Fall winds were thought to disturb the path of the *eidōla* on their way to sleepers. Again, Plutarch and most of the participants avoided this solution, which encroached on the domain of demonology. At the very least, divine beings did not belong to the kind of banquet discussion Plutarch wanted to represent.

Several reasons might explain this avoidance. Plutarch might have feared that the style of banquet discussion was doubly inappropriate for theology. First, explanations in his dialogues usually reduced phenomena to natural philosophy. Discussing theology in this context might have been perceived as confusing genres or, worse, as implying that the actions of divinities could depend on material considerations (a problematic implication for a Platonist). Second, theological discussions might have seemed too solemn for a banquet or too learned for those present. Reading Plutarch's cautious discussion of the evil eye from the critical point of view given by Lucian in *On Hired Companions* also suggests that Plutarch was aware that discussing anything related to *mageia* (such as demonic beings) could be dangerous. The connection between the souls of the "untimely dead" and ancient Greek and Latin forms of cursing was never explicitly stated in ancient sources, but it remains likely that many believed that such souls could be used to curse others.[14] Plutarch's remark closing the discussion cautiously avoided discussing this eventuality. He also made his intentions clear by stating that he

---

[10] *Life of Dion*, 2. On Plutarch and evil divine beings, see *On Isis and Osiris (De Iside et Osiride)*, 361b and Timotin 2012: 163–190.

[11] See 4.5–6, 5.3, 5.10, 8.1, 8.8, 8.10.

[12] See *On Isis and Osiris*, 65–67 (377b–378a).

[13] 4.5 (671b): εἰ δὲ δεῖ καὶ τὰ μυθικὰ προσλαβεῖν.

[14] See Ogden 1999: 16–23 and Johnston 1999: 71–80.

did not want his audience to think that he could invoke (*apagonta*) living and thinking *eidōla*, i.e. that he could manipulate the spirits mentioned by Gaius. That he feared being associated with cursing activities is even more likely considering that he proved to Florus (at Florus' own request) that he could find explanations for the most far-fetched observations.

In sum, both Lucian and Plutarch would have agreed that a client scholar had to be particularly careful with patrons—especially if their entourage included fellow scholars and clients. While answering his patron's question, Plutarch stressed that interest in the evil eye did not come from him and that his theory was a simple suggestion. Cutting short a public discussion on a delicate question, Plutarch could navigate the interests of his patron's family and avoid situations that might have been used by others to cast him as a sorcerer—or perhaps even worse, as the kind of client scholar Lucian would later describe as currying favor with a Roman patron by suggesting some extraordinary knowledge or ability.

Considering the number of Roman aristocrats who had been accused of cursing or of practicing *magia* in the first century CE, any scholar in Plutarch's situation would have stayed away from these topics as far as possible.[15] Ulpian, a Syrian jurist who worked with the Severan court (c. 205–223 CE) also thought that judges—like respectable men in general—should not pronounce themselves on the use of poisons and curses. Rather, he thought, they should destroy books dealing with these arts.[16] The opposition of the scholar and the sorcerer was axiomatic for Philostratus, writing his *Lives of the Sophists* one century after Plutarch. When defending two Greek-educated scholars from witchcraft accusations, Philostratus repeated a simple argument: a man who was rightfully recognized for his wisdom could not have been involved in witchcraft (523, 590). One of these two scholars, Adrian of Tyre (c. 110–190 CE), had been promoted secretary of the emperor just before the emperor's death (585–590).[17] Philostratus marked him as non-Greek (588) and Adrian appears to have emphasized his Syrian origins (587). He was also believed to have been a sorcerer (*goēs*; 590.5–7). Adrian's case appears to follow the pattern in which outstanding scholars from eastern backgrounds could easily be perceived as sorcerers.[18] Philostratus explained that Adrian's reputation came from the fact that he was mentioning fabulous things (*terateuomenos*) when

---

[15] See Tacitus, *Annals* 2.27–2.33, 12.22, 12.52 with Garosi 1976: 75–83.

[16] Digest 10.2.4.1: *Mala medicamenta et venena veniunt quidem in iudicium, sed iudex omnino interponere se in his non debet: boni enim et innocentis viri officio eum fungi oportet: tantundem debebit facere et in libris improbatae lectionis, magicis forte vel his similibus. haec enim omnia protinus corrumpenda sunt.*

[17] On dating Adrian, see Jones 1972: 480. On dating the award of his chair in Rome, see Swain 1990: 214–216. For a bibliography, fragments and testimonies see Amato 2009: 47–76.

[18] Christopher P. Jones (1972) argued that Adrian might have also been the unnamed target of Lucian's *Pseudologos*. The portrayal of the target of the *Pseudologos* is also comparable in many respects to the submissive client scholar of *On Hired Companions*.

speaking about the customs of the *magoi* (590.9–11). In retrospect, Plutarch appears to have been well advised not to speak in public about ghosts and curses.

Plutarch, however, was caught between two imperatives. On one hand, he had to answer the question of his patron concerning the evil eye and, potentially, those of his patron's stepson concerning demonic beings inducing curse-like effects. On the other, it was unbecoming and dangerous of him to speak of curses or *goēteia*. While chiding Gaius for bringing ghosts (*eidōla*) into the discussion, he nonetheless provided Florus with an answer. At the same time, however, he distanced himself from his claims by reminding his audience that his theory had been produced *ex tempore* and with the help of a copious amount of wine.[19] The two following case studies will show how scholars could imagine an entirely different course of action. Calasiris, a character of the *Ethiopica*, and Africanus rather emphasized their eastern origins and consciously or unconsciously provoked the same associations that Plutarch sought to avoid.

2. HELIODORUS' *ETHIOPICA*

The *Ethiopica* tells the adventures of Charicleia, the princess of Ethiopia, and of Theagenes, a young Greek aristocrat. The exact date of the novel is disputed but it is generally agreed that it must have been written at some point between the third or the fourth century CE.[20] Part of Charicleia's and Theagenes' fate was to be consecrated in Ethiopia as priestess and priest and, through that process, to stop the practice of human sacrifice in the country. Calasiris, a Memphite priest of Isis, plays a crucial role in the narrative by helping Theagenes and Charicleia escape Delphi through his use of trickery. Arrived in Delphi in search of the Ethiopian princess, Calasiris attracted the attention of many learned men and befriended a certain Charicles, priest of Apollo also described as "the first among the Delphians" (4.6). Thanks to his skill at interpreting human and divine signs, Calasiris gradually discovered that Charicleia, the adoptive daughter of Charicles, was the

---

[19] *Symposiacs*, 5.7 (682b10-c2).

[20] The only thing certain is that the *Ethiopica* was written before Socrates Scholasticus finished his *Ecclesiastical History* (438 CE), which mentions Heliodorus and his novel (5.22). I do not see any good reason to believe that Heliodorus' description of the siege of Syene (9.2–8, see esp. 9.4.2) was a direct borrowing from Julian's description of the siege of Nisibis in his panegyrics to Constantius II (see esp. *Orationes* 1.22 and 3.11.15–19 Bidez). As the argument is usually framed, the similarities between the two texts are so close that one writer must have borrowed from the other: if Heliodorus borrowed from Julian, the *Ethiopica* was written between the publication of Julian's orations and the publication of Socrates' *Ecclesiastical History*, so at some point between 357 and 438 CE; if Julian borrowed from Heliodorus, the borrowing would simply bring the *terminus ante quem* to 357 CE. For a survey of the literature on the question and arguments for a late-fourth-century dating, see Mecella 2014: 633–658, Bowersock 1994: 149–155 and Morgan 1996: 417–421. See also Ewen Bowie's (1996: 93, n. 19) short reply to Bowersock.

Ethiopian princess whom he had been charged to bring back to Ethiopia. Through his accurate interpretation of oracles and dreams, Calasiris also realized that Charicleia had been fated by the gods to escape Delphi with Theagenes (2.25–4.21). The interpretation of divine signs (or interpretation in general) is an important theme of the novel (if not the most important one)[21] and plays a crucial role in moving the plot forward.

While doubling as a holy man and scholar, Calasiris is also presented in the novel as a trickster.[22] His trickster-like character is most conspicuous in the subterfuges he uses to beguile Charicles (e.g. 2.29.1, 3.19.3) and to thwart the plans Charicles made to marry off his adoptive daughter. Since Calasiris' mission is motivated and justified by divine oracles, one could assume that the ideal reader of the *Ethiopica* would interpret Calasiris' trickery in a positive way. However, Calasiris' deceptive behavior makes his actions difficult to square with those typical of the holy man.[23]

While the ideal reader would not have taken Calasiris for a sorcerer, the novel obviously plays with the stereotype of the learned sorcerer. Arrived at the temple of Apollo, Calasiris attracted the attention of several philosophers who questioned him about Egypt and the true cause of the Nile's flooding. Claiming to relate the content of secret books from Egypt (2.28), Calasiris affirmed that waters contained in the Etesian winds traveled to a "torrid zone" (*diakekaumenē zōnē*) where heat stopped them and condensed their humidity. This process resulted in precipitation, which in turn produced the Nile's floodwaters. Composed of rainwater, these were said to be the sweetest (*glukutatos*). Calasiris also specified that the waters were particularly "soft to the touch" and explained this particularity by the fact that they retained some of the heat from the torrid zone.

As far as we can tell, Calasiris combines the Aristotelian theory for the flooding of the Nile with a theory that Diodorus of Sicily attributed to "some of the philosophers from Memphis."[24] Calasiris' theory also appears to have responded to other theories mentioned by Diodorus of Sicily. The favorite theories of Diodorus, like that of Calasiris and of most scholars after Aristotle, attributed the swelling of the Nile to rainfall.[25] Democritus, however, is reported to have claimed that the Nile's flood was produced by the condensation of the Etesian winds' humidity. Blowing southward during summer, these winds would have been blocked by a high mountain range south of Egypt and would have released their humidity there. The resulting rainfall would explain why the Nile flooded every summer.[26] Diodorus did not believe in the existence of these mountains but he did not offer

[21] See Winkler 1982: 93–158 and Dowden 1996: 267–285.
[22] On the duplicity of Calasiris see Winkler 1982 and Sandy 1982: 141–167.
[23] Morgan 2007: 21–51.
[24] *Historical Library*, 1.39–40: τῶν δ' ἐν Μέμφει τινὲς φιλοσόφων.
[25] See Bonneau 1964: 195–208.
[26] *Historical Library*, 1.39. See Bonneau 1964: 203–208.

any alternative theory to replace its explanatory function. The theory attributed to the philosophers from Memphis, however, contains elements that could play this role. It argues that the floodwaters came from an inhabited region (*oikoumenē*) in the southern hemisphere where seasons followed a course opposite to that of the northern region.[27] This would explain why the Nile flooded during the dry season. Through its travel from one region to the other, the floodwaters would have been heated by flowing through a "torrid (*katakekaumenē*) zone" situated between the two hemispheres. This would also have explained why the waters of the Nile were the "sweetest" of all river waters. Diodorus, however, was not satisfied by the explanation. He claimed that a river could not flow all the way into Egypt from an opposite region and that water altered by fire could not foster life as the waters of the Nile did.[28]

By keeping the detail about the sweetness of the waters, Calasiris' explanation appears to have borrowed from the Memphite philosophers while also avoiding the problems outlined by Diodorus. Calasiris mentioned that the waters of the Nile were sweet but explained this by observing that the floodwaters had been produced by rain, thus eliminating the problem perceived in theorizing a river that flowed into Egypt from the opposite hemisphere. In Calasiris' theory, this region still played a role but rather served the purpose of condensing the humidity of the Etesian winds. Rather than making the Nile waters sweet—as the Memphite philosophers of Diodorus claimed—Calasiris said that the heat made them soft. Calasiris' modification of the torrid-zone theory managed to explain a maximum of observations while also avoiding one problematic element of the traditional (Democritean) Greek theory, namely, the postulation of mountains high enough to have blocked the clouds. By keeping the Memphite climatic theory and by postulating a torrid zone, Calasiris could dispense with the mountain hypothesis and its explanatory role by claiming that the heat of the torrid zone stopped the winds and condensed their humidity. He also claimed that the explanation was found in secret books from Egypt. The theory Calasiris proposed at the same time responded to those attributed to Greek philosophers. However, rather than simply responding to these theories, Calasiris rather supplanted them by ascribing his explanation to Egyptian priests.

It is consequently obvious that Calasiris' theory was meant to air Egyptian sacred wisdom in a venue typical of Greek *paideia*. It is also thanks to the demonstration of his science that Calasiris attracted the attention of Charicles. His curiosity piqued by Calasiris' knowledge of Egyptian lore, Charicles asked if he could use some love-charm to convince his daughter Charicleia to abandon her vows of

---

[27] Pseudo-Plutarch, *Opinions of the Philosophers* (*Placita philosophorum*), 898b mentions that Eudoxus of Cnidus attributed the same theory to "the priests," whom he must have meant to be those of Egypt.

[28] Diodorus of Sicily, *Historical Library*, 1.40.

chastity and marry the man he had chosen for her. The reason for his request was that Charicles assumed Calasiris knew about a type of love-charm (the *iunx*) and was familiar with Egyptian wisdom (*sophia*) that could change her mind (2.33.6). The immediate juxtaposition of Calasiris' discourses about secret Egyptian lore with Charicles' request for a *iunx* suggests that Charicles interpreted Calasiris' access to primeval sources of wisdom as implying a knowledge of love-charms.

However, while Charicles was looking for a way to force his adoptive daughter to marry, Charicleia fell in love with a young man called Theagenes. This event, crucial for the development of the plot, is also a narrative element enabling the author to demonstrate Calasiris' interpretive skills—in this case, the knowledge of physiognomy through which he could determine that Charicleia and Theagenes had fallen in love with each other (3.5). Paralyzed by her chaste temperament, Charicleia pined away in her bed while Theagenes' showed the symptoms of a "melancholic" (i.e. manic-depressive) condition (3.10). Trying to hide the affair, Calasiris tricked Charicles into believing that Charicleia suffered from the evil eye (*baskania*). His purpose, as he gathered from oracles, was to bring Charicleia and Theagenes together and to precipitate their flight from Delphi. The episode parallels the same modification of the trope of Erasistratus and Antiochus' love for Stratonike found in the *Pseudo-Clementine Homilies*. The parallel suggests that Calasiris was represented as taking a role similar to that of Apion in the *Homilies*, i.e. as playing the role of a learned sorcerer and client.

Calasiris and the Evil Eye

Calasiris' discussion with Charicles concerning the evil eye is one more suggestion that his role in the Delphian episode was that of a Greek-educated scholar of foreign origin who exhibited his knowledge of *paideia* while also playing the role of a *magos*. There is little doubt that Heliodorus based his discussion of the evil eye (3.7-8) on Plutarch or on a very similar account. In both cases, the evil eye is explained with roughly the same examples, and the vocabulary of one of these examples is similar in both accounts.[29] Like the audience at Florus' banquet, Charicles also scoffs when Calasiris evokes the notion of the evil eye. The striking similarities of the two accounts led Matthew Dickie to argue that Heliodorus intended to present a parody of Plutarch's theory. It seems more likely that ancient readers who recognized the parallels would have interpreted the passage as an imitation of Plutarch's theory. Calasiris' theory could also have been seen as providing a serious explanation despite the fact that it was framed inside a narrative. This would not be stranger than the fact that Porphyry drew on a novel, Antonius Diogenes' *Incredible Things Beyond Thule*, as a source for his *Life of Pythagoras* (15).

Rather than focusing on the power of the gaze, Calasiris took a more explicitly

---

[29]Compare Plutarch, *Symposiacs*, 5.7 (681a5-9) with Heliodorus, *Ethiopica*, 3.7.5.4-8 and *Symposiacs*, 5.7 (681a10-b1) with *Ethiopica*, 3.7.5.1-4. See Dickie 1991: 17-29.

physical (and medical) perspective that attributed the evil eye to pneuma whether it came from the eyes or from other sources.[30] Both explanations accepted the principle that bodily "emanations" (*aporrhoiai tōn sōmatōn*) such as smell, voice and breath can penetrate other bodies and affect them. Plutarch concentrated on the eyes as the main emitter and receiver of emanations. He described the eyes as "particularly predisposed to movement" (*polukinetoi*) and as shooting out a "wonderful power" (*thaumastē dunamis*). He also argued that this power was emitted by the eyes thanks to pneuma and that this pneuma also sent out "fiery beams" (*augē purōdēs*).[31] Calasiris focused rather on the role of air and pneuma in transmitting evil intentions (*phthonos*) and in producing a disease (*nosos*):

> When the air that surrounds us slips in—reaching deep inside us and bringing[32] outside qualities through the eyes, the nose, the throat and other openings—it implants passions similar to itself into those who receive it. Accordingly, one that looks at beautiful things with evil intentions fills up the space around him with a harmful quality and disperses a bitter pneuma (i.e. breath) on his neighbors. Since it is tenuous, it infiltrates all the way into the bones and the marrow itself. In many people, evil intentions become a sickness, which is properly called *baskania*.[33]

As in the *Symposiacs*, love was used as an example for the theory:

> Prove this explanation to yourself with nothing else than the production of erotic desires. Their cause is produced by objects of vision, which, "swift as the wind" (*hoion hupēnema*), shoot passions through the eyes and into the soul. This is entirely to be expected since, of all our openings and senses, the eyes are the warmest and the most predisposed to movement (*polukinētos*). They are also apt to receive emanations by sucking in the movements of erotic desires with their fiery pneuma.[34]

---

[30] Dickie (1991: 24–29) argues that: 1) the fact that Calasiris would have failed to mention the role of the eyes in his theory suggests that the theory was made up; 2) Heliodorus consciously distorted Plutarch's theory of the role of the eyes so as to make it sound implausible to readers; 3) the example of the χαραδριός and of the basilisk, both of which imply that noxious emanations can be sent through the eyes, would be out of place in Calasiris' explanation since his theory would have been strictly related to airborne contagions (in Dickie's reading, pneuma only refers to breath); 4) saying that βασκανία was not necessarily intentional, Heliodorus added another unnecessary detail that made the incoherence of the theory obvious. Again, this would suggest that Calasiris was shown "simply having some fun at Charicles' expense."

[31] Plutarch, *Symposiacs*, 5.7 (681a). See the text of n. 8 above.

[32] Συνεισφερόμενος. The term is used in a similar way by Soranus (*Gynaecology*, 1.33.3) to speak about the "contribution" of external and internal causes to sexual desire.

[33] Heliodorus, *Ethiopica*, 3.7.3: Ὁ περικεχυμένος ἡμῖν οὗτος ἀὴρ δι' ὀφθαλμῶν τε καὶ ῥινῶν καὶ ἄσθματος καὶ τῶν ἄλλων πόρων εἰς τὰ βάθη διικνούμενος καὶ τῶν ἔξωθεν ποιοτήτων συνεισφερόμενος, οἷος ἂν εἰσρεύσῃ τοιοῦτο καὶ τοῖς δεξαμένοις πάθος ἐγκατέσπειρεν· ὥστε ὁπότ' ἂν σὺν φθόνῳ τις ἴδῃ τὰ καλά, τὸ περιέχον τε δυσμενοῦς ποιότητος ἀνέπλησε καὶ τὸ παρ' ἑαυτοῦ πνεῦμα πικρίας ἀνάμεστον εἰς τὸν πλησίον διερρίπισε, τὸ δὲ ἅτε λεπτομερὲς ἄχρις ἐπ' ὀστέα καὶ μυελοὺς αὐτοὺς εἰσδύεται καὶ νόσος ἐγένετο πολλοῖς ὁ φθόνος, οἰκεῖον ὄνομα βασκανίαν ἐπιδεξάμενος. Cf. Plutarch, *Symposiacs*, 5.7 (680f–681a).

[34] Heliodorus, *Ethiopica*, 3.7.5: Τεκμηριούτω δέ σοι τὸν λόγον εἴπερ ἄλλο τι καὶ ἡ τῶν ἐρώτων

Like Plutarch, Calasiris mentioned that the eyes could receive the erotic emanations coming from onlookers together with a "fiery pneuma" (*pneuma empuron*, rather than the *augē purōdēs* sent by pneuma in Plutarch). Unlike Plutarch, he did not concentrate on the role of the eyes as senders of noxious emanations but rather on their capacity to attract them, an assumption also shared by Plutarch.

It is difficult to tell how ancient readers would have evaluated the plausibility of the two theories. Broadly speaking, they were both based on the same principle: the exchange of extremely fine emanations through openings in the human body and especially through the eyes. According to Dickie, the fact that Calasiris does not mention the role of the eyes in *sending off* emanations indicates that Heliodorus wanted to parody Plutarch. Aelian's (c. 200 CE) description of the curselike effect of the breath and gaze of a type of toad shows that the exact origin of the emanations was not particularly important in this kind of explanation. While the theoretical part of the explanation for the toad's toxicity relies solely on the gaze of the animal, the actual description of the effect implies that the breath and the gaze produced it at the same time.[35] Aelian's work was one of compilation, not of natural-philosophical explanation.[36] Similarly, neither Plutarch nor Heliodorus was writing a work of natural philosophy in which one might have expected systematic natural theories.

Moreover, the fact that Calasiris was tricking Charicles with his explanation of the evil eye does not necessarily imply that his explanation was meant to be parodic or that it emphasized Calasiris' deviousness. This is especially true since Charicles figures as a particularly inept interpreter of signs. Calasiris' explanation of the evil eye proposes a model describing a sickness and explicitly applies it to love as an example, thus suggesting Charicleia's real affection and hiding it in plain sight. An exchange of pneuma had triggered her natural instincts, which, at the same time, would also lead her to fulfill the will of the gods. To claim as Calasiris did that the disease that had struck Charicleia was in the order of things (and indeed, of the gods) resonated with the main plot of the novel. There is also irony in the fact that a priest presiding over an oracle of Apollo—supposedly an expert

γένεσις, οἷς τὰ ὁρώμενα τὴν ἀρχὴν ἐνδίδωσι οἷον ὑπήνεμα διὰ τῶν ὀφθαλμῶν τὰ πάθη ταῖς ψυχαῖς εἰστοξεύοντα. Καὶ μάλα γε εἰκότως, τῶν γὰρ ἐν ἡμῖν πόρων τε καὶ αἰσθήσεων πολυκινητόν τε καὶ θερμότατον οὖσα ἡ ὄψις δεκτικωτέρα πρὸς τὰς ἀπορροίας γίνεται, τῷ κατ' αὐτὴν ἐμπύρῳ πνεύματι τὰς μεταβάσεις ἐρώτων ἐπισπωμένη.

[35] *Characteristics of Animals*, 17.12: Γένος τι φρύνης ἀκούω καὶ πιεῖν δεινὸν καὶ πικρὸν ἰδεῖν.... ἰδεῖν δὲ ἡ φρύνη κακόν ἐστι τοιοῦτον. ἐάν τις θεάσηται τὴν θῆρα, εἶτα αὐτῇ ἀντίος ὁρῶν προσβλέψῃ δριμύ, καὶ ἐκείνη κατὰ τὴν ἑαυτῆς φύσιν ἰταμὸν ἀντιβλέψῃ, καί τι καὶ φύσημα ἐμπνεύσῃ ἑαυτῇ μὲν συμφυές, χρωτὶ δὲ ἐχθρὸν ἀνθρωπίνῳ, ὠχροὺς ἐργάζεται ("I have learned that there is a type of toad that is dangerous to drink and painful to look at.... The gaze of the *phruē* is harmful in this way. If someone sees the creature and then faces it, looking at it sharply, and that the creature, looking back intensely at the person—as according to its nature—blows a breath that is natural to itself but harmful to the human skin, this person will become sickly pale").

[36] *Id*., prol.

in the interpretation of signs—was blind to natural and divine signs. Fooled by appearances, Charicles first laughed at Calasiris' suggestion that Charicleia had been struck by the evil eye (3.7.2) but he could not decipher Calasiris' explanation. Charicles could recognize Charicleia's symptoms in Theagenes' behavior but he did not interpret them correctly (3.11). Again, when he misinterpreted a dream concerning the escape of his daughter, Calasiris commented on the irony that Charicles, "a priest of the most prophetic of all gods," was unfit for dream interpretation (4.15). It is only at the very end of novel that Charicles finally understood the divine oracle that announced that his adoptive daughter would travel to Ethiopia (10.41).

Charicles serves as a foil for Calasiris in different ways. Through this comparison, the latter emerges as the only real and achieved scholar of the novel. Calasiris not only manages to read portents, oracles and dreams correctly, he is also a proficient reader of non-Greek forms of writing (2.28, 4.8, 4.12) and of physiognomic signs (3.5). Calasiris also demonstrates his knowledge of Greek disciplines. His deciphering of Theagenes' love for Charicleia also refers to medical theories on the effect of excess pneuma in the body (3.10.4–5).[37] In his explanation of the origin of the Nile's flooding, Calasiris implicitly referred to the theories of Greek philosophers and proposes a new theory that convinces Greek-educated scholars. The same thing can be said of his explanation of the evil eye. Rather than a spoof theory, ancient readers were more likely to read it as a credible theory and, perhaps, as a clever way to hide Charicleia's love to Charicles while indicating it to them.

Calasiris: Priest, Sorcerer and Scholar

Calasiris, however, never explicitly referred to Greek learning. He rather pointed out that some of his theories came from Egyptian sacred books (2.28, 3.8). The same attention to the Egyptian origin of his knowledge can be found in his claims that Homer wrote about theology, that he came from Thebes, and that he was the son of Hermes (3.12–14). There was apparently only one small step between making Homer a student of the Egyptians[38] and attributing to him Egyptian ethnicity. Such an attribution would not have surprised readers.[39]

In many ways, Calasiris' knowledge and perception surpasses that of the Greeks. Speaking to an Athenian, Calasiris explains that he expects that those

---

[37] See Aristotle, *Problems*, 4.30 (880a), 30.1 (953a10–955a27 and esp. 953b23–954a9), Rufus of Ephesus, *On Melancholy*, fr. 73 in Pormann 2008. On the role of pneuma in producing "melancholia," love and inebriation, see the introduction to Pigeaud 1988.

[38] See Diodorus of Sicily, *Historical Library*, 1.96–98

[39] To claim that Homer was not Greek was relatively common in post-Hellenistic biographies. Homer is said to be from "hundred-gated Thebes" in the *Greek Anthology* (7.7); a biography attributed to Plutarch mentions that Aristotle wrote that Homer was the son of a δαίμων (Pseudo-Plutarch, *Life of Homer*, 1.3–4); Meleager of Gadara claimed that Homer was Syrian (Athenaeus, *Learned Banqueters*, 4.157b); Lucian referred (mockingly) to the theory of a Babylonian Homer (*True Stories*, 2.20).

impressed by his knowledge of Egyptian lore would also think him capable of producing love-charms. This is the occasion for Calasiris to describe the Greeks' misconception of Egyptian sciences or "wisdoms" (*sophiai*). In truth, he states, there are two *sophiai*, a "people's wisdom" (*dēmōdēs*) and one that is "truly" (*alēthōs*) wisdom. Those like Theagenes, he says, "suffered from the condition of the masses, which err, thinking wrongfully that Egyptian wisdom is one and the same." He describes the "people's wisdom" as "the handmaiden of ghosts, crawling on the ground and gathering around the body of the dead." Pointed in the opposite direction, the true wisdom "look(s) at heaven." It was an "association with the gods" and a "participation in the nature of higher beings." He also associates the true Egyptian wisdom with astrology and says that it pursues "what is good and helpful for humans" (3.16.3–4).

In his meetings with Charicles and Theagenes, Calasiris' exposition of the "true" wisdom is always a prelude to the (mock) exposition of the "people's" wisdom. Noting that the source of his science was Egyptian, Charicles thought that Calasiris was able to make love-charms (2.33.6) and to dispel the evil eye (3.19). Having invited Charicles to a banquet, Theagenes meets Calasiris and is visibly interested when he hears that he is an Egyptian priest (3.11.3). Very early the next day, Theagenes meets with Calasiris in private and asks him to win over Charicleia on his behalf (3.17.3). The request is vague, leaving to Calasiris the responsibility of imagining how he is supposed to help Theagenes. Playing the role of an Egyptian *magos*, Calasiris confidently responds that Charicleia will not be stronger than "his *sophia*," describing it as an "art" that "knows how to constrain even nature" (3.17.5). Calasiris was not simply aware of the misperception of the Greeks, he exploited it.[40]

Calasiris condemned the conflation of the two wisdoms but also scrupulously kept to his different roles: healer (3.9, 3.19, 4.5.3), diviner (3.17.1), maker of curses (4.6.4, 4.15.3), remover of curses (4.5.3) and wonder-worker (5.13.2).[41] The fact that Calasiris interpreted the symptoms of Charicleia's love correctly through his mastery of medical physiognomics but that her adoptive father failed to do so are two distinctive elements of the topos picturing a scholar solving a problematic love triangle in a noble family. Seen through reformulations of the same topos in various literary genres, Calasiris appears in the

---

[40] That love-charms are implied remains implicit even when Calasiris later chides Theagenes for insinuating that his τεχνή could not force Charicleia's will (4.6.4). Together with Plato's description of "orphic purifiers" knocking at rich men's doors to offer purifications and curses (*Republic*, 364e–365a) and that of Apion in the *Pseudo-Clementine Homilies* (5.3–8), this scene is perhaps the closest we can get to an ancient representation of a person having recourse to a religious professional in order that a curse be made. It is noteworthy that the exchange is not represented as a transaction (no compensation was asked), that the exchange occurs between a man posturing as priest and scholar and an aristocratic man, and that the love-charm is not explicitly requested or even mentioned.

[41] On these roles, see Sandy 1982: 141–147, Winkler 1982: 129–132.

Delphic episode in a role similar to that of the physician Erasistratus in the paradigmatic story of Antiochus' love for Stratonike.[42]

It is not fortuitous that Apion played the same role in an adaptation of this topos in the *Pseudo-Clementine Homilies* (4–6). In both cases, the exchanges taking place between a learned man and an aristocrat share elements with Lucian's stereotypical description of scholarly patronage. First, Theagenes and Charicles, said to be "first among the Delphians," were described in ways suggesting aristocratic status.[43] Secondly, they misunderstood the true nature of Calasiris' wisdom just as the stereotypical patron misunderstood *paideia* as Lucian conceived it. Moreover, like Lucian's client scholar, Calasiris accepted playing the role of *magos* for a patron. In the *Homilies* and in the *Ethiopica*, Greek-educated Egyptians who were credited with the power of making love-charms are placed in a common narrative structure (that of Erasistratus and Antiochus) where they play the role of a Greek-educated client scholar.

Like Plutarch's ideal philosopher, who saw the role of client scholar as an opportunity to teach philosophy to aristocrats, Calasiris is presented as a scholar whose actions ultimately taught the art of interpretation to Charicles, represented as his patron in the Delphian episode. To bring humans to a deeper understanding of important matters is also what Plutarch recommended in *That a Philosopher Should Converse Especially with Rulers* and what Calasiris described as the "true" Egyptian *sophia*: to avoid "terrestrial evils" and to pursue "what is good and helpful to humans" (3.16.4).

The role of client scholar as described by Lucian and Juvenal, which could encompass different roles such as teacher, philosopher or poet, also appears more appropriate to Calasiris than the figures of the philosopher, holy man or sorcerer. Calasiris' use of lies, even if noble, does not correspond to the accounts of holy men or women.[44] Accounts were usually one-sided. Individuals presented as exceptionally upright or divine were in other cases presented as cheats or sorcerers. For instance, Lucian presented Peregrinus "Proteus" as a whimsical and shape-changing quack while Gellius described him as a serious and "steadfast" (*constantem*) philosopher.[45] The figure of Calasiris is also difficult to square with the largely negative representations of Egyptian priests and *magoi* found in other

---

[42] See Robiano 2003.

[43] Theagenes is the leader of the Thesssalians' procession in the function of master of the cavalry (ἵππαρχος, 3.3); he claims to be the descendant of Achilles and is described as divine in appearance (2.34); he hosts an important banquet attended by Charicles (3.10).

[44] See Sandy (1982: 154) who argues that Calasiris represents an "authentic type of holy man in late antiquity." As Dickie (1991) remarked, the concept of the "pagan holy man" as described by Garth Fowden (1982) leaves little room for deceptive characters such as Calasiris. For a similar interpretation, see Baumbach 2008: 167–183.

[45] See Lucian, *On the Death of Peregrinus* (*De morte Peregrini*) and Gellius, *Attic Nights*, 12.11.

novels.[46] In contrast to these characters, Calasiris was Greek in the type of themes he discussed, Egyptian in his references and a sorcerer by pretense.

Even though Calasiris made sure to highlight the Egyptian origin of his learning, he did so while discussing questions of natural philosophy. That is to say that the foreign background of Calasiris became an advantage only if it was expressed according to the rules dictated by *paideia*. In sum, Calasiris was represented as an Egyptian priest playing the role of a client scholar who took advantage of the stereotypes imposed on Greek-educated scholars of eastern backgrounds. Unlike the client scholars of Lucian and Juvenal, Calasiris agreed to play the *magos* not for his own advantage but rather to fulfill the will of the gods.

3. JULIUS AFRICANUS

The fragments of the *Kestoi* of Julius Africanus (c. 160–240 CE) show the work of a client scholar whose preoccupations must have seemed very close to *mageia* for many ancient readers, especially for those who thought like Pliny and Apuleius' accusers.

Africanus is primarily known as the first author of a Christian chronicle. His *Chronography* ran up to the last year of Elagabalus and was probably completed shortly after that time (222 CE).[47] He is also known as the author of two letters concerning philological problems in Christian literature.[48] In the *Kestoi*, Africanus collected recipes dealing with a variety of topics. Many of those preserved were meant to be used in war and the full collection of recipes appears to have dealt with several arts related to nature: agriculture, cosmetics, parturition, divination, etc. The fact that the recipes covered multiple topics and that they pretended to tap into the surprising powers of nature might explain the name of the work. This name, as Africanus wrote, was a reference to Aphrodite's embroidered breast band (*kestos himas poikilos*), described by Homer as the fount of all her charms.[49] The fact that the *Kestoi* were written in a sophisticated style shows that the work was meant to be more than a simple collection of recipes.[50]

---

[46] On these comparisons, see Sandy 1982: 147–154 and de Salvia 1987: 343–365. In contrast with Paapis in the *Mysteries Beyond Thule* and Nectanebo in the *Alexander Romance*, Zatchlas, the Egyptian priest of Apuleius' *Metamorphoses* (2.28–30), is not described as deceptive and harmful to his allies but nonetheless practices necromancy. This again stands in contrast with Calasiris, whose disapproval of this art (3.16) was validated later in the novel by the death of a woman who called back the soul of her dead son and died shortly thereafter (6.15).

[47] Syncellus, *Chronography*, 123.11–12.

[48] See Reichardt 1909, Wallraff et al. 2007, Guignard 2011.

[49] See the comments in Wallraff et al. 2012: xvii–xviii. Unless otherwise noted, all following references to T, F and D are made to the corresponding sections of this edition.

[50] On Africanus' style, see Wallraff et al. 2012: xxv–xxvi and the comments of Vieillefond 1970: 50–52.

Africanus is one of the best examples of a successful client scholar from the Roman Empire.[51] He probably came from Jerusalem, which he called an "ancient fatherland" (*archaia patris*).[52] First known as a courtier of king Abgar the Great of Edessa (179–216 CE),[53] Africanus may subsequently have frequented the Severan court since his *Kestoi* were dedicated to the emperor Alexander. Africanus claimed to have "personally supervised" the construction of a library for the emperor.[54] Africanus also exchanged letters about the authenticity of the Book of Daniel with Origen, who was also in contact with the Severan court through Julia Mammaea, Alexander's mother.[55] Contacts with this court are also suggested by Africanus' successful embassy to Rome for the city of Emmaus in 221.[56]

The Kestoi

Since the *Kestoi* were not preserved in their entirety, it is difficult to judge whether the collection emphasized certain types of recipes over others. The introduction to the seventh book can give us some idea of Africanus' plan:

> It is according to reason or law or fate or chance that affairs turn out as they do, both production and decay, mutation and healing. It is good to know each one of them, thereby gathering from them all a harvest of various kinds of benefit: treatment of maladies, secret knowledge or beauty in speech. These, at least in my estimation, have been accomplished to the best of my modest ability in what precedes and follows.[57]

Preserved fragments cover a broader range of matters. Reflecting the work's diverse subject matter, Georges Syncellus (c. 800 CE) wrote that the *Kestoi* dealt in nine books with the "properties of medical, natural, agricultural and alchemical agents."[58] The most extensive description of the content of the *Kestoi* is found in Michael Psellus' summary of the work:

1. Recipes related to procreation:
    - How to choose the sex of a baby
    - How to induce the production of breast milk
    - How to prevent breasts from swelling with milk after childbirth[59]

---

[51]On Africanus as *pepaideumenos*, see Adler 2004: 547–548.
[52]F10.50–51.
[53]F12.20.
[54]T3, F10.
[55]T5a. See Eusebius, *Ecclesiastical History*, 6.21.3–4.
[56]See Jerome, *On Famous Men*, 63, Eusebius, *Chronography*, 221 CE (=214h Helm).
[57]F12.Pr (trans. Wallraff et al.).
[58]Syncellus, *Chronography*, 439.18–20: Ἀφρικανὸς τὴν ἐννεάβιβλον τῶν Κεστῶν ἐπιγεγραμμένην πραγματείαν ἰατρικῶν καὶ φυσικῶν καὶ γεωργικῶν καὶ χυμευτικῶν περιέχουσαν δυνάμεις Ἀλεξάνδρῳ τούτῳ προσφωνεῖ.
[59]Different recipe with same goal in PGM VII.208–209, *Geoponica*, 8.19 and Pliny, *Natural History*, 26.163.

- Recipe for female contraception
- How to ease labor pains
- How to promote childbirth
2. How to stop bleeding with the bough of a mulberry tree
3. How to dye hair white with litharge
4. How to train one's voice with the help of natural ingredients
5. How to produce gold rust[60]
6. How to make an antidote
7. How to find a thief
8. Agricultural techniques:
   - How to graft a white poplar on a mulberry tree and get white mulberries
   - How to draw certain designs on the pit of a peach to grow a peach tree that produces red peaches[61]
9. How to stop a plague
10. How to prepare artificial wine
11. How to create artificial gemstones[62]
12. How to cure asp bite
13. How to cure cataracts
14. How to make a woman urinate, a man defecate or somebody laugh with the dung or the urine of a mated cow
15. How to make a field fertile again or remove its fertility
16. How to make selenite with dew and moon rays
17. How to keep people drinking all night from getting drunk[63]
18. How to make use of turtles, of the sexual organs of bears and of other animals
19. How to make a slimming cure
20. How to kill parasites on a plant
21. Discussion of the *gorgonion*, a subterranean plant which rises to observe a young woman having intercourse
22. How to make mascara[64]
23. How to bring back virginity in a woman
24. How to put a parasite (*parasitos*) to sleep
25. How to stop having dreams
26. How to facilitate the expulsion of a placenta
27. How to make blue eyes brown

---

[60] Similar recipe in PGM XII.193–204.

[61] Similar recipes are attributed to Democritus in *Geoponica*, 10.14–15.

[62] Recipes for the production of artificial gemstones can also be found in *P.Holm.* and *P.Leid.*

[63] Similar recipe in PGM VII.167–186 and *Geoponica*, 7.31.

[64] Related to the recipes of Pliny (33.102, 107), who mentions how antimony (*stibi*) and *spuma argenti* (called litharge by Dioscorides, 5.87) were used in cosmetics.

28. How to get rid of varicose veins
29. How to make "night-light" (*nuktiphaes*)
30. How to make aphrodisiacs and anaphrodisiacs
31. How to make white hair brown
32. How to make white hair black[65]

It is possible that the version of the *Kestoi* read by Psellus had been augmented with several other recipes during its transmission. It is also possible that he read a different set of recipes. Book 7, for example, was preserved in its entirety in a collection of works on military matters. It deals with topics not discussed by Psellus: armament, covert assaults, surgery, healing techniques, the handling of horses and draft animals and other techniques meant to be used in war. The end of an eighteenth book, preserved by a single third-century papyrus, details the spoken part of the necromantic rite (*nekuia*) of the *Odyssey*, which Africanus presented as the product of his inspiration.[66] Among fragments from the *Geoponica* and other manuscripts less securely attributed to Africanus, we can list a recipe against poisonous snakes (F55), a technique to change the color of horses (so as to steal them without being detected, F61), a discussion on the conversion of measures (F62), another on cinnamon (F75), several recipes concerning the use of dyes cited by authors of Greek alchemy (F69–74), medical recipes (F76–77) and a mention of divinizing a falcon by drowning it (F78).[67]

Considering Africanus' bold claims—e.g. that he could correct "a fault of nature by a technique (*technē*) of nature" (F12.6.21)—or his description of the "Homeric" necromantic incantation (F10), of amulets (e.g. F10), of odd and dangerous contraptions (F12.2.76–87), scholars have assumed that the *Kestoi* could not have been written by a Christian scholar of importance due to the "pagan" or "magical" quality of the compilation.[68] Ancient scholars such as Pliny would most probably have disapproved of the content in a similar way, but there are no reasons to believe that the *Kestoi* would usually have been thought to contain illegitimate rites or techniques. In the extent fragments, Africanus never relied on *mageia*, *goēteia* and cognates to explain the surprising powers of his recipes. When providing explanations, he evoked, rather, his knowledge of the special powers of natural products.[69] Once we look at Africanus primarily as a client scholar working inside

---

[65] See Psellus, Περὶ παραδόξων ἀκουσμάτων, 13–64 in Duffy 1992 (= T7).

[66] F10.48–49: ἅτε κύημα [πο]λυτελέστερον ἔπογκ[ο]ς αὐτὸς ἐνταυθοῖ κατέταξα ("I myself have arranged it here, seeing that I bear within me a very valuable fruit of inspiration"). By presenting himself as "pregnant" (ἔπογκ[ο]ς) with an "embryo" (κύημα), Africanus seems to imply that he had naturally produced the incantation. On the dating of the papyrus, see Wallraff et al. 2012: xxxiii-xxxviii.

[67] A similar practice is found in PGM I.1–64. Robert K. Ritner (1995: 3352, 3370) remarks that this practice was Egyptian and notes several other demotic examples.

[68] For a history of this problem, see Sestili 2015: 23 n. 57, Wallraff et al. 2012: xi-xii.

[69] See F12.10–5 and F12.6.21 with Wallraff 2009: 43–46.

royal and imperial courts and playing according to the rules of scholarly patronage, many apparent contradictions disappear.[70]

In as much as seeing Africanus' authorial identity as professional rather than religious can cut through the false problem of attribution, it still fails to explain why a client scholar of the reputation of Africanus could write about topics that would have been perceived as unscholarly. The necromantic invocation he attributed to Homer (and to himself at the same time) could readily have been identified as *goēteia*. This, however, would be ignoring how Africanus presented the text. Africanus' listing of Odysseus' lost necromantic incantation was not introduced as recipe but rather as a philological note meant to complete the text of the *Odyssey*. The invocation, he claimed, was not so much missing from the received text as from the "original" itself:

> Either this was the way it really stood, and the Poet himself omitted the superfluous (*periergon*) part of the incantation for the sake of the dignity of the subject matter; or the Pisistratids, when they were stitching together the other verses, excised these words, determining them to be incompatible with the verse ordering of the poem.[71]

Africanus' explicit intention was not to provide readers with a recipe but to supplement the defective text of the *Odyssey*. By saying that the passage was *periergon*—here meaning not simply "superfluous" but also "inappropriately inquisitive"—he implicitly recognized that the lines which Homer or the Pisistratids allegedly omitted were somewhat illegitimate.[72] Africanus appears to have operated in an intellectual environment where research into foreign philosophies and text (notably into those of the Hebrew prophets) was a legitimate scholarly pursuit as long as it was kept within the limits of *paideia*.

Africanus' presentation of a sleep-deprivation technique is more revealing in that regard. Known sleep-depriving techniques (*agrupnētika*) from the *Greek Magical Papyri* and from Pliny's Book 30 on the techniques of the *magi* confirm that the "bird of night," referred to by Africanus as "lying at the end in pentagon 9," was in fact the bat (F12.17.34–37). Pliny attributed the following techniques to the *magi*:

> To make sleep possible, [wear] the beak of a heron in the skin of a donkey tied on the forehead. They (i.e. the *magi*) think that the beak by itself has the same effect if it is dipped in wine. Conversely, tying on the dried head of a bat wards off sleep.[73]

[70] For similar arguments, see Adler 2004, 2009, Wallraff 2009. For a reactualization of the problem, see Guignard 2011: 7–9.

[71] F10.45–48 (trans. Wallraff et al. with some modifications).

[72] The use of περίεργος to describe illegitimate pursuits—especially the inquisitive—can be seen in the use of τὰ περίεργα in early Christian texts, see, e.g., *Acts* 19.19. Origen (*Against Celsus*, 2.51.32) used the adjective περίεργος of incantations controlling evil δαίμονες. *P. Yale* 299 also showed the Egyptian prefect of 198/199 CE using the term περιεργία in a letter banning the use of divination. See Rea 1977: 151–156.

[73] Pliny, *Natural History*, 30.140. The ἀγρυπνητικά of PGM IV.2943–2966, VII.652–661 and XII.376–397 also involve bats.

Pliny's book dedicated to the techniques of the *magi* included two more recipes similar to recipes from the *Kestoi*.⁷⁴ Considering that many of Pliny's sources for Book 30 were Greek, it is likely that a well-read audience would have made the association with *mageia*.

Africanus' use of a rudimentary encryption method indicates that he intended his work for an educated audience. In several recipes, Africanus did not spell out words, plants or animals but rather referred to an appendix where notices identifying these words or substances were placed inside geometrical forms, which were in turn identified with musical notations. The appendix was lost but the remaining text of the *Kestoi* indicates that each geometrical form must have been identified with the musical notations mentioned in the recipes. The technique can be exemplified by a recipe for poisonous bread, which required one to mix the remains of two animals previously sealed together in a vessel:

> Let us make bread, which is to nourish the final day of life, from animals that are represented at the end, in pentagon <1>, in which the signs of the proslambanomenos of the Lydian mode are lined up, imperfect zeta and upside-down tau.⁷⁵

Since Greek education is all that was required to decipher Africanus' references, it is unlikely that Africanus used them as an encryption method. The signs could also function as a learned game as Africanus suggested in the case of the *agrupnētikon*, since he implicitly but quite clearly identified one of the animals found in the tables (F.12.17.43–44).

Africanus' Self-Representation

The association of Africanus' *paideia* with *mageia* was reinforced by his self-representation. Africanus took a pro-Roman stance (F12.1.1–5) and indicated that he did not identify ethnically as Greek by saying his people ("we") called the Greek measure unit *chous* a *kabos*, a Semitic term (F62.49).⁷⁶ Calling Jerusalem the *colonia Aelia Capitolina* and describing it as the "fatherland," he appears to have located his origins in Roman Palestine (F10.50–51, see also F75).

Besides naming Egyptian gods in the incantation he supplied for the *Odyssey*, Africanus also affirmed having purchased the sacred book of a fourth-dynasty

---

⁷⁴Compare D27.15–19 with Pliny, 30.91 (stones from the stomach of young swallows stop epilepsy) and D41 with Pliny 30.119 (the brain of a dog in a linen plaster helps against cranial fractures).

⁷⁵F12.2.53–61 (trans. adapted from Wallraff et al.). The second part of the sentence reads: ζῷα ἅπερ ἀνάγραπτα ἐπὶ τέλει κεῖται ἐν πενταγώνῳ <πρώτῳ> ᾧ κατὰ τὸ γραμμοειδὲς ἔγκειται Λυδίου τρόπου προσλαμβανομένου σημεῖα, ζῆτα ἐλλιπὲς καὶ ταῦ ὕπτιον. Other extant examples show that the symbols were always drawn inside or outside (F12.6.25, 11.16–17) of the geometrical shapes, sometimes as a line (here, κατὰ τὸ γραμμοειδὲς), or sometimes in the shape of a "pyramid" (F.12.4.7: κατὰ τὸ πυραμοειδὲς). For the other examples, see F2.106, 4.7, 5.3, 6.25, 9.3, 11.16–17, 12.2.77, 17.44, 61.5.

⁷⁶χόας ὀκτὼ οὓς δὴ "κογγία" λέγουσιν "κάβους" δὲ ἡμεῖς. On the κάβους, see Septuagint, *Kings*, 4.6.25.3 and Epiphanius, *Treatise on Weights and Measures* in Dean 1935: 73b.

pharaoh called *Suphos*.⁷⁷ Showing how to poison wells or the food of an enemy army, he justified his advice by informing readers that the "Eastern barbarians" did not ignore these practices since they themselves committed "vicious acts against attackers."⁷⁸ Africanus explicitly presented himself to a Roman emperor as a broker of "Eastern" techniques. The conclusion of the book on military techniques emphasized his connection with the Edessan court of Abgar and displayed the extraordinary marksmanship of Syrmos "the Scythian," Bardesanēs "the Parthian" and Abgar's son Mannos.⁷⁹

Africanus was presenting himself to Romans as a Greek-educated foreigner from Jerusalem who could show them how to fight those of "inner Asia"⁸⁰ with their own weapons. While it is admittedly impossible to prove that Africanus intended to suggest his knowledge of *mageia*, it is hard not to imagine that he ignored the likelihood that offering secret recipes to the emperor (one of which consisted in a secret poison used by the Parthians) would have made other courtiers suspicious.

CONCLUSION

Africanus' self-representation is a good point at which to stop and sum up the argument. The previous chapter showed that figures of learned sorcerers emphasized a scholar's knowledge of *mageia* or *paignia*—i.e. forms of learning that were peripheral or antithetical to *paideia*. Like the mercenary scholars of Lucian, Apion, Simon and Pancrates were not simply represented as sorcerers but also as scholars who misused their Greek education, e.g. by indulging in the "overly curious" (*periergos*) use of necromancy for philological purposes; in the choice of *paignia* or tricks over learned conversation at dinner; in the use of love-charms instead of wise match-making (as in the case of Erasistratus); in flattery instead of counsel; in opting not for the "hard" road to rhetorical excellence but the "new" and "easy" one.

Up to the present chapter, the search for figures of client scholars depended almost entirely on polemical texts. This should not be surprising considering that teaching contracts are absent from papyrological evidence and that scholarly patronage was normally described as friendship. Plutarch's self-representation in the *Symposiacs* showed that the ideal client scholar and philosopher avoided discussing topics that could potentially associate him with *mageia*. Calasiris' exploitation of the stereotypical expectations of aristocrats illustrates the wider diffusion of the

---

[77] Africanus, *Chronography*, F46.53–55 in Wallraff et al. 2007.
[78] F12.2.93–99: μὴ ἀμαθεῖς δέ τις ἐς ταῦτα νομίσῃ τοὺς τῆς ἀνατολῆς βαρβάρους· καὶ αὐτοὶ πολλάκις τοὺς ἐπερχομένους κακουργοῦσιν.
[79] F12.20: τὰ ἄνω τῆς Ἀσίας ἔθνη.
[80] F12.1.1–5.

literary figure of the learned sorcerer as well as its possible rehabilitation. Finally, Africanus is the closest representative of the kind of client scholar who might have inspired the figure of the learned sorcerer. He was a relatively well-known scholar in his time, a client of Abgar of Edessa and perhaps of Alexander Severus. The content of his *Kestoi* and his self-representation as a purveyor of special poisons used by the eastern enemies of the Romans would certainly have made some think that he played the role of *magos* for the emperor.

Representations of client scholars as learned sorcerers suggest in turn that emphasizing one's extraordinary powers could attract the attention of some patrons. We should not rule out the possibility that some patrons were interested in hiring professional curse-makers and diviners. Assuming that the complaints voiced by Lucian and Juvenal were based on an actual change in the nature of scholarly patronage in Rome during the first centuries CE, we could also try to read their texts by translating their value judgments into observations. We could then say that Roman patrons were hiring certain individuals (who came from the eastern parts of the Empire, following Juvenal) in lieu of specialists of *paideia* precisely because these individuals offered intellectual products that were not theoretically part of *paideia*. What could this rival *paideia* have consisted in? Juvenal produces a long list of characters, most of whom appear to have been specialized artists and artisans of different types. Lucian also pointed out that playing the role of *magoi*, *manteis* or writing erotic poetry was likely to ingratiate a scholar with his patron. *Mageia* reappears insistently among the texts studied in chapters 3 and 4 as a form of anti-learning. As a matter of fact, the respectable status of *mageia* in the work of several post-Hellenistic philosophers suggests that it was likely that patrons who followed the development of Greek philosophy in the first centuries of the Roman Empire would be interested in "philosophical" *mageia*.

There is evidence that this movement was met with resistance. Diogenes Laertius, our main source for the kind of narratives found in Sotion's books on the succession of the philosophers, was also an opponent of the theory that Greek philosophy ultimately derived from eastern philosophies.[81] To a certain extent, the limits of *paideia* must have been contested at all periods, but we can assume that the lists of "approved" (*enkrithentes*) poets, orators, historians and philosophers that were compiled in the Hellenistic age were stable.[82] Speaking strictly in terms of literary respectability, it remains difficult to explain how foreign authors could acquire a status similar to that of Homer or Plato.

Lucian made a simple point that can provide part of the answer: unlike the ideal (i.e. aristocratic) scholar, the client scholar was more likely to suit his work to the expectations of patrons. While those who cared to maintain the status of scholar needed to show some respect for the norms of *paideia*, an aristocrat with-

---

[81] Diogenes Laertius, *Lives of the Philosophers*, prol.
[82] On these lists, see Pfeiffer 1968: 203–208.

out scholarly pretensions could afford idiosyncratic or anomalous scholarly interests. Consequently, by selling their work to patrons, client scholars also sold part of their function of gatekeeper, i.e. their right to decide what should and what should not be considered *paideia*. In other words, scholarly patronage could help introduce and transpose the scholarly interests of patrons into normative *paideia* whether their interests followed these norms or not. By accepting the challenge of being the "friend" of the powerful, client scholars of relatively modest origins could also secure or enhance their role as producers and reproducers of *paideia*.

If the influence of patrons on the gatekeeping role of scholars brought foreign traditions inside *paideia*, we can expect that scholars who participated in this change faced the disapproval of some of their peers. Forms of learning presented by these scholars were also likely to be perceived as incompatible with the preservation of strict and coherent standards of education and distinction. This can also explain why some used the stereotype of the learned sorcerer in an attempt to delegitimize new doctrines or tendencies that were perceived as potential game-changers. In sum, the continuing presence of the stereotype of the learned sorcerer in late antique sources suggests the persistent fear that client scholars could pervert a given scholarly tradition. Scholarly patronage is also likely to have played a role in legitimating new forms of scholarship within the domain of *paideia*. This last proposition can be confirmed by contextualizing the work of Zosimus of Panopolis.

CHAPTER 5

Zosimus of Panopolis and Ancient Greek Alchemy

The purpose of this chapter is to date the appearance of alchemy in antiquity by looking at texts mentioning or juxtaposing gold transmutation and soteriology, two concepts combined in the work of Zosimus and specific to alchemy. The ancient term for alchemy, *chēmeia* and variant forms, first appeared in non-alchemical texts and in other literature in the sixth century CE. Analyzing the uses of the term *chēmeutēs* and variants shows that the only term that could have designated an alchemist was rare and practically nonexistent in the Greek alchemical corpus (part 1). Gold transmutation is first considered as a potential reality in a panegyric written by Themistius to the emperor Valens (367 CE). A later evocation of the idea shows that it could be linked with arguments attempting to prove the possibility of a transformation of all matter during the resurrection. Contemporary papyri (from Nag Hammadi) as well as Gnostic and Hermetic literature suggest that processes meant to change the color of textiles, stones and metals served as a metaphor for the transformation of the self in the third century (part 2). Looking at explicit and implicit mentions of the afterlife in the works of Zosimus shows that his soteriology implied a similar transformation of the body and that his concern with the afterlife and the role played by matter in reaching the afterlife was shared by many late antique scholars (part 3). A major difference between Zosimus and other philosophers and theologians lay in the choice of source text. The next chapter will explain why he thought that tinctorial recipes concealed divine knowledge and that they were amenable to allegorical interpretation. Looking into the reasons why Zosimus wrote alchemical commentaries will bring the analysis back to the role of scholarly patronage in fostering and legitimizing peripheral and delegitimized types of scholarship.

1. REFERENCES TO ALCHEMY IN LATE ANTIQUE LITERATURE

Greek alchemy (*chēmeia*)[1] consisted in techniques called "tinctures" or "dyes" (*baphai*) used in the production or falsification of four categories of luxury products: gold, silver, gemstones and dyes.[2] These recipes took their source in ancient metallurgical and coloring techniques, many of which probably came from the Egyptian sacerdotal art of consecrating statues.[3] While the earliest Greek alchemical text is dated to the first century CE,[4] the practice of commenting on alchemical recipes was a late antique invention and its earliest representative is Zosimus of Panopolis.

A passage from John of Antioch's *Chronography* (c. 610–626 CE) now preserved in the *Suda* mentioned that Diocletian burned "books on the *chēmeia* of gold and silver" written by ancient Egyptians.[5] Assuming that nothing was added to the quotation of John of Antioch's *Chronography*, this would be the earliest attestation of a term for alchemy found outside of the Greek alchemical corpus.[6] The first use of a word directly related to *chēmeia* appeared about fifty years before in the *Chronicle* of John Malalas (c. 550 CE). Malalas reported that a certain John Isthmeus of Amida, "a *cheimeutēs* and a terrible cheat," was known to have

---

[1] Also written χημία, χυμεία and χυμία. See Halleux 1979: 45 n. 15. The form χειμεία is also attested. See, e.g., *Suda* X 227. For introductions to Greek alchemy, see Mertens 2006: 205–230 and Martelli 2016: 217–231.

[2] On this subdivision, see Martelli 2013: 13–18, Martelli 2014b: 1–22.

[3] A few texts suggest a connection between alchemy and Egyptian rituals for the consecration of statues: Syriac texts of Zosimus edited and translated by Martelli 2017: 202–220 (see ch. 6.2 below). Clement of Alexandria (*Protrepticus*, 4.48.4–6) reports a story told by the Stoic Athenodorus of Cana (or "Calvus," first century BCE) according to whom the pharaoh Sesostris asked a Greek artisan to make a status of Osiris. The Greek artisan mixed stones and metals together and colored the mixture dark blue, or "nearly black," as Clement says. The blackening of metal was a pre-existing feature of Egyptian statue making and metallurgy (Pliny, *Natural History*, 33.131). A Syriac text attributed to Zosimus discusses the blackening of copper, a technique used as early as the nineteenth century BCE in Egypt. See Martelli 2014b: 15. These reports suggest that Egyptian techniques used to color statues found their way into Greek alchemical literature. According to Philippe Derchain and François Daumas, inscriptions about the "atelier des orfèvres" from Dendera transmit the content of a book that dealt with the creation of statues, the ritual of the opening of the mouth and the act of "giving birth" (*msi*) to the gods (translation suggested by François Daumas). See Daumas 1980: 109–118 and Derchain 1990: 219–242. That gold was related to a ritual meant to give life to gods (i.e. statues) was most probably related to the vivifying powers attributed to the metal. See Daumas 1956: 9–13. See also Martelli 2013: 63–69.

[4] See Martelli 2013: 29–31.

[5] See John of Antioch, fr. 191 Mariev (= *Suda* Δ 1156, repeated at X 280). On a possible importance of his reign and of the seventh century for the diffusion of alchemy, see Mertens 2006: 220–222.

[6] The Ἐπιμερισμοί (*Partitiones*) attributed to Aelius Herodianus mention the words χειμεύω, χείμευσις and χειμία but no passage of the work can be safely attributed to Herodianus the second-century grammarian. See Dyck 1993: 792–793.

tricked bankers in Antioch by selling counterfeit gold. Brought before Anastasius (r. 491–518 CE), Isthmeus offered the emperor a horse-bit made of solid gold (*holochruson*) with a muzzle covered with pearls. The emperor believed this to be another trick and sent Isthmeus to die in jail.[7]

A search on the *Thesaurus Linguae Graecae* shows that it was particularly unusual to use the term *cheimeutēs* and variants as a title.[8] Besides occurrences found in the anecdote about Isthmeus, which all appear to be derived from Malalas, the term was also used by Anastasius of Sinai (seventh century) in his commentary on the book of Genesis.[9] Commenting on the mention of gold and precious stones in paradise, Anastasius of Sinai asserted that the scriptures "did not want to teach us to become goldsmiths (*chrusochoos*), gem-cutters (*lithourgos*) or *cheimeutas* of stones inlaid with gold."[10] The first two crafts referred to the gold and the stones mentioned in the commented text while the art of the *cheimeutēs* may have referred to the use of enamel.[11]

The first attestations of Syriac and Arabic transliterations of *chēmeia* are dated to the eighth century.[12] Zosimus was mentioned outside of the alchemical corpus

---

[7] See John Malalas, *Chronography*, 16.5 (= 395 Dindorf, 323 Thurn), Georges Cedrenus, *Compendium historiarum*, 1.629.9, Constantine VII, *De ceremoniis aulae Byzantinae*,, 1.163.8 and Theophanes Confessor, *Chronographia*, 150.12. All sources appear to have derived their version from Malalas. See Letrouit 1995: 56–57. Mischa Meier and Johannes Thurn (2009) suggested that this John Isthmeus might be the same as the Ioannes *scholasticus* of Amida mentioned by Pseudo-Zachariah, *Ecclesiastical History*, 7.1 (this is the Ioannes 39 of PLRE II, 603), who prophesied that Anastasius would later become emperor.

[8] Textual searches in the TLG (May 2018) for the root χιμ(μ)-, χειμμ-, χυμμ- or χημμ- show that Χημμι, Χιμμι and Χιμνουθ(ι) were names (or words) used in invocations (see Weinstock 1953: 9.2, 161.16 and PGM IV.2019, XVI.12, XIXa.8). Searches for χειμευ- brought the title of χειμευτής as found in the reports about John Isthmeus discussed above. No term referring to a titles was found when searching for χημευ-. A search for χυμευ- showed that Theophanes Confessor, mentioned above, called John Isthmeos an ἀνὴρ χυμευτής. It also brought up the only variant of χειμευτής found in the Greek alchemical corpus (see n. 32 below). Archives from monasteries on Mount Athos also show that Χυμευτή and Χυμευτός could be used as proper names much later in the 14th and the 15th centuries. See Oikonomidès 1984: 310.62, Guillou et al. 1977: 150.198, Kravari 1991: 196.64.

[9] Anastasius Sinaita, *In Hexaemeron*, 8.3.2–6, commenting on *Genesis*, 2.11–12.

[10] *Id.*, 8.3.6: οὐ γὰρ δὴ χρυσοχόους ἡμᾶς καὶ λιθουργοὺς καὶ χειμευτὰς χρυσοκολλήτων λίθων ἀπεργάσασθαι ἡ γραφὴ βουλομένη καὶ παιδεύουσα ταῦτά φησιν.

[11] I am informed by Shannon Steiner that the adjective χειμευτ- in texts from the ninth century CE and later can refer to enameled works (e.g. in the common construction χειμευτὰ ἔργα). See e.g. Constantine VII, *De cerimoniis aulae Byzantinae*, 2.581.9 Reiske. For similar uses, see e.g. Trapp 1971: 5.2227: δύο εἰκόνας χυμευτὰς ἁγίων Θεοδώρων; Διήγησις περὶ τῆς Ἁγίας Σοφίας, 17.13 in Preger 1901: κίονας … ὁλοχρύσους μετὰ λίθων πολυτελῶν καὶ χυμεύσεων. See Kondakov 1892: 70–71, 101–105 (http://nrs.harvard.edu/urn-3:DOAK.RESLIB:11337459?n=105), and Shannon Steiner's forthcoming dissertation, *Byzantine Enamel and the Aesthetics of Technological Power, Ninth to Twelfth Centuries*. It is consequently possible that Anastasios was referring to enameling when mentioning the χειμευτὰς χρυσοκολλήτων λίθων.

[12] See Martelli 2014a: 191–214.

and associated with *chēmeia* from that point on.[13] The alchemical compilation of the *Marcianus Graecus* 299 and a few entries in the *Suda* show that alchemical texts were considered c. 1000 CE as a discrete body of doctrines that concentrated on the preparation of gold and silver.[14]

Since the word *cheimeutēs* implies the existence of a term like *chēmeia*, we can further assume that alchemy was known when Malalas wrote his *Chronography* around 550 CE. However, the term *cheimeutēs* does not appear to correspond very well with the modern "alchemist." Like almost all alchemical writers, Zosimus was not called a *cheimeutēs* nor was he designated by any professional title more specific than *philosophos*. There are good reasons to believe that the uses of the term *cheimeutēs* referred primarily to artisans who imitated or counterfeited gold or jewelry.

The counterfeiting of gold and silver was a reality for all those who used coinage. Roman silver coinage was drastically debased in the period 50–300 CE. Techniques were used to hide these measures but the debasement of coinage was common knowledge.[15] In some cases, the techniques used to mint debased coinage appear to have been similar to those found in alchemical recipes.[16] Late antique goldsmiths also attracted suspicion.[17] In late antique works of literature, they are seen mainly in cautionary tales such as that of Isthmeus. For instance, John Moschus' *Spiritual Meadow* (c. 600 CE) tells the story of an aristocrat who brought a mass of gold to a goldsmith to be worked into the form of a cross that would be given to a church. Discovering that the weight of the cross was greater than that of the original mass of gold, the aristocrat accused the goldsmith of embezzlement. In fact, the goldsmith's apprentice revealed that he had added some of his own gold to the mass of metal, knowing that the cross would be offered to a church. Recognizing a faithful Christian in the apprentice, the aristocrat decided to make him his heir.[18] With two different endings, the story of Isthmeus and of

---

[13] George Syncellus, *Chronography*, 14.14, Photius, *Bibliotheca*, 170 (117a.28–29 Bekker): τῶν χειμευτικῶν Ζωσίμου λόγων (Θηβαῖος δ' ἦν οὗτος Πανοπολίτης).

[14] *Suda* X 227 and 280: ἡ τοῦ ἀργύρου καὶ χρυσοῦ κατασκευή. The *Suda* also has an entry for Zosimus of Panopolis (who, it says, is "from Alexandria"): Z 168 and other articles connected with alchemy: A 559, Δ 250, 1156. For later sources, see Mertens 2006: 224–228.

[15] Walker 1978. On debasement of coinage being public knowledge, see the *Lex Cornelia de falsis* (81 BCE) in the *Digest*, 48.10.1.8, Pliny, *Natural History*, 33.312.

[16] Keyser 1995–1996: 209–234. Studies showed the trace of mercury in debased silver coinage, implying that it was used for amalgam plating. See Vlachou et al. 2002: II9.2.1–9. Zosimus also mentioned that a recipe could be used on coins (MA 8.62–63).

[17] Like other ancient crafts, the work of ancient goldsmiths is not well known. For the status of goldsmiths in late antiquity, see Jones 1964: 863–864. For mentions of goldsmiths on papyri or stone, see Reil 1913: 50–59, Burford 1972: 90, 180–182, Ogden 1990: 93–103. Hübner 2005: 92 noted epigraphic evidence for twelve goldsmiths in the Cilician town of Corycos for the period between the fourth and the seventh centuries CE, one of whom was a πρεσβύτερος.

[18] John Moschus, *Spiritual Meadow*, 200.

the goldsmith apprentice tapped into the fear that those dealing in gold might take advantage of their clients. Closer to ancient lived experience, a letter written by an Egyptian goldsmith to a client who accused him of fraud (probably from Heracleopolis in the fifth century CE) also exemplifies the common suspicion that goldsmiths could debase the precious metals handed in by customers.[19]

Symbolically, gold was connected to imitation and falsification. Working with gold also appears as a quintessential act of deception in three texts from the second and the fourth century CE. According to the *Interpretation of Dreams* attributed to Artemidorus of Daldis (second century CE), to witness the casting of gold in a dream signified trickery because of the "salary" or "cut" taken by goldsmiths for their work (*ta hupokeimena tōn ergōn*). The text mentioned that dreaming of molding, of wood-engraving (*puxographein*) or of the working of metal—and of the making of statues—was good for "adulterers, orators, those forging documents and deceivers in general" since these arts were all considered as representing "what does not exist as if it existed."[20]

A similar association was used by Gregory of Nyssa in 380 CE to attack Aetius of Antioch (c. 310–367 CE), the originator of the heteroousian (or Neo-Arian) doctrine. According to Philostorgius, a historian sympathetic to the heteroousian movement, Aetius worked as a goldsmith at night to support his work as theologian.[21] Noting with disapprobation that Aetius worked as a "foundry worker" (*kamineutēs*), Gregory of Nyssa used the opportunity to associate his teachings with common suspicions concerning the goldsmith's art.[22] Aetius allegedly tricked a woman who had left a piece of jewelry for repair and substituted for it a gilded piece of bronze using a "superficial tincture" (*di' epipolaiou baphēs*). "The woman was tricked by the appearances," Gregory stated, concluding that "through the 'sophisms' of the art," Aetius "was good at cheating those he dealt with in metal-working as well."[23] Other accusations of sophistry directed against Aetius also compared him to a parasite and to a mercenary scholar.[24] The image used by Gregory of Nyssa might have been a relatively common rhetorical figure since Irenaeus compared true and false theology to real and false silver or emeralds.[25]

---

[19] See *Papyrus Erzherzog Rainer* (Vienna: Hollinek, 1983) No. 161 (= *Corpus Papyrorum Raineri*, 33 Vols. [Vienna: Hollinek, 1895–2015] 5.22). See http://papyri.info/ddbdp/p.rain.cent;;161. German translation available in Kreuzsaler et al. 2010: 152–153.

[20] Artemidorus, *Interpretation of Dreams*, 1.51.32–37.

[21] See Philostorigus, *Ecclesiastical History*, 3.15–20.

[22] Gregory of Nyssa, *Against Eunomius*, 1.38.

[23] *Id.*, 1.40: δεινὸς γὰρ ἦν καὶ τῇ χαλκευτικῇ διὰ τῶν τῆς τέχνης σοφισμάτων τοὺς χρωμένους παραλογίσασθαι.

[24] See Gregory of Nyssa, *Against Eunomius*, 1.44, 1.48, Theodoret, *Ecclesiastical History*, 2.28.9, Sozomen, *Ecclesiastical History*, 3.15.7.

[25] Irenaeus, *Against Heresies*, prol., 1.20–27. This image might go back as far as Plato's image of a touchstone that could be used to test souls (*Gorgias*, 486d). When discussing the heteroousian doctrine, Epiphanius, *Panarion*, 76.2.8–10 used the same comparison to illustrate how the likeness of the

In the *Mathesis* (c. 334 CE), Firmicus Maternus associated the four techniques traditionally connected with alchemy—the use of *baphai* (dyes) for the coloring or manufacturing of gold, silver, gems and textile dyes—with the working of metal and the art of making statues under the same astrological events. Those born when the moon moves from Mars to Venus, Firmicus wrote, make adulterers and people preoccupied by sexual activities and seduction. The same astrological conjunction also produces people dealing in seduction and sensual pleasure: "they will practice arts, either of painting, perfumery, or work with jewels or pearls; often they will become dyers or merchants in metals ... or they may be innkeepers, or prepare things necessary for food and drink in a successful business" (4.11.2). When the same conjunction implied Venus with Mercury rather than Mars, celebrated orators, poets and inventors were supposed to be born. Again, the trades described generally involved seduction, imitation and care for the body. As examples, Firmicus listed "discoverers of paints or colors or medicines," "workers in precious stones" and those "working with their own skill on costly tunics." Finally, the same astrological event was also thought to produce other professionals dealing in imitation and sensual pleasures: organ players, actors, dancers and singers (4.14.17).

Firmicus came closer to conceptualizing alchemy as a whole when describing the effect of the waning moon moving during the day toward Venus on the Midheaven or on any house except the tenth one:

> This combination ... makes natives of mediocre talents and those working in metal. Or they may be furriers, perfumers, or polishers of precious stones, or those who give stones a different color by using various types of pigments; it produces adorners, sculptors or makers of images/statues; it makes those who sing sacred songs in temples or temple pipe-players as well as those who know heavenly secrets or who easily learn hidden and secret things and make a living from this.[26]

This last list of associations implies a selection of techniques similar to that found in the *Book of Enoch* (cosmetics, the preparation of metals, precious stones and tinctures) and more precisely to those found in Zosimus' version of the myth

---

components of the trinity did not entail their identity: "Silver is like tin too, gold is like bronze and lead like iron, and precious stones are imitated by glass; and likeness does not show nature, but resemblance." Aetius may have used metallurgical metaphors to discuss theological concepts, as did the "Sethians" before him. See *Refutation of All Heresies*, 5.21.1–6 and Burns 2015, Charron and Painchaud 2001.

[26] Firmicus Maternus, *Mathesis*, 4.14.20: *Si vero in ceteris geniturae locis fuerit ista coniunctio, mediocres in facultatibus facit et qui artes metallicas exercere consueverint. Facit plerumque coriarios et qui aromata mercari consueverint, facit etiam eos politores pretiosarum gemmarum vel qui gemmis ex vario pigmentorum genere aliam speciem coloris adpingant, aut ornatores aut sculptores simulacrorum aut fabricatores efficiet aut in templis sacra carmina precantes aut tibicines templorum faciet et qui habeant rerum caelestium notionem vel qui sciant secreta caelestia vel qui res absconsas et abditas facili ratione perdiscant, ut ex his occasionibus vitae illis subsidia quaerantur.* Trans. Bram modified.

since both he and Firmicus connected secrecy with a similar group of practices. In contrast, those born when the moon is waning and moving during the day toward Venus on Midheaven or in the tenth house will be "builders of temples or consecrators of shrines, or they will be temple attendants or chief priests, with important duties."[27]

The conjunction is obviously connected to the kind of work done at temples: the creation or preparation of images/statues (*ornatores aut sculptores simulacrorum aut fabricatores*),[28] musicians singing or playing sacred songs and the knowledge of "heavenly secrets" (*secreta caelestia*) or of secret things. The contrast with the other similar conjunctions makes the connection with temples clearer. While the first conjunction mentioned produces staff attending to the work done in temples, the second creates individuals involved in the same kind of activities but with more important responsibilities. The description of the skills of the first group also indicate they are similar to those that were involved with alchemy. While all this is admittedly not a proof that Firmicus conceptualized these skills as one single category of techniques, namely alchemy—if so, we could expect him to have given it a name[29]—it shows that he assembled practices to form an astrological type that bore many similarities to the characteristics that collected around the terms *chēmeia* and *cheimeutēs*: the working of metals (especially for the making of statues), the coloring of gems and the knowledge of "heavenly secrets." Adding to this suggestion, Firmicus is also the only source outside of the alchemical corpus to attest the common alchemical saying that "(a) nature is defeated by another nature."[30]

The paradigmatic quality of the goldsmiths' tales told by Malalas, Moschus and those who repeated the story of Isthmeus also appears to have gained salience by tapping into anxieties about wealth, gold and counterfeiting. We can conclude that the term *cheimeutēs* was applied to Isthmeus in a context where the working of gold and the use of tinctures (*baphai*) was usually vilified and used to represent other acts of deception.

Several conclusions can be derived from the preceding. The notion of *chēmeia*, first found in a work by Zosimus c. 300 CE, spread to non-alchemical literature during the three following centuries. The term *chēmeia* first appeared in non-alchemical literature in the work of John of Antioch, c. 600 CE. Malalas' use of

---

[27] *Id.*, 4.14.19: *Si vero per diem minuta lumine ad Venerem feratur et <in> MC. vel in decimo ab horoscopo loco fuerit ista coniunctio, sacri certaminis palmas coronasque largitur aut sacris certaminibus facit esse praepositos aut templorum fabricatores aut simulacrorum consecratores facit aut certe neocoros aut principes sacerdotum aut magna in templis officia tractantes.*

[28] For similar expressions, all clearly related to the making of the statues of gods, see *Mathesis*, 3.5.33.

[29] The genethlialogical link between the moon in the house of Saturn and the *scientia alchemica* found in *Mathesis*, 3.19 is a medieval interpolation. See Diels 1965: 121–122.

[30] See Firmicus Maternus, *Mathesis*, 4.22.2 (*natura alia natura vincitur*) who attributed the saying to Nechepso, also known as the author of the second-century BCE *Astrologoumena*.

the term *cheimeutēs* suggests that educated readers would have known something about *chēmeia* half a century before that date.

As already noted, the term *cheimeutēs* first appeared in the works of Malalas and Anastasius of Sinai and referred to somebody involved with precious objects made of gold and/or gemstones. Considering that this title is a cognate of *chēmeia*, it is likely that it referred to a practitioner of alchemical recipes. The term is found only once in the Greek alchemical corpus and appears in a treatise on alchemy and music by an "anonymous philosopher," probably writing in the eighth or ninth century CE.[31] Concluding his treatise, he quoted a recipe attributed to "the first *chum(m)eutēs*."[32] Except for this single occurrence of the term in the corpus, all authors of Greek alchemy are called *philosophoi*. We can conclude that the use of the term *cheimeutēs* to designate authors of alchemical texts was exceptional while Anastasius and Malalas used it pejoratively to refer to individuals making use of the imitative techniques associated with *chēmeia*.

2. GOLD TRANSMUTATION IN NON-ALCHEMICAL LITERATURE

While references to basic metallurgical processes are fairly common in ancient and late antique texts, the mention of gold transmutation is rare.[33] To my knowledge, there are only three texts discussing this idea and they are all late antique. These three short passages strengthen the hypothesis that there was no term for, and perhaps no clear concept of, a practitioner or commentator of alchemical recipes as the tradition was taking shape in late antiquity.

Themistius

In a speech dated to 367 CE, Themistius wrote to praise emperor Valens' use of moderation in stopping the rebellion of Procopius and for forgiving those who rallied with him. In as much as he had transformed enemies into friends, Themistius claimed, Valens was comparable to Circe, Medea, Xerxes and Autoly-

---

[31] See Letrouit 1995: 63.

[32] CAAG 3.441.21.

[33] For examples, see *Ezekiel*, 22.17–22 and *Jeremiah*, 6.27–30 (description of smelting/parting of metals, processes which are compared to the purification of Jerusalem), Plato, *Statesman*, 303e (the act of distinguishing between categories compared to the parting of gold from other substances), Aristotle, *Meteorologica*, 3–4 and Theophrastus, *On Stones* (production of stones and metals in the earth; gold-testing), Dioscorides, *De Materia Medica*, 5 (on various mineral substances and their uses), Strabo, 3.12–14 (gold mining and parting), Diodorus Siculus, 2.52 (natural production of stones in the earth), Seneca, *Letters to Lucilius*, 90.33 (coloring of stones), Vitruvius, *De architectura*, 7.8.1–4, 7.9.4 and Pliny, 30.32, 33.64–65 (use of mercury in refining; see also Pliny, 33–37 *passim* for various substances and their uses), *Anthologia Graeca*, 6.92 (description of a goldsmith's tools and activities). See also Irby-Massie and Keyser 2002: 226–254.

cus—legendary figures who were all credited with powers of transformation.[34] Valens, Themistius added, could have subdued all rebels without any bloodshed if men could have invented "a technique to change bronze into silver or silver into gold."[35] However, unlike Xerxes and the others, he used a divine power that was not a form of rivalry with nature.[36]

Proclus

Gold transmutation is also described as an unlikely way to reproduce the work of nature in Proclus' *Commentary to Plato's* Republic (c. 450 CE):

> Those who prepare astronomical tables (*parapēgmata*) with the help of calculations imitate nature, which was created "over there" (i.e. before being), before calculations and before thoughts. Also, nature produces the simple (i.e. unmixed) species of gold before any of the mixing of species mentioned by those who claim to make gold.[37]

To calculate the movements of the stars, Proclus argued, astronomers combined horizontal and vertical movements but could not replicate the movement of the stars just as they occurred. Nature rather produced these movements all at once "without thinking." In a more tangible way, Proclus argued, the same was true of gold. The implication was that gold could not be produced by the combination of elements.[38]

Looking into Plato's theory of metals can help flesh out the argument's implications. Corrosion, Plato wrote in the *Timaeus* (58d–59c), was the process by which particles of earth separated from the particles of water composing metals. This implied that all corroding metals contained earth and, conversely, that non-corroding metals (gold and silver) were solely made of water particles. This is also why Plato called gold a "class made of a single species" (*monoeides genos*)—i.e. a natural species made of a single element. Echoing this theory, Proclus called gold a "simple species" (*eidos hen*).[39] The logic of Proclus' argument was that one would

---

[34] Themistius, *Orations* 7, 145.12–26. The mention of Xerxes probably refers to his crossing on foot of the Hellespont (and hubristic attempt to turn the sea into a slave: Herodotus, *Histories*, 7.35), presented by Themistius as a transformation of "sea and land." Autolycus is a proverbial thief (*Odyssey*, 10.254) said by Ovid to have been able to make white black and black white (*Metamorphoses*, 11.311–314).

[35] *Id.*, 146.1–11.

[36] *Id.*, 145.26–146.1.

[37] 2.234.14–19.

[38] On this passage, see Viano 1996: 202–206.

[39] Aristotle similarly described gold as the only metal that did not contain earth although he claimed that metals were formed by humid exhalations rather than water (*Meteorologica*, 3.378b1–5). The theory that metals were essentially water also needs to be assumed from Proclus' claim that the influence of astral bodies determined the type of metal produced by water crystallizing under the earth. See Proclus, *Commentary to the Timaeus*, 1.43.1–21. See also his *Commentary to the First Book of Euclid's Elements*, 105.16–18.

never manage to produce gold by mixing elements since gold was not a composite but rather, a substance solely composed of particles of water. Following this theory, gold-making would have been possible through the removal of the elementary earth found in corroding metals, not by the mixing of composite substances.

Aeneas of Gaza

Aeneas of Gaza, a younger contemporary of Proclus, a Christian and a professor of rhetoric, provides the third late antique attestation of the notion of gold transmutation found outside of the alchemical corpus.[40] In the *Theophrastus*, published toward the end of the fifth century CE, Aeneas dramatized a philosophical discussion between Euxitheos, a former student of the Platonist Hierocles, Theophrastus (the Peripatetic philosopher) and Aegyptus. The first part of the dialogue ends with a refutation of the doctrine of reincarnation (4–42) and the second with a defense of the doctrine of resurrection (52–66). The two sections are bridged by the description of a radical eschatology in which the world would be transformed into an incorruptible version of itself (43.10–15).

To defend this theory, Euxitheos compared the transformation of the resurrected body with other forms of transformations. Among several examples, he proposed a thought experiment in which a bronze statue of Achilles would be cut down into pieces. Imagining that "the wise craftsman" (*ho sophos dēmiourgos*) had melted and recast all the pieces while at the same time turning the bronze into gold "thanks to some wisdom and power," Euxitheos remarked that the new statue would still be "an Achilles." Just as "the wise craftsman" could change the metal of the statue, Euxitheos added, the creator of the world would make the bodies of the chosen to be "pure, light and immortal" (59.19–25).

Euxitheos' second example strengthened the comparison by demoting the demiurgic figure to that of a human craftsman:

> Change of matter to a better state is not implausible, for among us too, experts in materials, taking silver and tin, making their form disappear, melting them down together and coloring them, and so changing the matter into something grander, have produced excellent gold.[41]

This surprising claim might actually refer to cementation, a parting technique principally used to separate gold from silver. While the cupellation technique was used to separate gold and silver from other metals, it could not separate gold and silver. Before the discovery of gold-dissolving acids, the cementation technique

---

[40] On Aeneas, see Champion 2014: 9–11.
[41] 62.26–29: Καὶ οὐκ ἀπίθανος ἡ πρὸς τὸ κρεῖττον τῆς ὕλης μεταβολή, ἐπεὶ καὶ παρ' ἡμῖν οἱ περὶ τὴν ὕλην σοφοί, ἄργυρον καὶ καττίτερον παραλαβόντες καὶ τὸ εἶδος ἀφανίσαντες καὶ συγχωνεύσαντες καὶ χρώσαντες, ἐπὶ τὸ σεμνότερον μεταβαλόντες τὴν ὕλην, χρυσὸν κάλλιστον ἐποίησαν (trans. Dillon and Russell).

appears to have been the only one used in the parting of gold and silver.[42] The ancient process of cementation as it was applied to gold parting consisted in combining some gold and silver alloy with salt and other substances inside a closed ceramic pot. Under intense heat, the chlorine in the salt reacts with the silver and forms silver chloride, which is absorbed by the porous walls of the pot.[43] The fact that Diodorus of Sicily and Pliny reported this technique suggests that it must have been relatively common c. 100 BCE–100 CE.[44]

Diodorus' reported that the artisans involved in this process found gold in the bottom of the jar and nothing else. A modern reproduction of the technique described by Diodorus showed that this was possible provided that one ignored all ingredients from the recipe except for the alloy and the salts.[45] This suggests that misinterpretation or misrepresentation of a similar technique could have been at the origin of the claims Proclus attacked and which Aeneas' character Euxitheos presented as a fact, i.e. that gold could be produced by mixing metals together.

In sum, the techniques involved in the purification of precious metals—known from archaeology and from Diodorus' *Historical Library*—could explain how the notion of gold transmutation could receive some evidential basis. However, it does not explain why Aeneas chose it to form part of Euxitheos' argument. In this case the notion of gold transmutation acquired salience because it could be used to argue for the transformative resurrection of the body.

The notion of gold transmutation appears to have preceded that of the *cheimeutēs*. As it appears in Malalas and Anastasius, this term did not refer to individuals who thought they could transmute substances into gold. They rather used *cheimeutēs* pejoratively to refer to individuals dealing with gold or gemstones (or perhaps with enameling). Considering that only one author of alchemical texts ever used this term and that these authors referred to each other as philosophers, there is no evidence that authors of alchemical texts were recognized as a group of scholars distinct from that of philosophers before the use of the term *cheimeutēs* by the Anonymous Philosopher in the eighth or ninth century CE. Overall, the evidence suggests that authors of alchemical texts such as Zosimus represented themselves as philosophers rather than alchemists.

---

[42] See Pliny, 33.84 (the same process is evoked at 68–69), Diodorus of Sicily, 3.14, Strabo, 3.2.8. See Craddock et al. 1998: 111–121 and Forbes 1964: 172–176.

[43] On cementation, see Forbes 1964: 175–176, Craddock 2010: 115–119, 285.

[44] Pliny, *Natural History*, 33.25, Diodorus of Sicily, *Historical Library*, 3.14 citing Agatharcides of Cnidus. Part of the text of Agatharcides was also preserved by Photius and two alchemical compilations. See Martelli 2013: 65 n. 381.

[45] See Notton 1974: 50–56.

3. THE SOTERIOLOGY OF ZOSIMUS OF PANOPOLIS[46]

Discussing the possibility of self-transformation after death, Zosimus used the image of the transformation of copper into gold in a series of five allegorical visions called *Lessons* (*praxeis*). Postponing the contextualization of Zosimus' scholarship in its social context to the next chapter, I will here first describe how the visions of the *First Lesson on Virtue* hinted at his soteriological ideas, which were part of a larger late antique trend in discussing the future life of the soul and its relation with matter.

The Visions of Zosimus

The portion of the *First Lesson on Virtue* translated and analyzed here can be separated into five sections. The text starts with a list of ideas emphasizing the paradoxical multiplicity and simplicity of matter. At first, the list might appear disjointed but it corresponds with the content of the visions described and points the attention of readers to nature as a whole and to the theme of embodiment and disembodiment (section 1 of the translation below). In the next section, Zosimus describes a vision in which he met a priest called Iōn who was sacrificed inside an altar shaped in the form of a bowl (2). In the second vision, Zosimus explores the same bowl-altar, now described as a vast space (ambiguously called *taricheia*),[47] accompanied by a guide calling himself a pneuma and a guardian of pneuma. In the same vision, Zosimus meets another figure called the "master of the house" (*oikodespotēs*) and learns from him that Iōn, now described as a "copper human," is "the sacrificer as well as the sacrificial victim" (3). After waking up from the second vision, Zosimus lists different processes of exchange, some taking place between humans, others between parts of the universe (4). Zosimus then concludes the two visions and their interpretations with an allegorical recipe introduced as a summary of the preceding text (5). The final section of the *Lesson* (not translated here) provides readers with remarks, advice and a gold-making recipe.

The *First Lesson on Virtue* lends itself to at least two different and compatible interpretations. Concisely presented, the visions describe how human beings, sometimes described as metallic humans (e.g. *chalkanthrōpos*), are undergoing sacrifices or punishments (*kolaseis*) transforming them into pneuma. The first type of interpretation consists in reading the "punishments" as metaphors for tinctorial processes. As Zosimus wrote, the first vision concerned the "*thesis* of the water*," an expression translated by Mertens as "repos des eaux." The reason for the second vision was the so-called "divine water" (*to hudōr ... to theion*).[48] It

---

[46] This section expands on Dufault forthcoming a.
[47] Meaning both "maceration," as used in the conservation of foodstuff, and also "embalming" or "mummification." See Lampe, s.v. ταριχεία.
[48] MA 10.2.41–42: Μὴ οὕτως ἀρά ἐστιν ἡ τῶν ὑδάτων θέσις; MA 10.4.75–78: Τίς ἡ αἰτία τῆς ὀπτασίας ταύτης; μὴ ἄρα τοῦτό ἐστιν τὸ ὕδωρ τὸ λευκόν, τὸ καὶ ξανθόν, τὸ κοχλάζον, τὸ θεῖον; Καὶ ηὗρον ὅτι μᾶλλον καλῶς ἐνόησα.

is obvious that this water played an important role in tinctures but it is not clear what Zosimus meant by this expression. Throughout the corpus, the term sometimes designates a sulfurous liquid (*theiou hudōr*) used to color metals.[49] In Zosimus' short treatise "On the Divine Water" (MA 5), it appears, rather, to describe mercury. Besides these explicit references to alchemical substances, Michèle Mertens analyzed many other passages from the *Lessons* to show that the different "punishments" and "sacrifices" can be read allegorically as the representations of substances or of alchemical processes. This is suggested by the fact that the punishments (*kolaseis*) visited by Zosimus took place in a "bowl-altar" (*phialobōmos*)—*phialē* being a name used for parts of the alchemical apparatus.[50] I refer readers to Mertens' rich commentary for examples of the first type of reading.

The punishments and sacrifices can also be read as transformative processes applied to humans. Before analyzing the different elements of this text hinting at processes of human transformation and at Zosimus' soteriology, it will be helpful to anticipate some elements of the analyses of the treatise *On the Letter Omega* and the *Teleutaia apochē* presented in the next chapter.

In his treatise *On the Letter Omega*, Zosimus described the origin of human beings in a way reminiscent of anthropogonies associated with Gnosticism. According to Zosimus, the "interior" and "pneumatic human" whom he called *Phōs* (i.e. "light") was without body and originally resided in heavens. "Blown through by fate," he was persuaded by unnamed beings to clothe himself in "their Adam" (i.e. the body).[51] Citing Hermes, Zosimus wrote that by accepting fate rather than attempting to curb it, one could see the son of God "become everything for the sake of holy souls, to draw her (i.e. each soul) from the realm of fate up into the realm of the incorporeal." In the same treatise, he also described the soteriological role of Christ as advising his people to "exchange the Adam," i.e. the body. Proceeding to this exchange, as Zosimus wrote, humans "cut" and "killed" the body.[52]

The connection of alchemical practice with the extraction of the soul from the body is implied in a passage of the *Teleutaia apochē* (usually translated as the "*Final Count*"). Theosebeia, he wrote, would "reach the true and natural (tinctures)" by ceasing to wander in search of God, rectifying herself (*dieuthunousa*) and using the sacrifices that avert *daimones*. He then added that she should do this

---

[49] See Mertens 1995: 162–167, Martelli 2009.

[50] For descriptions of the φιαλοβωμός (or βωμὸς φιαλοειδός, MA 10.19) as the site of κολάσεις, see MA 10.3.63, 11.1.2, 2.41 and 12.2.14–18. On the φιάλη, see Mertens 1995: 35 n. 6. Association between the characters met by Zosimus and minerals are less implicit in MA 11 and 12. See, e.g. MA 12.2.11–14.

[51] MA 1.11: Ὅτε ἦν Φως ἐν τῷ παραδείσῳ διαπνεόμενος ὑπὸ τῆς εἱμαρμένης, ἔπεισαν αὐτὸν ὡς ἄκακον καὶ ἀνενέργητον ἐνδύσασθαι τὸν παρ' αὐτῶν Ἀδάμ, τὸν ἐκ τῆς εἱμαρμένης, τὸν ἐκ τῶν τεσσάρων στοιχείων.

[52] MA 1.13.126–132: συλῶν τοὺς ἑαυτοῦ συμβουλεύων αὐτοῖς ... καταλλαγὴν ἔχειν τοῦ παρ' αὐτῶν Ἀδὰμ κοπτομένου καὶ φονευομένου παρ' αὐτῶν ... τὸν ἑαυτῶν Ἀδὰμ ἀποκτείνουσι. On Adam symbolizing the four elements, see MA 1.9.

until she perfected her soul.[53] The practice of tinctures is directly connected with the perfection of the soul but it is not clear whether this perfection was a result of the discipline required to obtain the true and natural tinctures or of the performance of the same tinctures.

The implication for the first *Lesson* is that the "punishment" (*kolaseis*) of the humanoids and of their subsequent transformation into pneuma must be connected to Zosimus' conception of human nature and to his soteriology. A translation of sections 1–5 will help readers follow the analysis below:[54]

> (1) Thesis of the waters, movement, increase, disembodiment, embodiment, extraction of pneuma from a body, binding of pneuma to a body; these are not (coming) from natures that are foreign or brought from outside. Rather, uniform nature possesses the hard shells of the minerals as well as the soft pulp of the plants itself and only in respect to itself (lines 1–6).

Manuscript traditions give two different readings for the following paragraph:

> (Version A) The rich variety of the universe—which consists in many materials—and the research take shape (*schēmatizetai*) in this uniform and multicolor species. Hence the fact that it establishes (*hupoballei*) the abatement (*lēxin*) and the increase (*auxēsin*) by which nature flees (*hupophugei*), nature being under the temporal influence of the moon (7–16).

> (Version B) The rich and diverse research of all things is preserved in this uniform and multicolor shape (*schēmati*). Hence the fact that it establishes (*hupoballetai*) the cessation and the increase by which nature rides (*hippeuei*), nature being under the temporal influence of the moon (7–16).

> (2) As I was saying these things, I fell asleep: I see a sacrificer (*hierourgon*) standing before me above an altar shaped in the form of a libation bowl (*bōmou phialoeidous*). The altar was at the top of fifteen ladders (*klimakes*) and a priest (*hiereus*) stood there. I heard a voice coming from above saying:

>> "I have accomplished the action consisting in going down the fifteen ladders of shining darkness and going up these ladders of illuminating light. The sacrificer is now changing me (*kainourgōn*) by shedding away the density of my body. Consecrated by force I accomplish myself as pneuma" (17–25).

> After I had heard the voice of the one who stood in the bowl-altar, I asked wishing to know from him who he was. He answered saying with a weak voice:

>> "I am Iōn, the priest of the inner shrines and I undergo an intolerable violence. At sunrise, someone came running and mastered me, dividing me with a large knife (*machairai*), pulling me apart according to the structure

---

[53]See André-Jean Festugière's 1950 edition (367–368) and translation (280–281) of the *Teleutaia apochē*, following the fragment found in M for §8.

[54]The translation follows the text of MA 10 as edited by Mertens 1995: 34–42.

of the assemblage and skinning my head with the sword he possessed.[55] He intertwined the bones with the flesh and burned (them) with the fire from his hand until I learned to become pneuma by changing (my) body. This is the intolerable violence I endure" (25–36).

As he was talking to me and I was urging him to speak, his eyes became like blood and he vomited all his flesh. And I saw him as a small, mutilated human, chewing himself with his own teeth and collapsing upon himself (*sumpiptonta*). Frightened, I woke up and I wondered: "Would not that be, perhaps, the *thesis* of the waters?" And I was resolved to believe that I had truly understood (36–43).

(3) And I fell asleep again. I saw the same bowl-altar, which was infinite in size, with boiling water on the top part and a large population inside. There was nobody I could interrogate outside of the altar. I climb to look at the sight inside the altar and I see a small razor-wielding and grey-haired human (*pepoliōmenon xurourgon anthrōparion*) saying: "What are you looking at?" I answered that I was amazed by the agitation of the water and by the humans who burned together and yet lived. He responded to me saying: "The sight which you see is the entrance, the exit and the transformation (*metabolē*)." I interrogated him further: "What transformation?" He replied, saying: "(This is) the place of the exercise which is called "embalming" (*taricheia*) since humans who wish to reach virtue enter here and become spirits (*pneumata*) after having escaped their body." Then I said to him: "And are you a spirit?" And he answered, saying: "Both spirit and guardian of spirits" (44–59).

As we discussed these things and the boiling increased and the people screamed, I saw a human of copper (*anthrōpon chalkoun*) who held a lead tablet in his hand and who declared aloud, looking at the tablet: "I command to all those who are in the punishment to be burned,[56] to take each a lead tablet in their hand and to

---

[55] τῷ ξίφει τῷ ὑπ'αὐτοῦ κρατουμένῳ could mean several things: "with the sword he held," "the sword he mastered," and "the sword he [had] acquired." My reading of the text suggests that the sword symbolizes a tool used on matter in tinctorial processes as well as a tool used by the alchemist on him-/herself. In this sense, the "sword," i.e. the tool, is not simply held but "possessed" or "mastered." This reading can be justified by looking at Zosimus' use of the verb κρατεῖν in MA 1.7. Describing the attitude of the pneumatic human toward the divine and toward nature, he uses the verb in the sense of intellectual mastery: the pneumatic human lets fate follow its course and "searching for himself and knowing god, he/she masters the nameless triad/trinity intellectually (κρατεῖν τὴν ἀκατονόμαστον τριάδα)." It should be noted that this passage comes from a summary of a Hermetic treatise περὶ ἐναυλίας but there seems to be little chance that it was a verbatim quotation. The use of the expression κρατεῖν τὴν ἀκατονόμαστον τριάδα—which is similar to one used to describe the Trinity by Gregory of Nyssa (*Against Eunomius*, 2.3)—is consequently likely to come from Zosimus (see Bull 2018c: 402–404). Considering this example and the interpretation of MA 10 proposed here, the sword in Iōn's narrative might represent two things at the same time: a tool meant for separating alchemical products and an epistemological tool meant for understanding oneself (the topic of the passage of MA 1.7 just mentioned). This might also explain why the "pneuma guardian of pneuma" of the second vision is wielding a razor (ξυρουργόν). The use of the term μάχαιρα could be a reference to Jesus by way of a *logion* found in the *Gospel of Matthew* (10.34). See n. 96 below.

[56] Following the reading of M (καθευθῆναι) and translating as an infinite passive of καθ- εὔω (rath-

write with the (other) hand turning the eyes upwards and the mouth open until the uvula grows." And the action followed the word. And the master of the house (*oikodespotēs*) tells me: "Did you look, stretch your neck upwards and see what was accomplished?"[57] And I said that I saw and he said to me: "the one you have seen as a copper-human (*chalkanthrōpon*) is the sacrificer and the one who is sacrificed and who vomited his own flesh. He was given control over this water and over those who are chastised" (59–73).[58]

(4) And after I had these visions, I woke up again and I said to myself: "What is the cause of such a vision? Is this not the water which is white and which is yellow, the boiling, the divine?" And I found that I understood better and I said that it was good to speak and good to hear, good to give and good to take, good to be poor and good to be rich. How does nature learn to give and to take? The copper-human gives and the liquid-stone takes. The metal gives and the plant takes. The celestial bodies give and the flowers take. The sky gives and the earth takes. Thunderclaps give of the revolving fire (74–85).

Everything is woven together and everything is unwoven. Everything is mixed and everything is put together (again). Everything is blended and everything is separated. Everything is inundated and everything is dried, everything blooms and everything loses its bloom in the bowl-altar; for everything (exists) according to method, according to a measure and according to the minute measurement of the four elements. The weaving and unweaving of all things and the interconnection of the universe do not occur without method. Method is natural; it breathes in and out and it takes care of the orders [prob. the "order of things"],[59] increasing (*auxousa*) and abating (*lēgousa*). And, to summarize, if method is not left behind, all things being harmonized through separation and union transform nature (*ekstrephei*). Transformed (*strephomenē*), nature turns into itself (*eis heautēn strephetai*). This is the nature and interconnection of the virtue of the entire cosmos (85–99).

(5) In short, my friend, build yourself a monolithic shrine (*naon*) that is like white lead, like alabaster, like (marble) of Proconnesus, and which has neither beginning nor end in its construction. Inside, it has a source of the most pure water and a light shining like the sun. Seek diligently for the entrance of the shrine (*eisodos tou naou*), take a sword in your hand and search for the entrance. For the place where is the opening of the way is narrow and there is a snake lying next to the entrance, guarding the shrine. Once you have mastered it, first sacrifice it and, having skinned

---

er than καθεσθῆναι the infinitive passive of καθέζομαι or καθίζω). I would like to thank Donald J. Mastronarde for this suggestion. This copper-human is likely to be a representation of the "son of God" who teaches how to become pneuma through the use of "punishments." That Jesus was meant would make sense considering that he is described as "the sacrificer and the one who is sacrificed."

[57] Following the punctuation proposed by Berthelot and Ruelle (CAAG 2.110.1).

[58] The χαλκάνθρωπος appears to be the same as Iōn. Since he is said to be not only a "sacrificial victim" (ἱερουργούμενος) but also a sacrificer (ἱερουργῶν) he also appears to be identical with the sacrificer who stood over the bowl-altar in the first vision (l. 17 and 23).

[59] I accept the emendation of Michèle Mertens, who assumes that the versions of AL (τῆς μεθόδου) and of M (τὴν μέθοδον) are corruptions or unnecessary additions to the text.

it, divide its flesh and its bones part by part. After you have put back its parts one by one with the bones, make yourself a base next to the entrance of the shrine. Climb, enter and you will find there the thing sought for. For the priest, the copper-human, the one you see seated in the source and collecting the thing—you do not see him a copper-human (anymore). He has changed the color of (his) nature and has become a silver-human. If you wish, in a short time you will have a gold-human (100–118).

Several aspects of the visions suggest a voyage to a liminal space situated beyond the world of normal existence. Zosimus begins the first vision by describing a bowl-altar placed at the top of fifteen stairs or ladders (*klimakes*) and attended by an unnamed sacrificer. He also notices that he could hear the voice of Iōn but that he did not see what was happening. In contrast with the next part of the vision and with the second vision, Zosimus appears to have been situated below the bowl-altar. Iōn, who was inside it, mentions having climbed down and up the fifteen *klimakes* of light and darkness. Whatever Zosimus meant by these *klimakes*, he did not imagine them as parallel to each other but as forming a single path toward the bowl-altar.[60] The travel of Iōn down and then up to the bowl-shaped altar through 15 "ladders" of light and darkness suggests the rising and setting of the moon as well as its entire cycle (roughly two times 15 days). The moon and its influence on nature's growth and abatement are also referred to in the introduction to the *Lesson*. This reading is also reinforced by the fact that the moon cycle was sometimes depicted in Egyptian temples as a staircase with fourteen steps leading to a platform on which the moon was symbolized.[61]

A similar journey—also followed by the sight of punishments and located in an intermediary afterworld—can be found in the eschatological narrative closing Plutarch's *On Delays in Divine Vengeance* (*De sera numinis vindicta*). This narrative describes the vision of a man who fell unconscious and who visited the space between the Earth and the Moon in the company of the soul of a kinsman who acted as his guide. The afterworld of *On Delays in Divine Vengeance* is not described as the realm where souls stay after having stopped the cycle of reincarnation but as an in-between world where worthy souls could continue their journey to the moon (their final destination) while others reintegrate with the world.

[60] Mertens chose to translate κλίμακες by "marches" (See Mertens 1995: 35 n. 7). Since the main activities taking place in the visions are κολάσεις, it seemed preferable to translate κλίμαξ by "ladder," which suggests the "rack" used in torture (see LSJ, s.v. κλίμαξ, II and ἐκκλιμακίζω). Note that the Latin *gradus* would have been particularly appropriate in this context since it could be used for a step, stairs and an astrological degree (see, e.g. Manilius, *Astronomica*, 2.750–787, 4.119–121).

[61] Inscriptions found in the temples of Edfu and Dendara can also support the conclusion of Mertens. The moon phases are represented there by a staircase of 14 steps leading to a platform, the fifteenth step, on which rests an eye (= the moon). See von Lieven 2000: 127–132 (I would like to thank Joachim F. Quack for the reference). Zosimus could have read about Egyptian moon-symbolism in Greek texts. Plutarch mentioned that some associated Osiris with the lunar world and that the dismemberment of Osiris in fourteen parts was associated with the waning phases of the moon (*On Isis and Osiris*, 367c–368b). See also Derchain 1962: 25–26.

The visitor, a man renamed Thespesios by his guide, witnessed souls undergoing retributive tortures reflecting the nature of the crimes they had committed on earth. One of the punishments consisted in forcing souls to turn themselves inside out (*ektrepesthai*). Thespesios compared the movement of the soul to that of "sea-centipedes that have swallowed a hook and that turn themselves inside out (*ektrepousin heautas*)."[62] This punishment was meted out to those who pretended to be virtuous and recalls the experience of Iōn in Zosimus' vision. Considering that Zosimus described the goal of soteriology as the extraction of the "inside human" from the "outer human" (i.e. the separation of soul from body),[63] it is likely that the self-regurgitation of Iōn represented a similar process of punishment and purification (except that Iōn is also said to have absorbed himself afterwards). Other punishments described by Thespesios mimicked metallurgical processes:

> There were also pools placed one next to the other, one of boiling gold, one of icy lead and another of turbulent iron. Daimones attended these and, like blacksmiths, they were lowering and pulling back each of the souls of those who erred because of cupidity and greediness. Indeed, after the heat had started to make them glow and translucent, they threw them into the lead and immersed them (*baptontes*). When they solidified on the spot and became hard like hailstones, they moved them to the pool of iron. They became terribly black in there and, breaking down because of their extreme hardness, they were ground down and changed shape. They were then brought back to the gold, agonizing, as he said, from the painful changes to which they were submitted.[64]

The general idea is strikingly similar to that of Zosimus' vision: color-changes and metallurgical processes (immersion or "tinctures"—*baphai*) representing punishments (one consisting in a "reversion/transformation"—*ekstrephei, ektrepousin*) and taking place in an imaginary space. Considering that Zosimus saw a relation between the practice of alchemy and the extraction of the soul from the body, it is likely that he described the processes as "punishments" (*kolaseis*) because they recalled self-rectifying disciplines teaching humans to forget the passions of the soul and to abandon the body that produced them.[65]

The cultic imagery found in Zosimus' visions also has parallels in apocalyptic literature, where the heavens can be represented as a temple.[66] Zosimus' visions occur around or inside an altar (*bōmos*) shaped in the form of a bowl or a libation vessel (*phialē*). In the alchemical corpus, the *phialē* does not refer to a libation

---

[62] Plutarch, *On the Delays of the Divine Vengeance* (*De sera numinis vindicta*), 567b: τούτους (sc. the souls) ἐπιπόνως καὶ ὀδυνηρῶς ἠνάγκαζον ἕτεροι περιεστῶτες ἐκτρέπεσθαι τὰ ἐντὸς ἔξω τῆς ψυχῆς ... ὥσπερ αἱ θαλάττιαι σκολόπενδραι καταπιοῦσαι τὸ ἄγκιστρον ἐκτρέπουσιν ἑαυτάς.
[63] MA 1.10–15.
[64] Plutarch, *On the Delays of the Divine Vengeance*, 567c.
[65] See MA 1.7, 13–14, and Festugière 1950: 367 (translation: 280–281).
[66] See Himmelfarb 1993: 14–16.

vessel but to the top part of the alembic as well as to the receptacle for distillates.[67] It is also certain that the *phialobōmos* represented the alchemical apparatus and the sacrificial altar in one image.

The fact that the first vision (part 2 above) followed the format of eschatological narratives found in dialogues and revelations implies that Zosimus' visions could be read as tours of the afterworld occurring in a liminal space situated between the realm of normal existence and the state or place where salvation would be achieved. Eschatological narratives generally took place after a voyage through heaven and involved a divine guide describing and interpreting sights in the afterworld. These often included punishments.[68] Guides and punishments are also found in Zosimus' two visions, and both visions are separated by a linking formula ("I fell asleep as I was saying these things") similar to the one found at the beginning of the eschatological narratives of the *Zostrianos* from Nag Hammadi and to the first lines of the Hermetic *Poimenandres*.[69] The links between the *Lesson* and Hermetic symbolism studied in the next section suggest that Zosimus depicted the "bowl-shaped altar" as the site of a sacrifice of the body and of a radical transformation of the self.

Running Down into the Crater, Running up toward Poimenandres

In the first vision, Zosimus witnessed how Iōn "accomplished," or "perfected" (*teloumai*) himself as pneuma after he had been sacrificed by a third character called the sacrificer. The fact that Iōn was described as a "little human" (*anthrōparion*)—the same term used to describe the "razor-wielding" guide of the second vision—suggests that his ordeal effectively transformed him into pneuma. In the second vision, Zosimus sees the same bowl-altar (*ton auton phialobōmon*) but no sacrificer. Reaching for the bowl-altar, he sees a large number of people "in the punishments" (*en tais kolasesi*) who are "fleeing the body" and "becoming *pneumata*."[70] Zosimus moreover hears from the "master of the house" (*oikodespotēs*) that the copper-human who "vomited his own flesh," i.e. Iōn, was not simply the victim of a sacrifice but the sacrificer as well.[71]

The second vision confirms that what happened to Iōn in the first was a sacrifice and that this sacrifice transformed its victim into pneuma. Interpreting the visions from a technical point of view, Iōn would stand for a mineral substance and his "sacrifice" for an alchemical operation taking place inside the bowl-altar,

---

[67] See Mertens 1995: cxxi-cxxiii.

[68] For angelic guides in Apocalypticism, see Himmelfarb 1983: 50–60, 1993: 38–40, 55–57, 67–69.

[69] MA 10.2.17: καὶ ταῦτα λαλῶν ἀπεκοιμήθην. See *Nag Hammadi Codices*, VIII, 1.3.14–1.4.1 and *Corpus Hermeticum*, 1.1.

[70] MA 10.3.54–57.

[71] MA 10.3.69–72: λέγει μοι ὅτι τοῦτον ὃν εἶδες χαλκάνθρωπον καὶ τὰς ἰδίας σάρκας ἐξεμοῦντα, οὗτός ἐστιν ὁ ἱερουργῶν καὶ ἱερουργούμενος.

i.e. in an alchemical apparatus.[72] From a soteriological point of view, it also represented the process by which somebody would get rid of the body.

This double reading is first supported by the fact that the *Lessons* were concerned with the universe as a whole. The first six lines focus on nature and emphasize how it is self-enclosed and uniform—*monoeidēs*, i.e. the fact that it was made "of one species"—and the different activities and species it contained. The mention of the "hard shells of the minerals" and the "soft pulp of the plants," two distinct forms of natural species, obviously contrasts with the statement that nature was uniform.[73] Similarly, the conclusion of the second vision is also seen as an occasion to reflect on cosmic processes of change. Zosimus lists opposite notions beginning with moral terms and finishing with amoral ones: some humans speak, other listen, some give and some take; it is good to be rich and it is good to be poor. Similarly, the sky gives and the earth takes (lines 77–85), etc. The identification of moral processes of exchange with natural ones seem to aim at dissolving the human point of view. The juxtaposition of the two types of processes suggests that social oppositions and imbalances are not injustices but rather parts of the "orders" (*taxeis*), a term that appear to have referred to natural species (93–95). Similarly, the use of method—which Zosimus emphasizes elsewhere by preferring the correct use of tools, of "books with diagrams" or of "demonstrative reasoning" to the reliance on the good will of *daimones*[74]—can also be found in nature (93). "Natural" method guarantees the "weaving" and "unweaving" of all things (90–99). Zosimus expresses these processes by punning on the verb *(ek)strephein*: "turned inside out, nature turns into itself" (i.e. transforms itself).[75] The movement moreover recalls what happened to Iōn in the first vision. This universal process of cyclical changes and exchanges—which concerns humans as well—is what Zosimus calls the *aretē* (virtue, effect, wonder, glory) of the cosmos, hence the title of the *Lessons*.[76] Zosimus gives a final exhortation, which he describes as a "virtue" or "wonder" (*aretē*): "pay attention to the nature as you turn it inside out (i.e. as you transform it), and conceive what is made of a multiplicity of material as if it were made of a single material."[77]

This reading is supported by looking at the Hermetic notions evoked in the passage from the *Teleutaia apochē* mentioned above.[78] After explaining the histo-

---

[72]Zosimus discusses this analogy in the *Chapters to Eusebeia* (CAAG 2.170–171).

[73]This division between liquid and dry/solid substances (see also CAAG 2.170–171) also echoes the separation of the catalogues of reagents attributed to Democritus. See Martelli 2013: 26–29.

[74]See MA 1.2, 18.

[75]MA 10.4.98–99: ἡ γὰρ φύσις στρεφομένη εἰς ἑαυτὴν στρέφεται.

[76]MA 10.7.

[77]MA 10.7.133–135: ἐκστρέψας τὴν φύσιν ἐπίστηθι καὶ τὴν πολύϋλον ὡς μονόϋλον λογίζου.

[78]On Hermetic influence on Zosimus, compare the *Teleutaia apochē* in Festugière 1950: 1.367.18 with *Corpus Hermeticum*, 13.11.7–8. See also Festugière 1950: 1.365.15, 366.12; MA 1.4, 5, 7, 8, 15; CAAG 2.150.13, 156.8, 156.14–17, 157.2, 162.3, 169.9, 175.14–15, 188.19, 189.4, 198.3. Zosimus also referred to a Hermetic *Physika*. On this, see Bull 2018a.

ry of alchemy, Zosimus enjoins Theosebeia to avoid *daimones* and to obtain the "propitious, genuine and natural tinctures." He also exhorts her to "run down to *Poimenanēr*." "Having been immersed in the mixing-bowl (*kratēr*)," he writes, she will then "run up to [her] own kind."[79] The combination of *Poimenanēr/ Poimenandrēs* and the mention of an immersion in a mixing-bowl (*kratēr*) are clear references to Hermetic ideas and especially to *Corpus Hermeticum* 1 and 4. In *Corpus Hermeticum* 1, *Poimenandrēs* is called the "Intellect of the authority" (*nous authentias*) and the "Father-God" of the second Intellect (1.1.9–10, 1.9). In light of *Corpus Hermeticum* 1, "running down toward *Poimenanēr/-andrēs*" means getting knowledge that brings a "return to life" (21), which is acquired by recognizing oneself as being made of light and life. This process is also said to involve "leaving the body to alteration" and the body's dissolution (24). The final stage of the "return to life," or "rebirth" (*palingenesia*), is the heavenly ascent through the seven spheres up to the "Ogdoadic nature" (i.e. the eighth sphere), where the "Father-God" will be praised with hymns and finally integrated. This divinization is described as "the goal for those who possess knowledge" (25–26) and corresponds relatively well with Zosimus' soteriology, which emphasized the importance of losing the bounds uniting the "inner human" (soul)—which he describes by the name of "Light" (*Phōs*)—from the "outer human" (body).[80] This theological background, however, does not explain why acquiring the correct alchemical techniques should have helped Theosebeia become "perfect" and what the "immersion in the mixing-bowl" is supposed to refer to.

In *Corpus Hermeticum* 4, entitled *Hermes to Tat: The Mixing-Bowl, or the Monad*, it is said that God filled a crater with intellect and that he sent it down together with a herald bearing the following message: "you [feminine pronoun] who can immerse yourself in this mixing-bowl, you who believe that you will go back to him who sent the mixing-bowl, you who know why you were born"(4). The treatise explains that the immersion in the mixing-bowl is meant to "give intellect" to the heart (*kardia*), which is addressed by the herald. The intellect acquired in the mixing-bowl also brings knowledge of all things in the world, and this knowledge is thought to lead one to relinquish the world and to acquire immortality (5).

The two other "baptismal" images found in the Hermetic Corpus have generally been contrasted with that of *The Mixing-Bowl* since they are negatively connoted. In the treatise *To Tat on the Common Intellect*, the soul entering the body is said to step into and be immersed in pleasure and pain, which are compared to boiling humors.[81] The other text appears to strike an even more dissonant note: souls are

---

[79]Festugière 1950: 1.368.1–4: ὅταν δὲ ἐπιγνῷς σαυτὴν τελειωθεῖσαν, τότε καὶ <ἐπιτύχουσα> τῶν φυσικῶν τῆς ὕλης κατάπτυσον, καὶ καταδραμοῦσα ἐπὶ τὸν Ποιμένανδρα καὶ βαπτισθεῖσα τῷ κρατῆρι, ἀνάδραμε ἐπὶ τὸ γένος τὸ σόν.

[80]See MA 1.11–15.

[81]*Corpus Hermeticum*, 12.2: σώματος γὰρ συνθέτου ὥσπερ χυμοὶ ζέουσιν ἥ τε λύπη καὶ ἡ ἡδονή, εἰς

immersed (*bebaptismenai*) in flesh and blood, and this process is described as a punishment (*baptismou kai kolaseōs*).[82] In both cases, however, immersion in the mixing-bowl allegorizes embodiment.

The positive uses of the image of the immersion in the mixing-bowl found in *Corpus Hermeticum* 4 and in Zosimus' *Teleutaia apochē* are neither unrelated to the three so-called negative uses of the same image nor are they contradictory.[83] The tension perceived between worldly concerns or "technical" treatises on one side and rejection of the world or "philosophical" treatises on the other can be explained by the tendency for Hermetic texts to present knowledge of the world as a preliminary step toward rebirth.[84] That the one who wishes to achieve rebirth should first contemplate materiality is the topic of *Corpus Hermeticum* 5, entitled *That the Invisible God is the Most Visible*. Since God is invisible, Hermes stated, its contemplation should begin with its creation, the "visible God," i.e. the world. Remarking that climbing to heaven to study the most orderly part of creation is impossible, he suggests starting the contemplation of God with a study of the world below. The study of parturition also stands as a good way to achieve this contemplation since it is considered as the visible paradigm of universal creation.[85] The four references to immersion in the mixing-bowl referred to the same reality: the visible world, and more specifically, to the human body as a representation of the highest god.

From this perspective, the alchemical apparatus would seem like a fruitful site where one could reflect upon matter and its potential for transformation, get rid of passions and thus obtain rebirth. Reflecting the Hermetic image of rebirth as starting with an immersion in the mixing-bowl, Zosimus associates alchemical processes of purification with the place where salvation is acquired, i.e. the world. He is also probably thinking of the Hermetic mixing-bowl when he describes the second bowl-altar as a receptacle of infinite size as well as the "entrance, the exit and the transformation." The act of entering these structures implies embodiment and exiting them salvation, described as a transformation as well as embalming/maceration (*taricheia*). Zosimus' comparison of the formation of the human em-

---

ἃς ἐμβᾶσα ἡ ψυχὴ βαπτίζεται.

[82]SH 25.8.

[83]*Corpus Hermeticum*, 12.2, SH 25.8. Ephraim the Syrian (fourth century CE) also mentions a Hermetic teaching according to which a cup attracts souls into it and makes them forget where they came from. According to Ephraim's reading, the cup represents the body. See Mitchell 1921: 210 (= SH 22). See also Van den Kerchove 2012: 301–302, Edwards 1992: 55–64.

[84]Fowden 1993, Van den Kerchove 2012, Bull 2018c.

[85]*Asclepius* 20–21. For similar examples, see *Asclepius* 8, *Corpus Hermeticum* 5.1, 9.6–7, 9.21–22, 12.21, SH 23.3. Mahé 2009 also shows how an astronomical Hermetic treatise (SH 6) could have been conceived as a spiritual exercise in preparation for the flight of the "perfect" through the seven spheres. This is also similar to the comparison of the travel to the altar-bowl with the travel of the moon across the sky. On the study of heaven as a didactic travel going through several *gradus*, see Manilius, *Astronomica*, 2.750–787, 4.119–121 (here not only "steps" but also zodiacal "degrees") with Volk 2004.

bryo with the production of alchemical tinctures suggests the same association.[86]

The final allegory of the treatise (section 5 above) brings the notion of micro- and macrocosmic changes together. The snake must be sacrificed, flayed, its flesh separated from the bones "limb by limb" and its body recomposed bit by bit.[87] Placed in front of the opening of the shrine, the reassembled corpse is then used to find "the thing sought for," represented by the final transformation of the copper-human into a gold-human. Similarly, it is through the methodical dismembering of Iōn that transformation was achieved. Iōn said that his sacrificer first separated him apart with a sword or *machaira*, weaved (*suneplexen*) his flesh and bones together and burned him. This process transformed Iōn into an *anthrōparion*, that is to say, into a soul/pneuma. Zosimus also uses the same metaphor when describing the transformation of nature: it weaves (*sumplekontai*) and unweaves (*apoplekontai*) things with method (85–90), thus ensuring its union and its "virtue." Just like Iōn who turned himself inside out and reverted to his original self (pneuma), nature is said to be "turned inside out" (i.e. to change) and to "turn into itself."[88] It is consequently as a performer of alchemy that Iōn can be said to be a sacrificer, and it is as a sacrificial victim that he can be said to stand for a human being in the *phialobōmos* of nature.

The main lesson of his visions, which attributed a soteriological purpose to alchemy, is that escape from the world came at the cost of recognizing the power of necessity (*heimarmenē*) in alchemy as well as in one's life. In his treatise *On the Letter Omega*, Zosimus criticizes rival practitioners for ignoring technical books of alchemy and for relying on the good will of demonic beings. Their attitude, he claimed, testifies to their "lack of intellect" (*anoia*) and to the desire to dominate necessity. For Zosimus, success in alchemy can only come by respecting two principles. First, one must accept and understand the "bodily lessons" of nature (MA 1.4) and the necessity of natural processes, the "natural method" (MA 10.4). Second, one must avoid demonic beings and keep morally pure. Combining moral purity with the observance of the right (i.e. natural) alchemical practice, successful metallic "transmutation," or rather reversion (*ekstrophē*), means future success in the ultimate extractive process: the parting of the soul from the body.

CONCLUSION

Neither Zosimus nor Aeneas were original in using gold transmutation to discuss eschatological self-transformation. The association of metallurgical transforma-

---

[86] CAAG, 2.216.4–9.

[87] MA 10.5.108–113. In describing the separation and unification of bodies, Zosimus must have borrowed language from the Greek version of *Ezekiel* 37, which was interpreted by Origen and others as the reconstruction of the body of Christ. See Ramelli forthcoming.

[88] MA 10.4.97–98: ἡ γὰρ φύσις στρεφομένη εἰς ἑαυτὴν στρέφεται.

tions with moral purification echoed much older images representing or equating ethical and metallic purification.[89] Other examples can also be found in later literature. The idea of the theologian as "tester" (*dokimastēs*) of the true doctrine, or of the "pure" doctrine as gold, can also be found in the work of Clement of Alexandria and of Irenaeus of Lyon, who attributed it to an unnamed authority.[90] The *Commentary on Daniel* attributed to Hippolytus compared the body of Christ to the Ark of the Covenant, which was said to be gilded both inside and outside.[91] Plotinus, writing in the mid-third century CE, compared the pure soul to gold purified from all "earth-like material."[92]

Closer parallels with Zosimus' use of metallurgical metaphors can be found in Christian texts from the second century and later. A treatise on the resurrection attributed to Justin Martyr and written toward the end of the second century CE compared the resurrection to processes of parting and casting.[93] The *Refutation of All Heresies* mentions that a group he called the "Sethians" encouraged their students to read philosophical treatises about mixing and to observe how gold and silver could be separated from base metals. Such theories and techniques supported their claim that the three principles (light, pneuma and darkness) that were mixed when the universe came into being could later be separated. Some appear to have had the separation of soul and body specifically in mind since a certain "Sethian" (not identified in the text) interpreted the saying of Jesus according to which he came not to bring peace but a sword (*machaira*)[94] to mean that he came to separate the elements and bring them to their own place. The author of the *Refutation* noted that this interpretation of the *logion* was used to support eschatological beliefs.[95] This comparison of Jesus as sword and teacher of death is paralleled by Zosimus' interpretation of the salvific role of Jesus Christ:

> And both now and until the end of the world he [i.e. Jesus Christ] comes, both secretly and openly, to his own and communes with them by counseling them secretly

---

[89] See *Jeremiah*, 6.27–30, *Ezekiel*, 22.17–22, *Zachariah*, 13.9 and *Malachias*, 3.3.

[90] Clement, *Paedagogus*, 2.8.63.5, Irenaeus, *Against Heresies*, prol., 1.20–27. The metaphor had already been applied to the act of distinguishing the bad from the good ruler in Plato, *Statesman*, 303e.

[91] Hippolytus, *Commentary on Daniel*, 4.24.3. Irenaeus also made the same reading, see fr. 8 Harvey. The report that Simon the Samaritan also claimed to have been able to transform his body into gold (*Pseudo-Clementine Homilies*, 2.32) might reflect a similar idea since Simon is also known to have claimed to be god.

[92] Plotinus, *Enneads*, 1.6.5.50–53: καὶ ἔστι τοῦτο αἶσχος ψυχῇ μὴ καθαρᾷ μηδὲ εἰλικρινεῖ εἶναι ὥσπερ χρυσῷ, ἀναπεπλῆσθαι δὲ τοῦ γεώδους, ὃ εἴ τις ἀφέλοι, καταλέλειπται χρυσὸς καὶ ἔστι καλός, μονούμενος μὲν τῶν ἄλλων, αὑτῷ δὲ συνὼν μόνῳ ("This is the soul's ugliness, not being pure and unmixed, like gold, but full of earthiness; if anyone takes the earthy stuff away the gold is left, and is beautiful, when it is singled out from other things and is alone in itself") trans. Armstrong.

[93] Pseudo-Justin Martyr, *De resurrectione*, 6.11–12 Heimgartner.

[94] See the *Gospel of Matthew*, 10.34: οὐκ ἦλθον βαλεῖν εἰρήνην ἀλλὰ μάχαιραν, and the *Gospel of Thomas*, 16.

[95] *Refutation of All Heresies*, 5.21.1–6.

and through their minds to get rid of their Adam. By cutting off and slaying their Adam whose guidance is blind and who is jealous of the Man of spirit and light they kill their own Adam.[96]

Zosimus' soteriological concerns were reflected in Platonic discourses about the afterlife, and this places him alongside one influential and well-attested scholarly tradition. Zosimus also obviously borrowed Gnostic and Hermetic ideas found in roughly contemporary texts. Considering that the authors of alchemical treatises were only exceptionally described as alchemists, and that they do not appear to have constituted a definite body of scholars in late antiquity, it also appears that Zosimus must have been conceived primarily as a Christian scholar whose eclectic background included Hermetic, Jewish and Platonic literature. As the next chapter will show, Zosimus was also a client scholar who laid strong emphasis on the importance of *paideia* and of the Democritean corpus for the correct understanding of alchemy.

---

[96]MA 1.13.126–132 (trans. Jackson). In the metaphor closing the *First Lesson on Virtue* (MA 10.5.105), Zosimus also enjoins one "to grab a sword" with one's hands to carve a snake and to recompose its corpse so as to create a step leading to the discovery of the secret of transmutation. This is essentially the same role played by the figure of the μάχαιρα-wielding man who helps Iōn transform into pneuma in the *First Lesson on Virtue*. In the light of the interpretation of the *logion* of Jesus attributed to a certain "Sethian" by the *Refutation of All Heresies*, the sword in Zosimus' *Authentic Memoirs* is a metaphor for the son of God, whom he described as leading his people to "cut" and "kill" the "Adam" (which appears, like the snake, to mean both body and materiality; on "Adam" representing materiality in general, see MA 1.9, 11.106–107). See n. 55 above. On the parallels between the doctrine of the "Sethians" and the *Paraphrase of Shem*, see Burns 2015.

CHAPTER 6

Zosimus, Client and Scholar

At first sight, Zosimus' pioneering work on alchemical texts appears as an anomaly. Why would counterfeiting recipes attract such lofty considerations? Zosimus' conception of soteriology as the parting of the soul from the body provides part of the answer. Other reasons can be given for this peculiar choice of material. One reason was that the recipes he commented on were attributed to ancient and revered authorities.[1] More importantly, Zosimus also believed that the same authorities derived their knowledge from divine beings whose wisdom had been recorded in a book called the *Chēmeu* (hence, he claimed, the Greek name of alchemy, *chēmeia*).[2] Zosimus also thought that all traces from the *Chēmeu* would have been lost if it had not been for Democritus, who allegorized its content. This can explain why Zosimus took so much care in deciphering and analyzing many texts he attributed to Democritus.

This particular attention to Democritus can also explain why alchemical commentaries gained legitimacy in the eyes of later scholars—or, conversely, why Zosimus is the first known author of alchemical commentaries. The argumentation will start with the evidence concerning Zosimus' social milieu (part 1) and will proceed to his polemical works, which disclose precious information about his patroness and rival practitioners of alchemy. At least one of these rivals, whom Zosimus called a priest (*hiereus*), was connected to Theosebeia, the same aristocratic woman to whom Zosimus addressed several treatises and letters (part 2).

---

[1]Considering all of Zosimus' literary output preserved in Greek and ignoring the works Berthelot and Ruelle erroneously attributed to Zosimus, we find references to or quotations of recipes from Maria (76 instances), Democritus (74 instances, excluding those where he may have been referred to by the expression "the philosopher"), Hermēs (60), Agathodaimon (37), Ostanēs (19), Plato (10), Aristotle (9), Pēbichios (9), Moses (6), Apollon (6), Chu-, Chē- or Chimēs (5), Isis (3), Hesiod (3), Nicotheos (2), Pammenēs (2), Aratos (1), Poimēnandres (1), Bitos (1), Salomon (1) and Membrēs (1).

[2]See George Syncellus, *Chronography*, 14.2–14 Mosshammer and the Syriac Cambridge Mm. 6.29, fols. 49ʳ–50ʳ. See the edition and translation of Martelli 2014b: 12. Zosimus' history of alchemy will be discussed below.

According to Zosimus, his competitors practiced a form of alchemy comparable to the deceptive *mageia* of Zoroaster. Elsewhere, he also argued that his rivals invoked their personal *daimōn* to insure their success in the practice of alchemy. He claimed to be rather concerned with moral education and with Greek philosophical traditions and presented his opponents as base and ignorant. A similar contrast can be found in the Christian novels studied in chapter 4. In both cases, the protagonists are not just opponents; they are rivals competing for the attention of an aristocrat. Zosimus, I conclude, presented his rivals as learned sorcerers while claiming to bring *paideia* as well as ancient and exotic doctrines to bear on his patroness' interest in alchemy and on her ability to gain a peaceful afterlife (part 3).

1. THEOSEBEIA'S HOUSEHOLD[3]

On the Vaporization of the Divine Water that Fixes Mercury (= MA 8) was written by Zosimus at the request of Theosebeia, who was looking for a way to "whiten the bodies," i.e. to give a silvery color to base metals.[4] The introduction contains evidence about the nature of their connection:

> Lady, when I was staying at your house to instruct you, I was amazed by the entire work of the man whom you call a *strouktōr*. I was quite astonished by his work. I was ready to consider Paxamos a god and I thought that the purpose of each artisan consisted in producing something better by taking advantage of the few principles (*oligas aphormas*) left by predecessors. What really amazed me was the boiling of the chicken with a sieve. How is the content boiled by the vapor, the heat, as well as by the quality of the liquid, which also participates in the tincture? And, wondering at this, the mind is steered toward our goal. Is it indeed possible to boil and color our composite from the exhalation and vapor of the divine water?
>
> I searched whether one of the ancients had made mention somewhere of such an apparatus and nothing came readily to mind. I was consequently despairing but I consulted your books and found the diagram of this apparatus in the Jewish ones next to the apparatus that is "transmitted by the art"[5] and which is called the *tribikos*.[6]

---

[3] Elements from this section were taken from Dufault forthcoming a.

[4] MA 8.43-44: λευκάναι [sic] γὰρ βούλει τὰ σώματα. The four σώματα are copper, iron, tin and lead (CAAG 2.167.20–168.5). As noted by Michèle Mertens, mercury plays no role in the text. Θεῖον ὕδωρ, "divine water," carried a variety of meanings in alchemical texts and "the divine water that fixes mercury" was probably a circumlocution used to indicate what kind of divine water was meant. See Mertens 1995: 196.

[5] This translates τεχνοπαραδότου, an emendation suggested by Mertens to replace τεκνοπαραδότου found in M' (a second version of several texts of M contained inside M) and τεκνοδότου found in B, A and L. The only other occurrence of τεχνοπαραδότος in the *Thesaurus Linguae Graecae* is also found in a work attributed to Zosimus, MA 3, *On the Tribikos and the Tube*. It is used there in connection with the *tribikos* and Maria, which supports Mertens' correction of the reading of M'.

[6] MA 8.1–20.

Strouktōr is a transliteration of the Latin *structor*, meaning a servant or slave responsible for arranging meals.[7] Paxamos, known by ancient authors for his books on cooking, would have been the predecessor on whom Theosebeia's *structor* improved.[8] From the description of the first course of Trimalchio's dinner in Petronius' *Satyricon* (35–36; 39), it seems that *structores* were involved in the preparation of elaborate dinners. Trimalchio's *structor* designed a meal course hidden in a spherical vessel inscribed with the twelve zodiacal signs. He set appropriate pieces of food next to each sign (e.g. two fishes over Pisces) and placed a honeycomb on a piece of turf which lay on the top of the vessel. Finishing the scene, he ordered an Egyptian slave to walk around the spherical vessel while serving bread out of a silver oven. These were only meant as intellectual appetizers while the main course was contained in the vessel. The vessel and its presentation of the meal were also pregnant with metaphors. As Trimalchio explained, the entire meal represented life and death and was meant for lovers of literature: the spherical dish, as shown by the piece of turf, represented the earth ("round like an egg") and the honeycomb represented the goods it contained. "The world turns like a mill," Trimalchio concluded, "and always creates some evil, causing humans to be born or to die" (39). While Trimalchio did not explain why the Egyptian slave was carrying bread around (*circumferebat*) the guests in a silver oven, it seems that the oven was meant as a representation of the moon. This *tableau vivant* was also perhaps meant to include a flattering note: if the oven was the moon and the vessel the earth, the guests stood for the planets, that is to say, gods.

Theosebeia's use of a *structor* and the presence of a library in her house suggest that she was wealthy. Several elements also suggest that Zosimus was both client (i.e. friend) and teacher of Theosebeia. First, Zosimus was invited to a dinner in a household that belonged to Theosebeia and to other unnamed persons.[9] This was obviously not the only time that they interacted, since a large number of Zosimus' treatises or letters were addressed to Theosebeia. The mention that he came to her for her instruction (*dia tēn sēn akoēn*) and Zosimus' use of a professorial tone[10] also imply that he saw it as his responsibility to instruct her on tinctures.

Zosimus also wrote treatises in response to Theosebeia's questions concerning alchemy. The short text called *On the Synthesis of Principles (Peri aphormōn syntheseōs)* shows that some of Theosebeia's questions put Zosimus in a difficult position.[11] As it stands, this text appears as a letter introducing a work that was

---

[7] See Mertens 1995: 26 n. 2.
[8] On Paxamos, see Columella, *De re rustica* 12.4.2 and Athenaeus, *Learned Banqueters*, 9.19 (376d). The *Suda*, s.v. Πάξαμος (Π 253) attributed to him books on cooking (Ὀψαρτυτικά), on Boeotia (Βοιωτικά), on "the twelve techniques" (Δωδεκάτεχνον, which the *Suda* describes as περὶ αἰσχρῶν σχημάτων), on tinctures (Βαφικά) and on agriculture (Γεωργικά).
[9] See MA 8.1–2.
[10] See, e.g., Zosimus' *Teleutaia apochē* in Festugière 1950 vol. 1: 367.10–368.4 and MA 1.19 below.
[11] CAAG 2.204.

meant to unite "the separate syntheses of the ancients in one idea."[12] Zosimus warned Theosebeia that he could not include *ta teleia* ("the last things" or "doctrines")[13] in his work since he could not find them in the work of predecessors: "only to the extent that this seemed possible, I collected what had been dispersed and I interpreted what was allegorical. I did what was appropriate for a commentary."[14] Theosebeia's interest in alchemy is also evident from the last section of the treatise called *On the Letter Omega*, where Zosimus stated that Theosebeia asked for "things that ought not" to be mentioned.[15] Showing deference to the work of predecessors enabled Zosimus to find a honorable way out and to avoid providing Theosebeia with an answer to her questions. A Syriac translation of a lost work by Zosimus confirms that Theosebeia was more than a pupil and that she taught *chēmeia* herself:

> The philosopher (i.e. Democritus) claims: "they hid the writings on the natural substances under the multiplicity of matter." Perhaps they wanted to exercise our souls. Now, if they exercise the souls, well, philosopher, why to deny it? But you know how to exercise either the body or the soul, and it always leads you to achieve the perfection. In fact a wise saying reads: "studying is everything." And also Isidoros says: "studying increases your work." I know, this is not beyond your understanding (my lady), but you know it well, since you are one of those who would have liked to hide the art, if it had not been put in writing. For this reason you formed an assembly and administered the oath to each other.[16] But you (my lady) moved away from the various topics (of this book); you presented them in a shorter form and you taught them openly. But you claim that this book cannot be possessed unless in secret. Now, even though secrets are necessary, it is quite fair that anyone has a book of alchemy, since it is not kept secret for them.[17]

An explicit address to a woman is found in the next sentence (not copied above) and we can consequently assume that Zosimus was addressing himself to Theose-

---

[12]CAAG 2.204.9–10: ἡ περὶ ἀφορμῶν σύνθεσις, ὦ Θεοσέβεια, τὰς κατὰ μέρος τῶν ἀρχαίων συνθέσεις εἰς ἕνα νοῦν συνῆξεν. The text is found only in M (f.161ᵛ–162ʳ) and reads here ὡς θεοσεβειαν. Berthelot and Ruelle read ὦ Θεοσέβεια.

[13]See Lampe, s.v. τέλειος, II.D.

[14]CAAG 2.204.15–19.

[15]MA 1.19.193–199.

[16]The *Suda* (Z 168) mentions that Theosebeia was Zosimus' "sister" (ἀδελφή) and it has been argued on this basis alone that Theosebeia and Zosimus were part of an initiatory group. See, e.g. Reitzenstein 1904: 266 n. 2. The passage from the Syriac text partly confirms the theory while also suggesting that Zosimus was not part of Theosebeia's group. The salutation found at the end of a letter of Zosimus to Theosebeia (cited by a later Christian author) shows that she was part of a Christian group. CAAG 3.285.3–4: Ἔρρωσθε, φίλοι καὶ δοῦλοι Χριστοῦ τοῦ Θεοῦ ἡμῶν.

[17]Translation (and edition) by Martelli 2014b: 12. See also the translation of Rubens Duval in Berthelot et al. 1893: 238–239. The fact that Syncellus quoted the Greek version of the first part of this passage strongly suggests that the extended version in Syriac corresponds to the same work.

beia. It is noteworthy that Zosimus addressed her as a philosopher.[18]

Zosimus' situation combined most of the elements studied in the preceding chapters: he was a scholar invited to a banquet by an aristocratic friend to offer her treatises which he wrote in a professorial tone (e.g. MA 1.19). His role also appears to have been that of an instructor, which was typical for client scholars.

2. RIVALS AND SCHOLARS

Contrasting Zosimus' self-representation to the picture he drew of his rivals gives a better idea of the way he presented his work as commentator. In three polemical texts addressed to Theosebeia, Zosimus warned her not to listen to other individuals (men and women) involved in alchemy. In all cases, Zosimus described his opponents as unlearned and opposed their practice to the careful study of Greek literary traditions, notably that attributed to Democritus.

The Letter "On the Treatment of the Body of Magnesia"

The first example of Zosimus' polemics is found in a treatise *On the Treatment of the Body of Magnesia* and is directed against Neilos and other people connected to him. As with MA 8, the treatise is concerned with a whitening/silvering process, this time applied to the "body of magnesia." From a technical point of view, it presents a method for identifying the substance called *kōbathia* using Democritean texts as a reading key.[19] Zosimus argued that the "rind of purple (or Phoenician) *kōbathia*" (*lepuroi phoinikōn kōbathiōn*) mentioned in a recipe attributed to Hermes did not refer to real *kōbathia* but to sulfurous substances (*theiōdē*), and more precisely to arsenic, which, he wrote, "looks like *kōbathia*."[20] Zosimus' claim to have understood the actual meaning of the word in a Hermetic recipe was meant to explain the failure of a competitor. After claiming to have deciphered the recipe correctly and having warned Theosebeia against any reading that would contradict his,[21] Zosimus begins the polemical section of the treatise, addressing himself to Theosebeia:

> But you, blessed one,[22] cease with these foolish elements (*stoicheiōn*) troubling your understanding. For I have heard that you speak with the *parthenos* Taphnoutiē[23] as

[18] This, at least, is what I can conclude from Martelli's translation ("Now, if they exercise the souls, well, philosopher, why to deny it?"). Duval's translation rather reads: "or, s'ils instruisent les âmes, c'est qu'ils sont des philosophes. Si tu es philosophe, ne mens donc pas").

[19] That Zosimus referred to Democritus when he spoke of "the philosopher" at CAAG 2.189.12–17 is clear by his citing ἐν τῇ δευτέρᾳ τῶν λευκῶν ζωμῶν [βίβλῳ] ("in the second [book] of the white washes"). On the *Catalogues*, See Martelli 2013: 26–29.

[20] CAAG 2.189.

[21] CAAG 2.190.5–9.

[22] ὢ μακαρία is feminine and suggests that Zosimus was addressing Theosebeia.

[23] We know nothing more about Taphnoutiē and consequently we can not determine in what way

well as with some uneducated men and that you try to put their foolish and useless tales into effect. Enough then with those who are blind in their minds and are excessively burning![24] They too should be pitied and should hear the word of truth as much as they are worthy (to do so). For they are humans but they do not want to be helped. They do not tolerate being taught, boasting that they are teachers, and they would also like to be honored for their foolish and useless tales. When taught the steps of truth, they do not have patience for the art and do not digest (*peptousin*) it since they desire gold rather than formulas. Because of [their] hot temperament and great lack of intellect (*anoia*), they obtain no share of wealth nor formulas. If they were being guided by reason, then gold would follow and attend them, for reason is the master of gold. The one who prostrates before it, desires it and remains attached to it will find the gold that is covered in riddles and which lies before us.

Indeed, reason points the way to all that is good,[25]

Variant in M	Variant in Lb
just as [he] says somewhere in that respect that philosophy is the knowledge of truth.	just as the philosopher says somewhere in that respect that philosophy is the knowledge of existing things in as much as beings exist.

If someone receives reason, its possession will reveal the gold that lies before his eyes but those who have no patience for lessons never walk on sound foundations and try quite ridiculous things.[26]

---

she was said to have been a παρθένος (which can be translated as "virgin," "unmarried woman" or as "young woman").

[24] As far as we can tell from Zosimus' description of Neilos' procedure, his main error appears to have been the use of excessive heat. By saying that the minds of his rivals were burning, Zosimus might have been comparing his rivals to the product of their work. "Excessively burning in regard to the mind" (τὸν νοῦν καὶ ἄγαν καιομένων) also parallels the later mention of the rivals as "having a hot temperament" (ἀπὸ θερμότητος). Both were perhaps a pun referring to the fact that Neilos is said to have "kindled the fire ... all day long" (καίων ... πανημέριος). The same kind of symbolic equation between the maker of tincture and his or her work might explain why he wrote that Neilos "fled himself into 'the depth,' just like the whitening of the magnesia." These would not be the only two places where Zosimus identified makers of tinctures with the product of their art (see, e.g., MA 10.3.69–73).

[25] I have translated the text of M printed by Ruelle and Berthelot as well as that of Lb printed in the notes: φησὶν ὁ φιλόσοφος, ἡ φιλοσοφία ἐστι γνῶσις ὄντων ᾗ ὄντα ἐστί.

[26] CAAG 2.190.10–191.7: σὺ δὲ, ὦ μακαρία, παῦσαι ἀπὸ τῶν ματαίων στοιχείων, τῶν τὰς ἀκοάς σου ταραττόντων. ἤκουσα γὰρ ὅτι μετὰ Παφνουτίας τῆς παρθένου καὶ ἄλλων τινῶν ἀπαιδεύτων ἀνδρῶν διαλέγῃ· καὶ ἅπερ ἀκούεις παρ' αὐτῶν μάταια καὶ κενὰ λογύδρια, πράττειν ἐπιχειρεῖς. παῦσαι οὖν ἀπὸ τῶν τε τυφλωμένων τὸν νοῦν καὶ ἄγαν καιομένων. καὶ γὰρ κἀκείνους ἐλεηθῆναι δεῖ καὶ ἀκοῦσαι τὸν λόγον τῆς ἀληθείας, καθώς εἰσιν ἄξιοι. ἐπειδὴ καὶ αὐτοὶ ἄνθρωποί εἰσιν, ἀλλ' οὐ βούλονται ἐλέους ἐπιτυχεῖν, οὐδὲ παρὰ διδασκάλων ἀνέχονται διδάσκεσθαι, καυχώμενοι διδάσκαλοι εἶναι, ἀλλὰ καὶ τιμᾶσθαι βούλονται ἐκ τῶν ματαίων αὐτῶν καὶ κενῶν λογυδρίων. καὶ διδασκόμενοι βαθμοὺς ἀληθείας, τὴν τέχνην οὐκ ἀνέχονται, οὐδὲ πέπτουσιν, χρυσοῦ μᾶλλον ἢ λόγων ἐπιθυμοῦντες· καὶ ἀπὸ θερμότητος καὶ πολλῆς ἀνοίας, ἄμοιροι γίνονται τῶν λόγων καὶ τῶν χρημάτων. εἰ γὰρ ἡνιοχοῦντο

Zosimus' tone is that of a concerned master to a pupil and makes clear that the retrieval of formulas or doctrines (*logoi*) and gold are dependent on the submission of a pupil to the written tradition. The following, coming immediately after the part of the text just quoted, refutes Neilos on the basis of the analysis of the term *kōbathia* presented in the first part of the text:

> [But those who have no patience for teachings never walk on sound foundations and try quite ridiculous things...] Take as example the time when your priest Neilos aroused laughter by roasting *molubdochalkos* in a bread-oven; as if you could add some "bread" and achieve success by kindling the fire with *kōbathia* all day long![27] Blind in his bodily eyes, he did not think he would be hindered.[28] He was puffing (on the fire),[29] picked up the ash after it had cooled down and showed it off. He was asked where (was) the whitening and said in confusion that it had sunk "into the depth." He then added copper and colored the ash since there was nothing solid remaining. He was then confounded, stood up and fled himself "into the depth"—just like the whitening of the magnesia. Hearing this from her opponents, Taphnoutiē was distressed by the great laughing matter. Likewise, you all too are afflicted by a lack of intellect (*anoia*). Pass my greetings to Neilos, the *kōbathia*-burner.[30]

Zosimus' argument implies that Neilos would not have failed if he had read the literary tradition properly. The failure of Neilos in giving a silvery appearance to

---

ὑπὸ τοῦ λόγου, εἵπετο ἂν αὐτοῖς καὶ ἠκολούθει ὁ χρυσός· ὁ γὰρ λόγος δεσπότης ἐστὶν τοῦ χρυσοῦ, καὶ ὁ τοῦτον προσπίπτων καὶ ποθῶν καὶ προσκολλώμενος εὑρήσει τὸν χρυσὸν τὸν ἔμπροσθεν ἡμῶν κείμενον, σκολιῶς διακεκρυμμένον.

ὁ οὖν λόγος δείκτης ἐστὶν πάντων τῶν ἀγαθῶν, ὡς καθώς πού φησιν, ἡ φιλοσοφία γνῶσις ἐστιν ἀληθείας, εἰ ὄντα εἰσίν [Lb: φησὶν ὁ φιλόσοφος, ἡ φιλοσοφία ἐστὶ γνῶσις ὄντων ᾗ ὄντα ἐστί]· καὶ ἐάν τις τὸν λόγον δέξηται, ἕξει αὐτὸν δεικνύοντα αὐτῷ ἐν τοῖς ὀφθαλμοῖς κείμενον χρυσόν. οἱ δὲ μὴ ἀνεχόμενοι τῶν λόγων πάντοτε κενεμβατοῦσιν, γέλωτος ἰσχυρότερα ἔργα ἐπιχειροῦντες. For Berthelot and Ruelle's translation, see CAAG 2.186–187.

[27] My translation reads ὡς for ὥστε. As Matteo Martelli (2017) pointed out, ἄρτος ("bread") could also be used for slabs of "magnesia" (CAAG 2.192.1–2). The use of this term was most probably ironic considering that κλίβανοι could be used for baking, that Zosimus never used this word to speak of ovens and that he mocked his rivals for refusing to study books on ovens (see below).

[28] The translation of this sentence attempts to make the best of a difficult and probably corrupt passage (οὐκ ᾤετο τὸ βλαβησόμενον).

[29] As with the case above with ἄρτος, ἐφυσι<ᾶτο> was most probably ironic. I have settled for the literal meaning.

[30] CAAG 2.191.7–18 (with the punctuation and emendations suggested by Martelli 2017 and accepting Berthelot and Ruelle's proposed readings for ἐφυσιοῦτο and ἀκούσας): οἷόν ποτε γέλωτα ἐκίνησεν Νεῖλος ὁ σὸς ἱερεύς, μολυβδόχαλκον ἐν κλιβάνῳ ὀπτῶν· ὥστε, ἐὰν βάλῃς ἄρτους, καίων κωβαθίοις πανημέριος τύχοις· καὶ τυφλούμενος τοὺς σωματικοὺς ὀφθαλμούς, οὐκ ᾤετο τὸ βλαβησόμενον, ἀλλὰ καὶ ἐφυσι<ᾶτο>, καὶ μετὰ τὸ ψυγῆναι ἀνενέγκας, ἐπεδείκνυεν τὴν τέφραν. καὶ ἐπερωτώμενος ποῦ ἡ λεύκωσις, καὶ ἀπορήσας ἔλεγεν ἐν τῷ βάθει αὐτὴν δεδυκέναι. εἶτα ἐπέβαλεν χαλκόν, ἔβαπτεν σποδόν· οὐδὲν γὰρ στερρόν. εἶτα διατραπεὶς ἀνέστη καὶ ἔφυγεν αὐτὸς ἐν τῷ βάθει, καθὼς ἡ λεύκωσις τῆς μαγνησίας. ταῦτα δὲ ἀκούσα<σα> παρὰ τῶν διαφερόντων Ταφνουτίῃ, ἀπὸ τοῦ πολλοῦ γέλωτος ἐκακώθη, ὡς καὶ ὑμεῖς κακοῦσθε ἀπὸ ἀνοίας. ἄσπασαί μοι Νεῖλον τὸν κωβαθηκαύστην.

"the body of magnesia" (= *molubdochalkon*)³¹ is contrasted with his interpretation of the Hermetic recipe mentioning the *kōbathia*. This is also why Zosimus warns Theosebeia not to frequent Taphnoutiē and the "uneducated men" (*apaideutoi*) around her—an expression that appears to have targeted Neilos as well. In other words, Neilos allegedly lacked what Zosimus had, i.e. a sufficient acquaintance with the Greek textual tradition attributed to Hermes and Democritus. Zosimus' description of Neilos' ignorance also dovetails with his admiration of divine images as found in Zosimus' "sixth book" *On Copper and on the Working of Copper*, which is preserved in a fifteenth-century Syriac manuscript. Most recipes from this book appear to have been taken from the Egyptian art of preparing cult statues.³² While Zosimus discusses this art,³³ he also distances himself from the cult of the statues and refuses to interpret their symbolism.³⁴ Contrasting with his own attitude, Zosimus presents Neilos as an admirer of the statues of the gods:

> These are the images, statues, or idols of snakes and female serpents, of the good *Daimon*, of the good Fortune, and also other (statues) of Aphrodite, of (the daimons?) of the earth, of Capricorn, or of Nilos—that is Gihon (i.e. a river flowing from the Eden)—or of fruits, ears of wheat, and of those things that lead upset people to mistakes and illusions. I condemn Neilos' disciples, who are astonished and admire things that do not deserve admiration. Indeed, they are not expert; but he (Neilos) addressed them with the precept that says: "know thyself."³⁵

The passage immediately following suggests that Zosimus saw the admiration of the statues as a sign of the ignorance of Neilos and of his disciples:

> I think that the ancients were envious and did not write down these (tinctures), yet they revealed them only to priests in secret. People were frightened at the sight of these images/statues. They thought that they were something animated and that nature provided their bodies with the same natural colors of our bodies; for this reason they did not dare to fully look at these (images/statues), since they were afraid of the nature of their limbs and of the figure of the produced (images). Only a very few people thought that the images/statues had been produced by the medicine³⁶ and the

---

³¹ A lead and copper alloy that could be called "body of magnesia." Maria, an alchemical authority often cited by Zosimus and others, wrote that μολυβδόχαλκος ("lead-copper") and μελανὸς μόλυβδος ("black lead") could be called "body of magnesia." See CAAG 2.192.7–9.

³² See Cambridge Mm. 6.29, fol. 32ᵛ–45ᵛ and more esp. fol. 32ᵛ–34ᵛ. I am basing my interpretation of the text on the translation made by Rubens Duval in *La chimie au Moyen Âge* (Berthelot et al. 1893: 222–224) for fol. 32ᵛ–34ᵛ and on the translations of Matteo Martelli quoted below. Zosimus lists recipes for the coloring of statues on fol. 34xʳ (trans. Duval in Berthelot et al. 1893: 224–225) and 39ʳ (228).

³³ See fol. 39ʳ.

³⁴ See fol. 34ʳ⁻ᵛ (trans. Duval in Berthelot et al. 1893: 223–224).

³⁵ Cambridge Mm. 6.29, fol. 39ᵛ. Trans. Martelli 2017. Rubens Duval (Berthelot et al. 1893: 228) translated the last sentence as: "ils étaient en effet ignorants, et on leur appliquait la parole qui dit: 'connais-toi toi-même.' Cette parole même ils ne l'admiraient pas."

³⁶ ʼōsyūtō. See Martelli 2017: n. 53, who notes that this term means the "medical art," a "remedy," or a "cure."

work of human beings.[37]

The admiration of Neilos and his disciples for "things that do not deserve admiration" is most probably a reference to the statues enhanced by *baphai* ("tinctures"). Zosimus suggests in the two passages that Neilos and his disciples were similar to the ignorant people who, unaware of the presence of tinctures, believed that the statues were alive.

Zosimus calls Neilos Theosebeia's priest (*ho sos hiereus*) and it is possible that he meant that Neilos was a priest associated with an Egyptian temple.[38] However, if we assume that Zosimus believed the history of alchemy he told in the *Teleutaia apochē* (see below), Neilos could hardly have been one of these priests, since the text mentions that the temples had been deserted and the cults abandoned. It would also be strange that a priest associated with a temple be described as Theosebeia's priest rather than as the priest of a specific city, god or temple.

Philosophers like Porphyry of Tyre could also claim the title of priest (*hiereus*) in late antiquity[39] and Zosimus may have referred to Neilos in a similar sense. This could explain Zosimus' sibylline mention of the Delphic maxim in this context. That Neilos instructed his disciples to "know themselves" at the same time as they were marveling at statues suggests some form of teaching specific to late antique philosophy. Zosimus may have hinted at similar criticism in another text—also coming from the Syriac manuscript—where he uses the same formula and where he mentions a "spiritual mirror" of electrum. Gazing into the mirror, he writes, one can recognize oneself as the "divine intellect" and this also had the effect of diverting one's gaze from "those who bear the name of gods or demons."[40] Following this line of interpretation, Neilos may have been a rival scholar offering an alchemico-ethical doctrine similar to that of Zosimus.[41] Showing life-like statues of gods and saying "know yourself" also resonates with certain passages from Plotinus' work. The common experience of beauty, Plotinus argues, can lead one to the more unusual act of witnessing one's inner beauty. This can be achieved, he argues, by removing accretions clinging to the soul just as sculptors removed stone in order to create a (divine) image: "do not stop 'working on your statue' until the godlike magnificence of your own virtue shines out and until you see 'self-control seated on its holy throne.'"[42] Following the old philosophical principle that "like knows like," Plotinus also claims that one "ought first to become entirely godlike

---

[37] *Id.*, fol. 40ʳ. Trans. Martelli 2017.
[38] Martelli 2017.
[39] See Porphyry, *On Abstinence*, 2.49, *Letter to Marcella*, 16 and Marx-Wolf 2016: 100–125.
[40] See the translation from the Syriac Cambridge Mm. 6.29, fol. 85ʳ–87ᵛ by Camplani 2000: 76–80, 93–98.
[41] On the use of the Delphic maxim in Hermetic texts, from which Zosimus drew inspiration, see Betz 1979: 465–484 (the same idea is fundamental to the argument of *Corpus Hermeticum* 5).
[42] Plotinus, *Enneads*, 1.6.9.13–16.

(*theoeidēs*) and entirely beautiful if one is to contemplate God and beauty."[43] This vision, Plotinus warns, can be first exercised on the work of good men, not on the works achieved through their crafts.[44] Recognizing oneself in an image of the divine brought one close to recognizing/achieving one's own divinity (although Plotinus refers to moral activities rather than to worked objects). Neilos' activities have more affinities with Porphyry's *On Images* (*Peri agalmatōn*), a book on the interpretation of the colors, forms and attributes used in the representations of divinities.[45] While Neilos' identity remains difficult to establish, the fact that Zosimus accused him of ignoring the lessons of the Democritean tradition informs us about what Zosimus considered to be a crucial element of alchemical inquiry.

On the Final Abstinence

Zosimus' history of alchemy in the πρῶτον βιβλίον τῆς τελευταίας ἀποχῆς also implies rivalry with individuals who respected the gods of Egypt and their statues. This work is usually called the "Final Count," following Marcellin Berthelot and Charles-Émile Ruelle. André-Jean Festugière accepted the translation and suggested that the name of the treatise came from the fact that it finished a series of books.[46] This would be curious considering that it is called a "first book" and that it closes with Zosimus announcing that he will begin with his main subject. It is also unclear how the treatise could be considered an "account" or a "receipt," another possible translation for *apochē*. The text rather reads like a letter introducing a treatise. It also presents an argument in narrative form for the abstention (*apochē*) from the sacrifices offered to *daimones*. The *Final Abstinence* consequently seems like a better translation for *teleutaia apochē*.

The complete text of the *Final Abstinence* must be pieced together from two sources presenting different readings.[47] The following summary takes up only those elements common to both versions.

(1) Two arts (*technai*) are foundational to the kingdom of Egypt: one deals with "the propitious" (*kairikai*), by which we must understand the "propitious

[43] *Id.*, 1.6.9.33–35
[44] *Id.* 1.6.9.2–5. On the use of the Delphic maxim by Plotinus and Porphyry, see Courcelle 1974: 1.83–90.
[45] See fr. 351–360a in Smith 1993.
[46] Festugière 1950: 1.274.
[47] This tradition is mainly represented by A, fol.251ᵛ–255ʳ and L, fol. 235ʳ–240ᵛ, which is of a slightly later date and almost identical to A (but not necessarily its copy, see Mertens 1995: xxxviii-xlii). Paragraphs 1, 2 and 8 are also found quoted in a commentary on Zosimus attributed to Olympiodorus in M. The text preserved there shows substantial differences from the one in A and L. I follow the edition of Festugière 1950: 1.363–368 (trans. 1.275–281), which is, however, incomplete. For passages not edited by Festugière, I have transcribed the text from A, followed the subdivisions proposed by Berthelot and Ruelle and included cosmetic modifications to the text. The text up to the first sentence of par. 9 was also translated and annotated in Tonelli 1988: 113–123. For a summary and partial translation, see Ruska 1926: 18–23.

tinctures" (*kairikai katabaphai*) mentioned by Zosimus in the treatise *On the Letter Omega*.⁴⁸ The other art deals with the "sands" (*psammoi*), by which Zosimus might have meant pulverized ores. Pharaohs had a monopoly on the techniques dealing with metallic ores and tried to prevent them from being known.

(2) Neither Democritus nor the ancients revealed the art of extracting metals from ores since they were "friends of the kings of Egypt and claimed the first place in the prophetic (order)." Only the Jews revealed them, as can be read in Maria's book on ovens (*kaminographia*).⁴⁹

(3) The Greeks disclosed some of these techniques but did not reveal the propitious tinctures. Democritus is the only one to have revealed them although he did so only through allusions.⁵⁰ Zosimus attempts to demonstrate that Democritus alluded to the propitious tinctures by analyzing specific passages from the Democritean tradition.⁵¹

(4) Continuing his allegorical reading of the Democritean corpus, Zosimus argues that Democritus was writing about "all things" (*ta panta*) when he mentioned single products and multiple tinctures.⁵²

(5) Democritus was the only one to have written about these tinctures, albeit in covert ways (Zosimus repeats what had already been said in section 3).⁵³ The

---

⁴⁸There is a tension in Zosimus' vocabulary concerning tinctures. Since the "propitious tinctures" (καιρικαὶ καταβαφαί) were dependent on the will of demonic beings (Festugière 1950: 1.366.8–9) and since Zosimus argued against any form of contact with them, we could conclude that he was against the use of these tinctures. At the same time, Zosimus also approved of the "genuine and natural propitious [tinctures]" (Festugière 1950: 1.368.1: τῶν γνησίων καὶ φυσικῶν καιρικῶν) in the same book, where he designates tinctures simply as αἱ καιρικαί. It is difficult to reconcile these two positions except to say, as Daniel Stolzenberg (1999) argued, that Zosimus did not mean that the "genuine and natural propitious tinctures" were actually propitious. The reason for this might be that Zosimus thought that the entire art of tinctures had been monopolized by the terrestrial demons (Festugière 1950: 1.366.21–22: [οἱ ἔφοροι...] ἔκρυψαν <γὰρ> πάντα τὰ φυσικὰ καὶ αὐτόματα). From that point on, all tinctures were *de facto* καιρικαί, even the natural ones.

⁴⁹Maria is only known through short quotations from later authors. Zosimus often referred to her works. These quotations were collected by Patai 1994: 60–91.

⁵⁰Festugière 1950: 1.365.13–14.

⁵¹See, e.g., A, fol. 253ʳ, l.8–12 (CAAG 2.241.19–22): μᾶλλον δὲ ἀγαγὼν τῶν καιρικῶν μηνύσει τὰς βαφάς. Φησὶν γάρ· μίσυ ὠμόν· μίσυ ὀπτόν· σῶριν ξανθόν· ⚹ (= χαλκάνθον) ξανθῇ [sic]· καὶ τὰ ὅμοια· ἀλλ' οἰκονομηθέντα λέγει· εἰς τὰς τιμίας τέχνας καλῶς εἶπας ("What is more, he indicates the propitious [tinctures] when he reveals the tinctures. For [when] he says 'uncooked *misu*, cooked *misu*, yellow *sōrin*, yellow copper sulphate and similar things,' he truly speaks about the noble arts [i.e. the propitious tinctures] when he mentions the substances that are treated"). Festugière did not edit par. 3–4 in their entirety (CAAG 2.241.9–242.9).

⁵²A, fol. 253ʳ, l.15–17 (CAAG 2.241.25–26): Ἀλλ' ἐκεῖνος (CAAG: ἐκεῖνον) ἤδη ὅπερ ἐφρόνησε· καὶ ὅπερ ἔγραφεν δι' ἑνὸς συγγράμματος αἰνιγματοειδοῦς, τὰ πάντα αἰνίξασθαι ἠθέλησε ("And see that what he understood is what he wrote about in one single allegorical work. He wanted to signify all things allegorically").

⁵³Festugière 1950: 1.365.21: αὐτὸς δὲ μόνος ἀπέδειξεν ὁ Δημόκριτος εἰς τὸ σύγγραμμα καὶ ἠνίξατο. Festugière translated: "Seul Démocrite les a exposées dans son ouvrage et il en a fait mention." Zosim-

Egyptians used symbolic characters to encrypt the recipes and hid them inside shrines. The Jews hid theirs in underground chambers.

(6) Propitious tinctures are divided into two groups. "The local overseers" (*hoi kata topon ephoroi*) gave the first type to their priests. These techniques deal with the dying of clothes (*othonai*)[54] and were called *kairikai* since their efficacy was dependent on the moment (*kairos*) and the will of the overseers. The second type are the "natural" and "genuine" propitious tinctures but these were begrudged by beings described in the manuscripts as the *perigeioi* ϙϙ. These are the same as the overseers who are also said to be "terrestrial" (*perigeioi*).[55] Those who are initiated can chase the overseers away and reach their goal.

(7) In former days, powerful men kept the overseers at bay. In order to receive prayers, the overseers "hid" (*ekrupsan*) the art of natural tinctures and replaced them with a "non-natural" one (*aphusikon*), asking for sacrifices in exchange for success in these tinctures.[56] After a "revolution of the astrological zones (*klimatōn*)" and a war, the human race disappeared from "this zone" (*ek tou klimatos ekeinou*).[57] The temples were deserted and the sacrifices offered to the overseers were consequently neglected. Contacting those left as if in dreams and sending them omens, the overseers continued to exchange success in tincture for the offering of sacrifices.[58] Having reached the end of the history of alchemy, Zosimus then turns to Theosebeia to warn her of the overseers.

The text at this point reaches the passage of the *Final Abstinence* (par. 8 and the beginning of 9) discussed above in the context of Zosimus' soteriology. Having

---

us does not simply mean that Democritus "mentioned" the tinctures but that he wrote (about them) allegorically. The previous mention of a σύγγραμμα appears to have been a reference to Democritus' own work unless this book was understood as the ultimate source of Democritus' knowledge, which Zosimus considered to be the *Chēmeu*.

[54] Perhaps intended for liturgies. See Lampe, s.v. ὀθόνη.

[55] In all places in the text where modern translators assumed that something like *daimones* was intended, manuscripts show the symbol ϙϙ. A single koppa (written ϙ, or ♀) was used in manuscripts to symbolize copper or Venus (i.e. the planet *Lucifer*/Φώσφορος). This could explain why the symbol here was used to mean something like *daimones*. See symbol No. 6 in Zuretti 1932 (coming from M, fol. 6ʳ). In the manuscripts of the *Final Abstinence*, the double koppa referred to the "local" or "terrestrial overseers" (ἔφοροι περίγειοι) except in the marginal note of A, fol. 253ʳ (found in the running text of L, fol.237ʳ [= CAAG 2.242.5–6]). On local divinities said to be ἔφοροι and περίγειοι, see Iamblichus, *De Mysteriis*, 5.25 and Festugière 1950: 1.279 n. 2.

[56] Festugière 1950: 1.366.6–367.5.

[57] See LSJ, s.v. κλίμα, II.5 and Bull 2018b: 220 n. 62.

[58] Festugière 1950: 1.366.29–367.5: ἀλλ' ὅτε ἐγένετο ἄρα ἀποκατάστασις τῶν κλιμάτων καὶ διεφέρετο κλίμα πολέμῳ καὶ ἐλείπετο ἐκ τοῦ κλίματος ἐκείνου τὸ γένος τῶν ἀνθρώπων καὶ τὰ ἱερὰ αὐτῶν ἠρημοῦντο καὶ αἱ θυσίαι αὐτῶν ἠμελοῦντο, τοὺς περιλειπομένους ἀνθρώπους ἐκολάκευον ὡς δι' ὀνειράτων διὰ τὸ ψεῦδος αὐτῶν <καὶ> διὰ πολλῶν συμβόλων τῶν [τῶν] θυσιῶν ἀντέχεσθαι, αὐτὰς δὲ πάλιν παρεχόντων τὰς ψευδεῖς καὶ ἀφυσίκας ἐπαγγελίας καὶ ἥδοντο πάντες οἱ φιλήδονοι ἄθλιοι καὶ ἀμαθεῖς ἄνθρωποι.

laid out the history of the tinctures, Zosimus warns Theosebeia not to sacrifice to the overseers but rather to "stay home," "rectify herself" (*seautēn dieuthunasa*) and avert *daimones*. "Doing so," Zosimus adds, Theosebeia would perfect her soul and find the "natural, genuine and propitious tinctures."[59] The theology implied by the passage opposes a god who is everywhere to a multiplicity of local demons (*daimonia*),[60] who can be identified with the "local overseers."

(9) Finishing his moral exhortation, Zosimus concludes the discussion by turning to technical questions:

> As for me, I will turn to the question of your imperfection [...]. Listen to him when he says later that the two eggs ... is a single thing that becomes different. One is liquid and cold, one dry and cold, and the two make a single work.[61]

The subject of "he says" (*autou legontos*) is Democritus, whose book was quoted earlier in the treatise.[62] Zosimus also appears to pick up his reading of pseudo-Democritus where he left it at par. 3–4. Just as he said earlier that Democritus wrote "a single allegorical work,"[63] Zosimus understood here that Democritus spoke of multiple techniques and implied that the use of tinctures was "a single work." Zosimus recognized that Democritean texts discussed different types of tinctures, tools and products but he assumed that there was only "one tincture and one process."[64]

(10–11) Zosimus finally discusses the multiplicity of propitious tinctures and the different colors they produced.[65] To explain these, he refers Theosebeia to his

---

[59] *Id.*, 1.367.10–368.4 (M). The crucial passage is at 1.368.2–3: ὅταν δὲ ἐπιγνῷς σεαυτὴν τελειωθεῖσαν, τότε καὶ <ἐπιτύχουσα> τῶν φυσικῶν τῆς ὕλης κατάπτυσον καὶ καταδραμοῦσα ἐπὶ τὸν Ποιμένανδρα καὶ βαπτισθεῖσα τῷ κρατῆρι ἀνάδραμε ἐπὶ τὸ γένος τὸ σόν. The emendations proposed by Festugière are based on the last lines of a passage of par. 8 quoted in M (1.367.21: καὶ οὕτως ἐνεργοῦσα ἐπιτεύξῃ τῶν γνησίων καὶ φυσικῶν, καταπτύουσα τῆς ὕλης).

[60] *Id.*, 1.367.14–15 (A), 13–14 (M): θεὸς ... ἥξει πρὸς σὲ ὁ πανταχοῦ ὢν καὶ οὐχ ἐν τόπῳ ἐλαχίστῳ ὡς τὰ δαιμόνια.

[61] *Id.*, 1.281 n. 7: ἐγὼ δὲ ἐπὶ τὸ προκείμενον ἐλεύσομαι τῆς σῆς ἀτελειότητος [ἀλλ᾽ ὀλίγον ἐπεκτεῖναι καὶ ἀνενέγκαι χρή με τὸ ζητούμενον]. ἄκουσον αὐτοῦ λέγοντος καὶ μετ᾽ ὀλίγα· ἓν πρᾶγμά ἐστιν <τὰ> δύο ᾠὰ καταποτιζόμενα καὶ διαφόρως γενόμενον, τὸ μὲν ὑγρὸν καὶ ψυχρόν, τὸ δὲ ξηρὸν καὶ ψυχρόν, καὶ τὰ δύο ἓν ἔργον ποιοῦσιν. I read δύο ⊙⊙ (= ᾠὰ) κατ(ὑ/ἱ)ποτασόμενος in A and L where Festugière read δύο ᾠὰ καταποτασόμενος in A, which he corrected by καταποτιζόμενα. According to the table of symbols of L, the two circles stand either for ᾠα or for *ophthalmoi*. Festugière 1950: 1.281, translated "deux oeufs imbibés." The intended word could have been καθυποτασσόμενος, "found below" (following LSJ, s.v. ὑποτάσσω, III: "put after, subjoin, append") and might have referred to a table giving the meaning of the symbols.

[62] CAAG 2.241.12–16, 242.3, 8–9.

[63] CAAG 2.241.25–26.

[64] CAAG 2.242.1–3.

[65] CAAG 2.245.19–246.1–3.

book on colors and his book on furnaces (MA 1). The overview of the problems concerning the unity of the art (par. 9–11) followed Zosimus' exhortation to Theosebeia and served as a demonstration of the importance of study in the practice of alchemy. In other words, Theosebeia's "imperfection" appears in Zosimus' mind to be close to that which he attributed to Neilos, i.e. a lack of acquaintance with the Democritean corpus. In the conclusion, Zosimus repeats the main lesson of the text, which is that both experience and the perfection of the soul are necessary to obtain success in the tinctures:

> All that is sought for is accomplished by the art. Indeed, these tinctures have the power to rot/mature many things and few things, that is to say, to be created in small and large quantities in glass ovens, in large and small crucibles and in the various types of furnaces and fires. Experience will demonstrate (the results) together with the aid of perfection in everything concerning the soul. You have the exposition of the fires and of everything that is sought in the Letter Omega. Let me now begin, purple-clad lady.[66]

The fact that Zosimus points out the importance of experience (*peira*) also explains why he believes studying technical treatises is important.

Zosimus' history of alchemy in the *Final Abstinence* presents a historical argument against contemporary users of the "non-natural" tinctures and looks upon the works attributed to Democritus as a means to bypass the *daimones* who controlled them. While the critique is different, the solution is similar to that which Zosimus used to disqualify Neilos in *On the Treatment of the Body of Magnesia*. In both cases, Zosimus emphasizes his learned and literary approach to the practice of tinctures and contrasts it to the "lack of intellect" of Neilos and the others, claiming that "those who remained" after the abandonment of temple cults were ignorant (*amatheis*) and based their practice on the (deceitful) instructions they received from *daimones* rather than on the study of texts. Zosimus' conclusion to the *Final Abstinence* develops the implications of this history of alchemy by claiming that Democritus was the only author to have alluded to the ancient and genuine tinctures. Consequently, he thought, the only way to practice the original form of alchemy was to avoid *daimones* and to study the Democritean tradition. A similar argument was used in the letter *On the Treatment of the Body of Magnesia* seen earlier. Zosimus explains Neilos' failure in this letter by arguing that he could have avoided it if he had interpreted the Hermetic recipe by reading Democritus. The emphasis on the correct reading of Democritus was central to Zosimus' commentaries and it also distinguished his work from that of his rivals.

---

[66] CAAG 2.246.14–23: τὰ γὰρ ζητούμενα πάντα ἐν τῇ τέχνῃ κατώρθωσαν.᾽Έχουσιν οὖν φύσιν αὗται αἱ βαφαὶ καὶ πολλὰ σήπτεσθαι, καὶ ὀλίγα, τουτέστιν γίγνεσθαι καὶ ἐν καμινίοις ὑελοψικοῖς, καὶ ἐν χωνείαις μεγάλαις καὶ μικραῖς, καὶ ἐν διαφόροις ὀργάνων <διὰ> φώτων, καὶ ἐν ποσότητι αὐτῶν· καὶ ἡ πεῖρα ἀναδείξει, μετὰ καὶ τῶν ψυχικῶν πάντων κατορθωμάτων.᾽Έχεις οὖν τῶν φώτων τὰς ἀποδείξεις ἐν τῷ Ω στοιχείῳ, καὶ πάντων τῶν ζητουμένων· ἔνθεν ἀπάρξομαι, πορφυρόστολε γύναι.

Zosimus on the Origins of Alchemy

Zosimus' second history of alchemy provides further explanation for Zosimus' form of alchemical inquiry. Found in George Syncellus' *Chronography* (c. 800 CE) and in the Syriac translation of Zosimus cited above, this history explains that *chēmeia* had been brought to humans a long time ago by "a race of *daimones*" (*ti daimonōn genos*), also called *angeloi*, who descended to earth to mate with women. Zosimus claims that their knowledge, which encompassed "all works of nature," was recorded in a book called the *Chēmeu*.[67] As recorded by Syncellus, this list of techniques included the use of potions and incantations, the making of every instrument of war, the working of the products of mines and the making of jewelry out of gold and silver as well as the use of cosmetics, precious stones and tinctures (*ta baphika*).[68] As Matteo Martelli (2014b) noted, the list of Azael's techniques as found in Syncellus includes the four different types of tincture mentioned in the oldest texts related to the alchemical tradition.

Zosimus' story has a parallel in another alchemical text entitled *Isis to her Son Horus*, which is dated to the second century CE.[69] In both texts, the work of these divine beings could not have been entirely negative, since the arrival of these *daimones* or *angeloi* must predate the moment the overseers took over the practice of tinctures (i.e. after the "revolution of the zone") mentioned by Zosimus in the *Final Abstinence*. This would not be entirely surprising considering that Clement of Alexandria accepted that the "fallen angels" of the Enochian myth brought divine knowledge to humans. As noted by Annette Yoshiko Reed, Clement's conception of the fallen angel myth differed from that of many other Christians. Understanding the fallen angels' teachings as a "premature infusion of heavenly knowledge," Clement explained how philosophers could have known the (Christian) doctrine of Providence.[70]

Zosimus believed that the *Chēmeu* had been almost irremediably lost. "Those who came afterwards," he wrote, "divided the book in many parts," "damaged" and "hid" its content.[71] By "hiding the books," it is likely that Zosimus did not simply mean that the *Chēmeu* had been secreted away but that its content had also been allegorized. In the *Final Abstinence*, Zosimus rejects the sacrifices necessary for success in the "propitious tinctures" and consequently turns to Democritus,

---

[67] George Syncellus, *Chronography*, 14.2–14 Mosshammer and the Syriac Cambridge Mm. 6.29, fols. 49^r–50^r. See the edition and translation of Martelli 2014b: 12.

[68] George Syncellus, *Chronography*, 12.13–17 Mosshammer. Syncellus' account is similar to a corresponding section of the *Book of the Watchers* (as edited in Black 1985: 8.1) but replaces the mention of armlets (ψέλια) with that of gold and silver jewelry.

[69] On *The Prophetess Isis to her son Horus*, see CAAG 1.28–9.

[70] Clement of Alexandria, *Stromata*, 5.1.10.2. See Reed 2005: 181–184.

[71] This passage is only extant in the Syriac version. See Martelli 2014b: 12. Christian H. Bull (2018a) recently argued that the *daimones* who, according to Zosimus, had brought the *Chēmeu* should be identified with those who "hid" the alchemical tradition.

who, he claims, is the only author to have alluded to the original and unadulterated tinctures. While this is implicit, Zosimus' history of the *Chēmeu* justified his attempts at reading Democritus or other past authorities between the lines in order to recover the message he believed they contained. Incidentally, the history of the *Chēmeu* also justified the creation of novel content that had been allegedly hidden in alchemical recipes. His main criticism, as he highlighted in the letter *On the Treatment of the Body of Magnesia*, was that rivals apparently believed that they could afford to ignore Democritean literature.

On the Letter Omega

The same conclusion can be reached by reading the third and last of Zosimus' polemical writings. Like the *Final Abstinence*, *On the Letter Omega* is addressed to Theosebeia and serves as an introduction to a lost treatise.[72] Its main aim is to criticize the alchemical technique of individuals who had mocked a book on furnaces and tools. The core of the treatise (par. 5–16) is built according to a binary structure opposing different notions around the concept of fate (*heimarmēnē*). The content of these statements is embedded in the polemics of the text, which repeat the fundamental opposition between the learned disposition of Zosimus and the ignorance of his rivals.

After a preamble on the symbolic value of the letter omega (1), Zosimus explains that those who used "deep and propitious tinctures" (*kairikai katabaphai*) had achieved some success by receiving the help of demonic beings and had taken the opportunity to mock the book *On Furnaces and Tools*. Zosimus argues for a position supporting the role of "demonstrative reasoning" (*logos apodeiktikos*) and against resorting to one's personal (*idion*) *daimonion* (2). The reasoning at play also justifies why he believes that one should not attempt to change fate (*heimarmēnē*). The idea that the sacrifices of his rivals were meant to attract the good will of *daimones* is moreover suggested by his reference to the use of the *mageia* of Zoroaster as a means to modify fate.[73] As seen in chapter 2, Porphyry and Eusebius noted the same association between *mageia* (or in this case *mageiai*) and the propitiation of *daimones*. The mention of rivals waiting on the good will of personal *daimones* suggests individuals similar to "those who remained" (after the destruction of the "zone") and those who offered sacrifices to *daimones* in the last narrative part of the *Final Abstinence*.

Zosimus, however, teaches us little about those who mocked the book *On Furnaces and Tools*. We can see that the terms of the conflict were not about the efficacy of their practice, since Zosimus agreed that *daimōnes* could grant success in alchemy (2). The main thrust of the argument was rather ethical and based

---

[72] The most recent edition and translation of the text is MA 1 in Mertens 1995.
[73] MA 1.7.

on theological assumptions. The reliance on *daimones* in the use of "propitious tinctures" signaled the materialistic ethics of his rivals and their concern with the avoidance of fate. In contrast, approving the attitude of philosophers toward fate, Zosimus proposed several fundamental differences between himself and his rivals.

The first paragraphs of the treatise suggest that the main opposition revolved around the acceptance or denial of fate. The same axis opposes Zosimus' rivals to philosophers and God (3.25–26). Unlike philosophers, who were said by Hermes and Zoroaster to be "above fate" (5), Zosimus' rivals are "without intellect" (*anoas*, 4) and change their minds as "the *daimonion*" favors them without considering the "obvious facts" (3.26–30). These men simply follow fate for the goods it brings while at the same time vilifying it for its "bodily lessons" (*sōmatika paideutēria*, 4). Presenting his rivals as anti-philosophers, Zosimus then lists a series of oppositions associating them implicitly with mythological figures and concepts.

First, Zosimus claims, Hesiod opposed Prometheus to Epimetheus because the first refused the "gifts of fate" while the second rejoiced in them (6). Zoroaster, he writes, claimed that he could deter bad fate using *mageia* while Hermes taught one to accept necessity (7). The two oppositions, Prometheus vs. Epimetheus and Hermes vs. Zoroaster signal Zosimus' rhetorical technique and message. While Zosimus and his alchemical method were aligned respectively with philosophers and the acceptance of fate, his rivals and their practice were respectively aligned with *mageia* (a technique to change fate) and Zoroaster.

Zosimus also divides the human being into two parts. One is the material "outer human" (*exo anthrōpos*), who is also called Thoth or Adam (8–9). The other part is the "spiritual and inner human" (*esō anthrōpos ho pneumatikos*), whose common name is *Phōs* (i.e. "Light," 8–10). Originally residing in paradise, Phōs was "blown through by fate" and tricked through the agency of beings to "clothe himself with their Adam."[74] The structuring principle is still the axis of fate, separating those who, like Phōs, accept fate and those who attempt to bend it to their will (11).

Switching back to the allegorical interpretation of Hesiod, Zosimus adds that the first bond (*desmos*) with which Zeus shackled Prometheus was meant to represent the "outer man." Zosimus also mentions that Pandora/Eva was sent by Zeus as a second bond (12). "Prometheus," Zosimus comments,

> is also sometimes an image for the soul, sometimes the mind and sometimes the flesh because of the disregard of Epimetheus, which disregarded its own Prometheus [i.e. his own foresight]. Indeed our Nous says: "the son of God is capable of anything

---

[74] MA 1.11.104–107: ὅτε ἦν Φῶς ἐν τῷ παραδείσῳ διαπνεόμενος ὑπὸ τῆς εἱμαρμένης, ἔπεισαν αὐτὸν ὡς ἄκακον καὶ ἀνενέργητον ἐνδύσασθαι τὸν παρ' αὐτῶν Ἀδάμ, τὸν ἐκ τῆς εἱμαρμένης, τὸν ἐκ τῶν τεσσάρων στοιχείων. These unnamed beings seem to be identified with the ἀντίμιμος δαίμων in MA 1.14.133–134 where Zosimus wrote that he would trick humans "as before" (ὡς τὸ πρώην).

and can become everything he wishes when he decides to appear to each."[75]

Read allegorically, the two successive bonds of the "inner human," also called Prometheus, are Epimetheus (the body) and Pandora/Eva (one of the two gifts of fate, 6). Coming back to a narrative account in a prophetic mode, Zosimus opposes Christ (13) to the future "imitating (*antimimos*) *daimōn*," also called the "jealous one" (*zēlōtēs*). Christ's purpose, he claims, was to liberate humans from "their Adam" while the imitating *daimōn*'s purpose was to stop him (14–15).

Finally, returning to his contemporaries, Zosimus transposes the rivalry that opened the treatise to the field of medicine and thus creates another set of oppositions. Imagining a bone fracture, he opposes the "personal superstition" (*tēs idias deisidaimonias*) of a "bone-setting priest" (*hiereus osteodetēs*) to the diagrams found in the books of physicians (*iatroi*). Zosimus observes that one should not be left to die if no bone-setting priests can be found; a physician should rather be called for support (17–18). This opposition, as the text implies, is similar to that opposing Zosimus to his rivals: a man making use of books is contrasted to men using "*daimōn*-fearing" techniques (*deisidaimoniai*). The conclusion, obviously aimed at his rivals, refers back to the opening of the text, where Zosimus mentioned that rivals had mocked a technical book.

The sequence of opposition can be represented more succinctly in the following table:

Matter/Body	Intellect/Spirit
Processes	
Propitious tinctures (2)	Zosimus' method and the book *On Furnaces and Apparatus* (2)
Modifying fate with *mageia* (7)	Being "above fate" (5) "Proceed in the solitary search for oneself" (7)
The personal rites of the bone-setter priest (18)	The art of the physician, which is based on books (18)
Characters	
The First Human, also called "the first bond," the Adam of flesh (*sarkikos*) or Thoth (8–10), the "outer human" (12) and the earthly Adam (15)	Phōs, the "human within (the first human)," the "spiritual" human (10–11) and the luminous (*phōteinos*) human (15)

---

[75] MA 1.12.115–120: καὶ ποτὲ μὲν ψυχῆς ἔχει εἰκόνα ὁ Προμηθεύς, ποτὲ δὲ νοός, ποτὲ δὲ σαρκὸς διὰ τὴν παρακοὴν τοῦ Ἐπιμηθέως ἣν παρήκουσεν τοῦ Προμηθέως τοῦ ἰδίου <νοῦ>. Φησὶ γὰρ ὁ νοῦς ἡμῶν· ὁ δὲ υἱὸς τοῦ θεοῦ πάντα δυνάμενος καὶ πάντα γινόμενος, ὅτε θέλει, ὡς θέλει, φαίνει ἑκάστῳ.

Epimetheus, who accepts the material gifts of fate (beauty, wealth, 6), or earthly (*gēios*) Adam (16)	Prometheus, who rejects the gifts of Zeus (i.e. Fate) through philosophy (6); as mind (*nous*) counseling Epimetheus and identified in that sense with Phōs and Christ (16)
Pandora/Eve, the "bond" (*desmos*) of Prometheus according to allegorical interpretation (12)	"a single human," i.e. soul and body, or Prometheus and Epimetheus conceived as a unit according to allegorical interpretation (12)
The "imitating demon" (14), the "Imitator" (15)	Christ/Prometheus (13, 16), the Son of God (15)

As can be seen in the table, the point of Zosimus' argument was not simply to show that his rivals should accept technical books. Zosimus' anthropological and eschatological narrative placed him and his opponents on the opposite sides of a universal fault line.

The information about Zosimus' rivals in *On the Letter Omega* correlates with what has been said about the rivals of the other polemical treatises. The "unnatural" and propitious tinctures are attacked in the *Final Abstinence*, where they are presented as the creation of earthly and local *daimones* (i.e. the gods of the Egyptian temples). One can consequently conjecture that Neilos used a similar type of alchemy. Whether Zosimus' opponents formed a distinct group or not, his polemics confirm that he was engaging in rivalry for Theosebeia's ear, that he emphasized his knowledge of technical and literary traditions and that he criticized those who ignored or mocked these traditions.

Zosimus' response to the claims of his rivals was double. In *On the Letter Omega* and *On the Treatment of the Body of Magnesia*, he emphasized the importance of the study of "the ancients"—i.e. of the alchemical works attributed to Democritus, Maria, Hermes and others, which all appear to have been relatively recent (post-Hellenistic) and written in Greek. His second response can be found in the exhortative part of the *Final Abstinence*, where he played up the abstinence from sacrifice, the rejection of demons and the care for the soul.[76] The *Final Abstinence*,

---

[76]This was somewhat overemphasized by Festugière 1950: 1.274 and 282. In contrast to the versions found in A and L, the version of par. 8 found in M, fol. 169ʳ (edited in Festugière 1950: 1.367.10–24 [M] and CAAG 1.84.4–11) appears to have placed more emphasis on the role of self-knowledge. It does not mention the passions and the "twelve lots of death," and omits the references to apotropaic rituals of *Membrēs* and Salomon and the crucial conclusion of the passage: "spit on matter, run down to *Poimenandrēs*, be baptized in the crater and run up to your own kin." It also carries sentences not in the version of A and L: Theosebeia is told not to search for god to and fro, "knowing that there is one god and one art" (ἐπιγνοῦσα ἕνα θεὸν καὶ μίαν τέχνην). She is also told that "she will know the god who is truly one when she will know herself" (ὅταν δὲ ἐπιγνῷς σαυτήν, τότε ἐπιγνώσῃ καὶ τὸν μόνον ὄντως θεόν).

however, was not just a call for a final renunciation of traditional sacrifices and an exhortation to moral purification. By revealing the demonic origins of the propitious tinctures, Zosimus also underlined the necessity of studying Democritean writings to recover the "genuine and natural tinctures."

To sum up the argumentation thus far: 1) in the letter *On the Treatment of the Body of Magnesia*, Zosimus' most explicit rival was a certain Neilos, identified as Theosebeia's priest, whom he described as marveling with disciples in front of the statues of divinities. Neilos' activities as well as the mention that he was the priest *of* Theosebeia (and not that of a temple, a god or a city) suggest that he was not necessarily attached to an Egyptian temple. 2) In the historical narrative of the *Final Abstinence*, Zosimus described the alchemical practice of "those who remained" (the *perileipomenoi anthrōpoi*) as related to that of former Egyptian priests. The gods of the Egyptian temples had stolen control over the ancient tinctorial art a long time ago and had lured their priests into sacrificing to them. In exchange, the priests received success in a debased form of alchemy. After the "zone" (*klima*) had been laid to waste—by which Zosimus must have meant Egypt—its temples deserted and its rituals abandoned, the gods kept control over the tinctures by visiting "those who remained" in their dreams and by promising them success in tinctures in exchange for sacrifices. Zosimus does not appear to have imagined these to be the rites of the temples since he assumed that they had been abandoned after the "destruction of the *klima* (of Egypt)." Following this narrative, the contemporary practitioners of alchemy who sacrificed to the *daimones* were "those who remained," a group not necessarily the same as the ancient priestly class of Egypt. 3) The rivals mentioned in *On the Letter Omega* practiced propitious tinctures and were in contact with their personal *daimones*. These two characteristics suggest that the rivals of *On the Letter Omega* belonged to the group of "those who remained" described in the *Final Abstinence*. Since Zosimus attempted to discredit Neilos by showing his interest in the statues of the gods and that the wrong alchemical technique he described was dependent on sacrifices offered to the "terrestrial overseers" (i.e. local divinities), we can conjecture that Zosimus put all his rivals in the same group. It is also evident that what Zosimus calls the overseers are the traditional gods of Egypt, since he describes them as having resided in the temples before their desertion. The actual social identity of the practitioners imagined by Zosimus remains mysterious but he appears to have described individuals whose alchemical practice continued that of the Egyptian temples since it involved the offering of sacrifices to the (now delocalized) Egyptian gods. More importantly, Zosimus' description of his rivals emphasized his own mastery of the literature attributed to Democritus.

3. *MAGEIA* AND *CHĒMEIA*

Part of Zosimus' rhetorical tactic consists in describing his opponents as demon-worshippers. Drawing a comparison between their techniques and the "personal superstition" (*idia deisidaimonia*) of a "bone-setting priest" (*hiereus ostodetēs*), Zosimus claims that they would hardly have realized how problematic their methods were even if these had repeatedly failed them.[77] He also makes an implicit comparison between their technique and the *mageia* of Zoroaster,[78] which is associated in several texts with the control of *daimones*.

Fourth-century CE manuscripts discovered in an unknown location in the Theban region also provide evidence to claim that alchemical texts and *mageia* were somehow associated in antiquity. Scholars who worked on *P. Holmiensis* and *P. Leidensis* X, the two oldest books of Greek alchemy, usually agree that they were written by the same person who wrote *P. Leidensis* W (= PGM XIII), containing the "Tenth Book of Moses" and the two versions of the "Eighth Book of Moses."[79] It is also likely that these three recipe books were found together with several other books of recipes (usually concerned with divination and love charms) written in Demotic, Coptic and Greek and acquired in the nineteenth century by various European institutions.[80]

The "Books of Moses" found in the collection focus on acquiring the name of a god to provide their bearer with special powers. Many of these powers (e.g. fetching a lover, sending dreams, *charitēsia*) are typical of those allegedly found in the Theban archive. Some are similar to the practice of Zosimus' bone-setting priests[81] or to *paignia* (e.g. quenching fire, making "all types of winged creatures" die by speaking in their ear), which, as discussed in chapter 3, were found in connection with the figure of the learned sorcerer. Some of the recipes found in the books believed to form a single Theban archive also describe the power of recipes as *mageia*.[82] Whatever the writers of the recipes had in mind, many Greek-educated

---

[77] Compare MA 1.2.20–24 with MA 1.18.178–188.

[78] MA 1.7.

[79] On the handwriting, see Halleux 1981: 9–12 and PGM, 86. In his edition of *P.Holm.*, Otto Lagercrantz (1913: 50) remarked that the handwriting of *P.Leid.* X (= *P.Leid.* I 397, sometimes written J 397) and *P.Holm* were very similar and suggested that the author was the same.

[80] According to Dosoo (2016), these are PGM I, II, IV, V, Va, PGM/PDM XII, PGM XIII, PGM/PDM XIV, PDM Suppl., *P.Leid.* X and *P.Holm*. It is generally assumed that these books were used by priests trained in the scriptoria of the Egyptian temples, whether these priests were attached to temples or not. See, e.g. Frankfurter 2000, Dieleman 2005 and Love 2016. Considering that alchemical books were found in the so-called "Theban Magical Library," one could consequently infer that Neilos, whom Zosimus called a priest, had been trained in an Egyptian temple. It is, however, unclear what kind of priest Neilos was and it is possible that Zosimus' competitors could be perceived as priests, whether Egyptian or not, and so without having received the traditional training.

[81] See PGM XIII.244–245.

[82] Of the nine uses of *mageia* and cognates in the PGM, one (LXIII.4–5) is a conjecture from the ed-

scholars from the Roman Empire would have seen in the use of this vocabulary a confirmation of the suspicion that these were books of *mageia*.

It is also clear that *P.Leid.* X and *P.Holm.* would have been considered as alchemical and possibly also as books containing ancient prophetic knowledge (like the "Books of Moses"). Taken as a whole, they show the same fourfold subdivision of tinctures found in early alchemical texts (gold, silver, gems and textile dyes) and can consequently be tied to this tradition.[83] While Greek alchemical texts do not mention the kinds of recipes found in PGM XIII or in similar recipe books, PGM XII includes a recipe for "gold rust" (*iōsis chrusou*), for which equivalents can be found in the alchemical corpus.[84] This reinforces the impression that a person principally interested in recipe books such as PGM XIII could also be interested in alchemical recipes.

Alchemical literature itself does not suggest a link with *mageia* broadly considered but with *mageia* conceived as the wisdom of the Persian *magoi*. Democritus, who was considered one of the most important figures of Greek alchemy, was also commonly thought to have studied with *magoi*. One alchemical text claims that Democritus wrote his *Four Books* only after having been initiated by the *magos* Ostanes in Memphis. The connection of Democritean alchemy with *mageia* is also

---

[83] See Mertens 1995: 14.

[84] PGM XII.193–204. Zago (2010: 139–140) translates ἰός by "affinazione," Betz (1986: 160), by "tincture" or "reduction" and the PGM, 2.71 by "Läuterung." Halleux (1981: 165–166) suggested that the recipe was a παίγνιον based on the cementation (i.e. refining) of alloyed gold (although gold is not mentioned in the recipe itself). For a discussion of this argument, see Martelli 2013: 95 n. 46, commenting on a similar recipe found in the *Physica et Mystica*, 13.141–142. Psellus attributed a recipe for ἴωσις χρυσοῦ to Africanus (see Wallraff et al. 2012: T7). Pelagius, an alchemical author dated to the fourth century CE (Letrouit 1995: 46–56) also mentioned ἰός χρυσοῦ and specified that it was produced from copper (CAAG 3.255.9). The scrapings of residues from the furnaces of goldsmiths could be used as a drug (compare Dioscorides, *Materia Medica*, 5.75, Pliny, *Natural History*, 34.128–134). Since the ἴωσις χρυσοῦ recipe produced "scrapings" (λακήματα), it is possible that it was meant to produce a counterfeit remedy similar to the one discussed by Pliny, *Natural History*, 33.25.

---

itors and all others appear in PGM I and IV. In a recipe used to conjure a sumptuous dinner, Pnouthis the sacred scribe writes to his addressee as a μα[κάριε] μύστα τῆς ἱερᾶς μαγείας (127). A recipe showing how to invoke a divinity enjoins the invoker to ask περὶ οὗ θέλεις, περὶ μαντείας, περὶ ἐποποιίας, περὶ ὀνειροπομπείας, περὶ ὀνειραιτησίας, περὶ ὀνειροκριτίας, περὶ κατακλίσεως, περὶ πάντων ὅ[σ]ων ἐστὶν ἐν τῇ μαγικῇ ἐμπει[ρίᾳ]. The "magical craft" appears to be the name of a category including the types of divination mentioned. In PGM IV, a letter from Nephotes addresses pharaoh Psammetichus as μάγων καθη<γε>μών. A recipe for an invocation found in a letter of Pitus addressed to "king Ostanes" advertised its efficacy by mentioning that πλεῖστοι δὲ τῶν μάγων παρ' ἑαυτοῖς τὰ σκεύη βαστάξαντες καὶ ἀποθέμενοι ἐχρήσαντο αὐτῷ παρέδρῳ καὶ τὰ προκείμενα διὰ πάσης ὀξύτητος ἐπετέλεσαν (2083–2087). An invocation to the moon mentions the invoker's μαγείης τῆς ἐμῆς ... βέλος that could possibly compel the moon (2314–2315). The invoker is also said to impersonate Hermes μάγων ἀρχηγέτης (2283–2285). The last occurrences of cognates of *mageia* are found in an invocation attributed to the προφήτης Panchrates. He is said to have demonstrated τὴν δύναμιν τῆς θείας αὐτοῦ μαγείας to the emperor Hadrian, who is also said to have witnessed τὴν ὅλην ἀλήθειαν τῆς περὶ αὐτὸν μαγείας.

suggested by the notion that Democritus attempted to contact his dead master through a necromantic rite.[85]

In his extant works, Zosimus focuses on Democritus and cites Ostanes several times while at the same time dissociating himself from *mageia*. *Mageia*, he claims, is not comparable to what he practices nor does he see it as useful in any way. Zoroaster, he writes, had presumptuously presented *mageia* as a means to control one's destiny. Citing the authority of Hermes against Zoroaster, Zosimus asserted that one should not try to rectify fate through *mageia* or any other means.[86] It is also clear from the history of alchemy found in the *Final Abstinence* that Zosimus associated the use of "propitious tinctures," with the offering of sacrifices to *daimones*.[87] The nature of his accusations coincides with a marked tendency in late antiquity to associate demon-worship with *goēteia* or the wrong type of *mageia*.[88] Both Zosimus and Porphyry argued that philosophers should avoid blood sacrifice or ritualistic means to produce the return of the soul to the divine, i.e. that neither *mageia* nor *theourgia* could be effectively used for soteriological purposes.[89] Rather than siding with those who used *mageia* to change their fate (MA 1.7), Zosimus held demonology and ethical-soteriological principles that placed him in the middle of a large (third-century) scholarly consensus on the avoidance of blood-sacrifice.[90] Like contemporary philosophers and scholars, he claimed that his rivals made use of illegitimate rituals. Considering that alchemy appears to have been associated with *mageia*, this kind of accusation would have been useful for discrediting rivals while at the same time avoiding the suspicion surrounding *mageia*.

---

[85] See the *Physica et Mystica*, 3 and *The Philosopher Synesius to Dioscorus*, 1–2 in Martelli 2013: 82–85, 122–125 together with Martelli's introduction on the Persian elements in the alchemical works of Pseudo-Democritus (32–34, 69–73).

[86] MA 1.7.

[87] See the *Final Abstinence* in Festugière 1950: 1.367.24–27 (trans. 1.280).

[88] See, e.g., Porphyry, *On Abstinence*, 2.37–43, and more specifically 2.41.5. Porphyry argued against blood sacrifice in general but tolerated its use in apotropaic rituals (2.44). Augustine described the miracles of the *magi* who opposed Moses in Augustine, *De diversis quaestionibus 83*, 79.4 as proceeding from "individual contracts" (*per privatos contractus*) with "powers" (*potestates*) which he identified elsewhere with demons (*De doctrina christiana*, 2.20.30). On the growing association of illegitimate rites and demon worship in late antique Christianity, see Flint 1999: 277–348 and Sanzo, forthcoming.

[89] See the summary of Porphyry's doctrine concerning theurgy and soteriology in Augustine, *City of God*, 10.9. I do not see good reasons to dispute his claim that Porphyry did not consider theurgy effective in bringing the return of the noetic part of the soul to its source. Augustine's comments do not imply that Porphyry saw theurgy as the equivalent of *goēteia* but rather that he demoted theurgy in regard to the form of soteriological practice he reserved for himself and philosophers. For Porphyry's own description of the actions involved in the return of the soul, see Porphyry, *On Abstinence*, 1.57.2, 2.33–34. See Marx-Wolf 2016: 100–125. More generally on this question, see Addey 2014: 136–138, 150–157, 180–183, Van Liefferinge 1999: 176–190 and Tanaseanu-Döbler 2013: 83–88.

[90] See Marx-Wolf 2016. On Zosimus more specifically, see Camplani and Zambon 2002: 59–99, Knipe 2011: 59–69. See also Martelli 2017.

CONCLUSION

Zosimus described his opponents as uneducated (*apaideutoi*) while at the same time underlining his own *paideia* by emphasizing the importance of Democritus for the correct practice of alchemy. In Zosimus' vision of alchemy, the Democritean tradition—which could be conceived as an integral part of *paideia*—replaced the alchemy of his rivals, which he described as a form of *mageia* and an anti-philosophy.

In all three cases, Zosimus' response to the challenges posed by rivals was the same: one ought to bring literary traditions to bear on the practice of tinctures. For Zosimus, "extracting" the soul from the body and returning to the state enjoyed by Phōs before the fall involved ethical as well as scholarly exercises. Success in tinctures, he told Theosebeia, would only work if she rectified herself, gave up on the help provided by *daimones*, prayed to the one god and acquired practical experience (*peira*). Giving up on the help of *daimones* meant that piecing back together the traditions stemming from the *Chēmeu* was crucial to one's success in alchemical matters. According to Zosimus, interpreting Democritus was a necessary step in the reconstruction of the *Chēmeu*, which had been "damaged," "hidden" and "divided."

Zosimus thought that the correct and saving practice of alchemy was predicated on a moral and intellectual enterprise that was typical of *paideia* and more particularly of Greek philosophy. Since he was opposed to the form of alchemy that he associated with *mageia* and demon-worship, legitimacy for alchemical practice had to be found somewhere else. His history of alchemy implied that the study of Democritus was the only way one could reach back to the "genuine" and "natural" tinctures of the fallen angels. As far as we can tell, such a conception of alchemy was more aligned with the interests of Christian, Greek-educated scholars than with the alchemy of his opponents.

Conclusion

While discussing the figure of the learned sorcerer, I have abstained from commenting on the fact that many examples provided came from Christian literature. In constructing this figure, early Christian writers may have deployed a rhetorical tactic that had been previously used against Jesus. Often called a "teacher" by his followers, he was described as a "sophist" and a "sorcerer" (*goēs*) by those who opposed early Christians.[1] The apologetic works studied in chapter 3 turned the same rhetoric against the purported founders of competing Christian schools. This also suggests that the authors of the *Acts of Peter* and of the *Pseudo-Clementines* imagined the first evangelists and their enemies to have conducted their mission by borrowing social channels that had been previously created by scholarly patronage. The sociological imagination of these polemicists could consequently reflect the means by which third- and fourth-century Christian scholars evangelized some aristocratic houses.

The purpose of this book was not to bring readers to this conclusion but rather to show that Zosimus was a client scholar and that scholarly patronage contributed to the legitimation of alchemical commentaries. Those unaware of the alchemical tradition would most probably have heard of counterfeiting techniques and perhaps have seen collections of alchemical recipes such as those found in *P.Leid.* and *P.Holm.* On the other hand, those aware of the alchemical tradition as described by Zosimus or by the *Four Books* attributed to Democritus were also likely to have perceived such collections of recipes as the work of *magoi*. Considered merely as a derivative of this type of literature, Zosimus' work was unlikely to have been selected as worthy of memory by later scribes and scholars. More elements from Zosimus' work suggest that his commentaries would have been ignored by later

---

[1] See, e.g., Pliny the Younger, *Letters*, 10.96, Justin Martyr, *Dialogue with Trypho*, 69.7. On Jesus as σοφιστής, see Lucian, *Peregrinus*, 13, as *goēs*, see Origen, *Against Celsus*, 1.68 (citing Celsus' *True Discourse*, second century CE), Eusebius of Caesarea, *Against Hierocles*, 2.27 (citing Hierocles' *Lover of Truth*, late third century CE).

Christian scholars and copyists. His high regard for the visionary Nicotheus (described in the Bruce codex as a "perfect one" along with Marsanes) associated him with discredited Christian doctrines;[2] his emphasis on Hermes and the *Hermetica*, and the anthropogonic myth of *On the Letter Omega* also placed him outside of nascent Christian orthodoxy; and his disincarnated view of salvation contradicted the consensus on the resurrection of the body that developed among Christian scholars during his lifetime.[3] Through his choice of source material—unconventional, of purported Jewish or Egyptian origin, associated with *mageia* (at least through Democritus) and with trickery (i.e. counterfeiting) or *paignia*—Zosimus also shared characteristics with the learned sorcerer figure. However, the study of Juvenal, Lucian, Plutarch and Julius Africanus and Heliodorus showed that patrons did not necessarily see this as detrimental to the reputation of a scholar.

On the contrary, many Greek-educated scholars considered eastern learned traditions such as *mageia* to be legitimate topics of study. In the works of Philo of Alexandria, for example, the "true magical" art was a technique meant to interpret divine signs found in the world and to be of service to kings. However, like other Latin-speakers, Philo's near contemporary Pliny did not distinguish between a philosophical/positive type of *mageia* and a host of illegitimate rites and subtle forms of aggression. Overlaps between these two large categories of uses of the term *mageia* and cognates can explain why the association with *mageia* was problematic or desirable depending on the context. Contrasting the way Porphyry and Eusebius used the terms shows that polemics or misunderstandings could frame interest in eastern traditions as improper or dangerous "curiosity" in curses and divination.

Descriptions of learned sorcerers included elements typical of the life of client scholars. These, rather than religious professionals and/or philosophers, must have served as a template (and as a target) for the literary figure of the learned sorcerer. The figure of Apion in the *Pseudo-Clementine Homilies* is a particularly good example of this literary type. In contrast with his earlier depictions, the Apion of the *Homilies* shared several traits with the uneducated client scholar imagined by Lucian. A follower of Simon "Magus," he had also befriended a Roman aristocrat and offered love-charms to his son, Clement. He also stood for the corrupting influence of Greek myths and for scholars who attempted to rationalize myths through allegorical interpretation. From the perspective of the *Homilies*, his education (*paideia*) was like that of the client scholar who resorted to playing the role of *magos*. Apion's sorcery, however, was an empty show of verbal sophistry. As with Lucian's Pancrates and his explanation of the aristocratic expectation that client scholars could play the role of *mantis* and *magos*, the extraordinary powers of the learned sorcerer simply mimicked real scholarship. The figure of

---

[2] See MA.1.1, 10, with the commentary in Jackson 1978: 17 n. 4, 29 n. 50, 1990: 250–277.
[3] Bynum 1995.

the learned sorcerer was a rhetorical construct used to delegitimize certain ideas or scholars, and its oldest extant template was the figure of the "mis-educated" scholar described by Lucian and Juvenal. The stereotype suggests that some scholars were perceived as pseudo-scholars because they were supported by powerful patrons. Whether or not we might agree with him, Lucian testifies to the fact that the irritation and indignation they provoked came from their perceived ability to legitimate peripheral or undesired knowledge as proper to *paideia*.

Considering his interests, theological ideas and proselytism, Zosimus could well have been described as a learned sorcerer and his work would then have been delegitimized. This, however, never happened. Zosimus' work managed, rather, to sustain the interest of scholars from different linguistic and intellectual backgrounds for many centuries. One explanation for the success of his commentaries in the ancient Greek-speaking world was that, by squaring the attraction of eastern philosophies with the conservative forces of *paideia*, he made a virtue of necessity. As a Greek-educated scholar, Zosimus had to satisfy the requirements of *paideia* and of his patroness. By arguing that Democritus was the only author who spoke about the ancient and genuine tinctures and by discrediting the pretentions of his rivals, he turned his patroness' attention away from the Egyptian traditions and refocused it on Greek texts. Only Greek-educated scholars like himself, Zosimus tacitly claimed, could retrieve the ancient technology of the fallen angels through a careful interpretation of the Democritean corpus. Zosimus thus attempted to bind alchemical practice to the Greek commentary tradition. The attempt at annexing alchemical practice ascribed to Egyptians, Jews or Persians as a scholarly field within *paideia* can also explain how Greek alchemical commentaries found legitimacy in the eyes of later scholars. The patronage of Theosebeia played a role in this process by providing Zosimus' work with a venue, which helped its diffusion. The rivalry with Neilos and others also enabled him to voice a theological and soteriological position that broke with former religious practices while perpetuating and profiting from the fascination with Egyptian traditions.

BIBLIOGRAPHY

Addey, Crystal. 2014. *Divination and Theurgy in Neoplatonism*. London.
Adler, William. 1993. "Apion's 'Encomium of Adultery': A Jewish Satire of Greek Paideia in the Pseudo-Clementine *Homilies*." *Hebrew Union College Annual* 64: 15–49.
———. 2004. "Sextus Julius Africanus and the Roman Near East in the Third Century." *Journal of Theological Studies* 55.2: 520–550.
———. 2009. "The *Cesti* and Sophistic Culture in the Severan Age." In M. Wallraff and L. Mecella, eds., *Die Kestoi des Julius Africanus und ihre Überlieferung*, 1–15. Berlin.
Amato, Eugenio. 2009. *Severus Sophista Alexandrinus*. Berlin.
Ameling, Walter. 2014. "Some Remarks on Apion." *Scripta Classica Israelica* 33: 1–15.
Aune, David A. 2007. "'Magic' in Early Christianity and its Ancient Mediterranean Context." *Annali di Storia dell'Esegesi* 24: 229–294.
Armstrong, Arthur H., trans. 1966–1988. *Plotinus. Enneads*, 7 vols. Cambridge, Mass.
Armstrong, David. 2012. "Juvenalis Eques: A Dissident Voice from the Lower Tier of the Roman Elite." In S. Braund and J. Osgood, eds., *A Companion to Persius and Juvenal*. Oxford.
Bain, David. 1998. "Salpe's *paignia*: Athenaeus 322a and Plin. H.N. 28.38." *Classical Quarterly* 48: 262–268.
———. 2006. "Koiranides." In *Reallexikon für Antike und Christentum* 21: 224–232.
Barbara, Sébastien. 2014. "Le dentifrice d'Apulée (*Ludicra*, fr.2): Déviance coupable ou banalité frivole?" In P.-A. Deproost, ed., *Extravagances*, 133–170. Paris.
Baumbach, Manuel. 2008. "An Egyptian Priest at Delphi: Calasiris as *theios anēr* in Heliodorus' *Aethiopica*." In B. Dignas and K. Trampedach, eds., *Practitioners of the Divine*, 167–183. Cambridge, Mass.
Betegh, Gábor. 2004. *The Derveni Papyrus: Cosmology, Theology and Interpretation*. Cambridge.
Berthelot, Marcellin. 1885. *Les origines de l'alchimie*. Paris.
Berthelot, Marcellin, et al. 1893. *La chimie au Moyen Âge*. 3 vols. Paris.
Berthelot, Marcellin, and Ruelle, Charles-Émile. 1887–1888. *Collection des anciens alchimistes grecs*. 3 vols. Paris.
Betz, Hans D. 1979. "The Delphic Maxim γνῶθι σαυτόν in Hermetic Interpretation." *Harvard Theological Review* 63: 465–484.

———. 1986. *The Greek Magical Papyri in Translation*. Chicago.
Bidez, Joseph, and Cumont, Franz. 1938. *Les mages hellénisés*. 2 vols. Paris.
Black, Matthew. 1985. *The Book of Enoch*. Leiden.
Bompaire, Jacques. 1958. *Lucien écrivain: Imitation et création*. Paris.
Bonneau, Danielle. 1964. *La crue du Nil*. Paris.
Bonner, Stanley. 1977. *Education in Ancient Rome*. London.
Bowersock, Glen W. 1969. *Greek Sophists in the Roman Empire*. Oxford.
———. 1994. *Fiction as History*. Berkeley.
Bowie, Ewen. 1990. "Greek Poetry in the Antonine Age." In D. A. Russell, ed., *Antonine Literature*, 53–90. Oxford.
———. 1996. "The Ancient Readers of the Greek Novels." In G. Schmeling, ed., *The Novel in the Ancient World*, 87–113. Leiden.
Boyce, Mary. 1975. *A History of Zoroastrianism*. 3 vols. Leiden.
Bram, Jean Rhys, trans. 1975. *Ancient Astrology, Theory and Practice. Matheseos Libri VIII by Firmicus Maternus*. Park Ridge (N. J.).
Braund, Susanna Morton, trans. 2004. *Juvenal and Persius*. Cambridge, Mass.
Bremmer, Jan N. 1998. "Aspects of the *Acts of Peter*: Women, Magic, Place and Date." In J. N. Bremmer, ed., *The Acts of Peter: Magic, Miracles, and Gnosticism*, 1–20. Leuven.
———. 2002. "The Birth of the Term 'Magic.'" In J. N. Bremmer and J. R. Veenstra, eds., *The Metamorphosis of Magic from Late Antiquity to the Early Modern Age*, 1–11. Leuven. A previous version of this paper appeared in *Zeitschrift für Papyrologie und Epigraphik* 126 (1999) 1–12.
———. 2010a. "Pseudo-Clementines: Texts, Dates, Places, Authors and Magic." In J. N. Bremmer, ed., *The Pseudo-Clementine*, 1–23. Leuven.
———. 2010b. "Apion and Annubion in the Pseudo-Clementines." In J. N. Bremmer, ed., *The Pseudo-Clementine*, 72–91. Leuven.
———. 2014. *Initiation into the Mysteries in the Ancient World*. Berlin.
Bull, Christian H. 2018a. "Wicked Angels and the Good Demon: The Origins of Alchemy According to the Physica of Hermes." *Gnosis* 3: 3–33.
———. 2018b. "Hermes between Pagans and Christians: The Nag Hammadi Hermetic in Context." In H. Lundhaug and L. Jennott, eds., *The Nag Hammadi Codices and Late Antique Egypt*, 207–260. Tübingen.
———. 2018c. *The Tradition of Hermes Trismegistus: The Egyptian Priestly Figure as a Teacher of Hellenized Wisdom*. Religions in the Graeco-Roman World, v. 186. Leiden.
Burford, Alison. 1972. *Craftsmen in Greek and Roman Society*. Ithaca.
Burkert, Walter. 1983. "Itinerant Diviners and Magicians: A Neglected Element in Cultural Contacts." In R. Hägg, ed., *The Greek Renaissance of the Eighth Century B.C.: Tradition and Innovation*, 115–119. Athens.
———. 1992. *The Orientalizing Revolution*. Cambridge, Mass.
———. 2007. *Babylon, Memphis, Persepolis*. Cambridge, Mass.
Burns, Dylan M. 2014. *Apocalypse of the Alien God*. Philadelphia.
———. 2015. "μίξεως τινι τέχνῃ κρείττονι: Alchemical Metaphor in the *Paraphrase of Shem* (NHC VII,1)." *Aries* 15: 79–106.
Bury, Robert G., trans. 1933. *Sextus Empiricus. Outlines of Pyrrhonism*. Cambridge, Mass.
Busch, Peter. 2006. *Magie in neutestamentlicher Zeit*. Göttingen.

Busine, Aude. 2005. *Paroles d'Apollon: Pratiques et traditions oraculaires dans l'Antiquité tardive (IIe-VIe siècles)*. Leiden.
Butterworth, G. W., trans. 1919. *Clement of Alexandria: The Exhortation to the Greeks. The Rich Man's Salvation. To the Newly Baptized*. Cambridge, Mass.
Bynum, Caroline. 1995. *The Resurrection of the Body*. New York.
Calvo Martínez, José Luis. 2007. "¿Magos griegos o persas? Los usos más antiguos del término *magos*: Heráclito, Sófocles, Eurípides y el Papiro de Derveni." *MHNH: Revista Internacional de Investigación sobre Magia y Astrología Antiguas* 7: 301–314.
Camplani, Alberto. 2000. "Procedimenti magico-alchemici e discorso filosofico ermetico." In G. Lanata, ed., *Il Tardoantico alle soglie del Duemila*, 73–98. Pisa.
Camplani, Alberto, and Zambon, Marco. 2002. "Il sacrificio come problema in alcune correnti filosofiche di età imperial." *Annali di storia dell'esegesi* 19: 59–99.
Carastro, Marcello. 2007. *La cité des mages*. Grenoble.
Carlà, Filippo. 2016. "Dal *Perpetuum exilium* al taglio della mano: Falso in moneta e *maiestas* nel diritto tardoromano, bizantino e romano-germanico." In J. Chamerou and P.-M. Giuhard, eds., *Produktion und Recyceln von Münzen in der Spätantike*, 29–46. Mainz.
Chadwick, Henry, trans. 1953. *Origen. Contra Celsum*. Cambridge.
Champion, Michael. 2014. *Explaining the Cosmos*. Oxford.
Charron, Régine. 2005. "The Apocryphon of John (NHC II, 1) and the Greco-Egyptian Alchemical Literature." *Vigiliae Christianae* 59: 438–456.
Charron, Régine, and Painchaud, Louis. 2001. "'God is a Dyer,' The Background and Significance of a Puzzling Motif in the Coptic *Gospel According to Philip (CG II, 3)*." *Le Muséon* 114: 41–50.
Cirillo, Luigi, and Schneider, André. 2005. "Introduction." In P. Geoltrain and J.-D. Kaestli, eds., *Écrits apocryphes chrétiens*, vol. 2, 1593–1621. Paris.
Colinet, Andrée. 2000a. *Les alchimistes grecs. Tome X: L'anonyme de Zuretti*. Paris.
———. 2000b. "Le *Travail des quatre éléments* ou lorsqu'un alchimiste byzantin s'inspire de Jabir." In I. Draelants et al., eds., *Occident et Proche-Orient: Contacts scientifiques au temps des Croisades*, 165–190. Turnhout.
———. 2010. *Les alchimistes grecs. Tome XI: Recettes alchimiques (Par. Gr. 2419; Holkhamicus 109)—Cosmas le Hiéromoine, Chrysopée*. Paris.
Collins, Derek. 2008. *Magic in the Ancient Greek World*. Oxford.
Conche, Marcel. 1986. *Héraclite, Fragments*. Paris.
Coppola, Giovanna. 1994. *Cultura e potere*. Milan.
Corbeill, Anthony. 2001. "Education in the Roman Republic: Creating Traditions." In Y. L. Too, ed., *Education in Greek and Roman Antiquity*, 261–287. Leiden.
Côté, Dominique. 2001. *Le thème de l'opposition entre Pierre et Simon dans les Pseudo-Clémentines*. Paris.
———. 2006. "Les procédés rhétoriques dans les pseudo-clémentines, L'éloge de l'adultère du grammairien Apion." In F. Amsler et al., eds., *Nouvelles intrigues pseudo-clémentines*, 189–210. Geneva.
Courcelle, Pierre. 1974. *Connais-toi toi-même*. 3 vols. Paris.
Courtney, Edward. 2013. *A Commentary on the Satires of Juvenal*. Berkeley.
Craddock, Paul. 2010. *Early Metal Mining and Production*. London.

Craddock, Paul, et al.1998. "The Refining of Gold in the Classical World." In D. Williams, ed., *The Art of the Greek Goldsmith*, 111–121. London.
Cribiore, Raffaella. 2005. *Gymnastics of the Mind*. Princeton.
———. 2007a. "Lucian, Libanius, and the Short Road to Rhetoric." *Greek, Roman, and Byzantine Studies* 47: 71–86.
———. 2007b. *The School of Libanius in Late Antique Antioch*. Princeton.
D'Angour, Armand. 2011. *The Greeks and the New*. Cambridge.
Damon, Cynthia. 1995. *The Mask of the Parasite*. Ann Arbor.
———. 2008. "'The Mind of an Ass and the Impudence of a Dog': A Scholar Gone Bad." In I. Sluiter and R. M. Rosen, eds., *Kakos*, 335–364. Leiden.
Dandamayev, Muhammad A. 2011. "Arabia i. The Achaemenid Province Arabāya." In *Encyclopaedia Iranica* II.3, s.v. Arabāya. London (updated version available at http://www.iranicaonline.org/articles/arabaya-arabia-a-province-of-the-achaemenid-Empire).
———. 2012. "Magi." In *Encyclopaedia Iranica* (http://www.iranicaonline.org/articles/magi; accessed on 23 Oct. 2018).
Daumas, François. 1956. "La valeur de l'or dans la pensée égyptienne." *Revue de l'histoire des religions* 149 (1956) 9–13.
———. 1980. "Quelques textes de l'atelier des orfèvres dans le temple de Dendara." In J. Vercoutter, ed., *Livre du Centenaire, 1880–1980*, 109–118. Cairo.
Davidson, James. 1995. "Don't Try This at Home: Pliny's Salpe, Salpe's *Paignia* and Magic." *Classical Quarterly* 45: 590–592.
Dean, James E. 1935. *Epiphanius, Treatise on Weights and Measures. The Syriac Version*. Chicago.
De Salvia, Fulvio. 1987. "La figura del mago egiziano nella tradizione letteraria greco-romana." In A. Roccati and A. Siliotti, eds., *La magia in Egitto ai tempi dei faraoni*, 343–365. Modena.
DeFilippo, Joseph. 1990. "*Curiositas* and the Platonism of Apuleius' Golden Ass." *The American Journal of Philology* 111.4: 471–492.
DePalma Digeser, Elizabeth. 2012. *A Threat to Public Piety*. Cornell.
Derchain, Philippe. 1962. "Mythes et dieux lunaires en Égypte." In *La lune, mythes et rites. Sources Orientales V*. Paris.
———. 1990. "L'atelier des orfèvres à Dendara et les origines de l'alchimie." *Chronique d'Égypte* 65: 219–242.
Dickie, Matthew. 1991. "Heliodorus and Plutarch on the Evil Eye." *Classical Philology* 86: 17–29.
———. 1999. "The Learned Magician and the Collection and Transmission of Magical Lore." In D. R. Jordan et al., eds., *The World of Ancient Magic*, 163–194. Athens.
———. 2001. *Magic and Magicians in the Greco-Roman World*. London.
Dieleman, Jacco. 2005. *Priests, Tongues, and Rites*. Leiden.
Diels, Hermann. 1965. *Antike Technik*. Osnabrück.
Diels, Hermann, and Kranz, Walther. 1934–1938. *Die Fragmente der Vorsokratiker*. Berlin.
Dillon, John. 1985. "The Magical Power of Names in Origen and Later Platonism." In R. Hanson and H. Crouzel, eds., *Origenia Tertia*. 203–216. Rome.
Dillon, John and Russell, Donald, trans. 2014. *Aeneas of Gaza: Theophrastus with Zacharias of Mytilene: Ammonius*. London.

Dosoo, Korshi. 2016. "A History of the Theban Magical Library." *Bulletin of the American Society of Papyrologists* 53: 251–274.

Dowden, Ken. 1996. "Heliodorus: Serious Intentions." *Classical Quarterly* 46: 267–285.

Dufault, Olivier. 2015. "Transmutation Theory in the Greek Alchemical Corpus." *Ambix* 62: 215–244.

———. 2017. "Transmutation Theory and the Dating of the Alchemical Recipe 'On the Same Divine Water.'" In A. Le Moli and L. Alexidze, (eds). *Prote Hyle: Notions of Matter in the Platonic and Aristotelian Traditions*, 67–84. Palermo.

———. Forthcoming a. "Lessons from the Body." In I. Ramelli and S. Slaveva-Griffin, eds., *Lovers of the Soul, Lovers of the Body: Platonic Perspectives on the Soul and Body in Late Antiquity*. Cambridge, Mass.

———. Forthcoming b. "Mōt in the Phoenician History of Philo of Byblos as a Reference to the Egyptian Goddess Mut." In R. A. Díaz Hernández, M. C. Flossmann-Schütze and F. Hoffmann, eds., *Antike Kosmogonien. Beiträge zum internationalen Workshop vom 28.-30. Januar 2016*, 15–24. Vaterstetten.

Duffy, John M. 1992. *Michael Psellus, Philosophica minora*. 2 vols. Leipzig.

Dyck, Andrew. 1993. "Aelius Herodian: Recent Studies and Prospects for Future Research." In *Aufstieg und Niedergang der Römischen Welt* II.34.1: 772–794.

Edwards, Mark. 1992. "The Vessel of Zosimus the Alchemist." *Zeitschrift für Papyrologie und Epigraphik* 90: 55–64.

———. 1997. "Simon Magus, the Bad Samaritan." In M. Edwards and S. Swain, eds., *Portraits*, 69–91. Oxford.

Eidinow, Esther. 2017. "In Search of the Beggar-Priest." In R. L. Gordon et al., eds., *Beyond Priesthood: Religious Entrepreneurs and Innovators in the Roman Empire*, 255–275. Berlin.

Elm, Susanna. 2015. *Sons of Hellenism, Fathers of the Church: Emperor Julian, Gregory of Nazianzus, and the Vision of Rome*. Berkeley.

Eshleman, Kendra. 2012. *The Social World of Intellectuals in the Roman Empire*. Cambridge.

Estiot, Sylviane. 2012. "The Later Third Century." In W. E. Metcalf, ed., *The Oxford Handbook of Greek and Roman Coinage*, 538–560. Oxford.

Festugière, André-Jean. 1939. "L'expérience religieuse du médecin Thessalos." *Revue biblique* 48: 45–47.

———. 1950. *La révélation d'Hermès Trismégiste*. 4 vols. Paris.

———. 1967. "La création des âmes dans la Korè Kosmou." In A.-J. Festugière, ed., *Hermétisme et mystique païenne*. Paris.

Filoramo, Giovanni. 1990. *A History of Gnosticism*. trans. A. Alcock. Oxford.

Flint, Valerie. 1999. "The Demonisation of Magic and Sorcery in Late Antiquity: Christian Redefinitions of Pagan Religions." In B. Ankarloo, S. Clark, eds., *Witchcraft and Magic in Europe: Ancient Greece and Rome*, 277–349. Philadelphia.

Fögen, Marie Theres. 1993. *Die Enteignung der Wahrsager*. Frankfurt.

Forbes, Robert J. 1964. *Studies in Ancient Technology*. Leiden.

Fowden, Garth. 1982. "The Pagan Holy Man in Late Antique Society." *Journal of Hellenic Studies* 102: 33–59.

———. 1986. *The Egyptian Hermes: A Historical Approach to the Late Pagan Mind*. Princeton.

———. 1993. *The Egyptian Hermes*. Princeton.
Frankfurter, David. 1998. *Religion in Roman Egypt*. Princeton.
———. 2000. "The Consequences of Hellenism in Late Antique Egypt: Religious Worlds and Actors." *Archiv für Religionsgeschichte* 2: 162–194.
Fraser, Kyle A. 2004. "Zosimos of Panopolis and the Book of Enoch: Alchemy as Forbidden Knowledge." *Aries* 4: 125–147.
———. 2007. "Baptised in Gnosis: The Spiritual Alchemy of Zosimos of Panopolis." *Dionysius* 25: 33–54.
Freu, Christel. 2017. "Lucien à la lumière des papyrus: Un philosophe en apprentissage dans l'*Hermotimos* 80–82." *Cahiers des études anciennes* 54: 11–34.
Friedrich, Hans-Veit. 1968. *Thessalus of Tralles, De virtutibus herbarum*. Meisenheim am Glan.
Fronterotta, Franceso. 2013. *Eraclito, Frammenti*. Milan.
Frontisi-Ducroux, Françoise. 1975. *Dédale. Mythologie de l'artisan en Grèce ancienne*. Paris.
Gaillard-Seux, Patricia. 2003. "Sympathie et antipathie dans l'*Histoire naturelle* de Pline l'Ancien." In N. Palmieri, ed., *Rationnel et irrationnel dans la médecine ancienne et médiévale*, 113–128. Saint-Étienne.
Ganschinietz, Richard. 1913. "Hippolytos' Capitel gegen die Magier." In A. Harnack and C. Schmidt, eds., *Texte und Untersuchungen zur Geschichte der Altchristlichen Literatur* 39.2: 7–77. Leipzig.
Garosi, Raffaella. 1976. "Indagini sulla formazione del concetto di magia nella cultura romana." In P. Xella, ed., *Magia: Studi di storia delle religioni in memoria di R. Garosi*, 13–93. Rome.
Geissen, Angelo. 2012. "The Coinage of Roman Egypt." In W. E. Metcalf, ed., *The Oxford Handbook of Greek and Roman Coinage*, 561–583. Oxford.
Gemoll, Wilhelm. 1884. *Nepualii fragmentum Περὶ τῶν κατὰ ἀντιπάθειαν καὶ συμπάθειαν et Democriti Περὶ συμπαθειῶν καὶ ἀντιπαθειῶν*. Striegau.
Geoltrain, Pierre. 2005. "Introduction." In P. Geoltrain and J.-D. Kaestli, eds., Écrits apocryphes chrétiens, vol. 2, 1175–1187. Paris.
Glucker, John. 1978. *Antiochus and the Late Academy*. Göttingen.
Gold, Barbara K. 1987. *Literary Patronage in Greece and Rome*. Chapel Hill.
Goldhill, Simon. 2002. *Who needs Greek? Contests in the Cultural History of Hellenism*. Cambridge.
Gordon, Richard. 1987. "Aelian's Peony: The Location of Magic in Greco-Roman Tradition." *Comparative Criticism* 9: 59–95.
———. 1999. "Imagining Greek and Roman Magic." In B. Ankarloo and S. Clark, eds., *Witchcraft and Magic in Europe: Ancient Greece and Rome*, 161–275. Philadelphia.
Goulet-Cazé, Marie-Odile. 1982. "L'arrière-plan scolaire de la Vie de Plotin." In L. Brisson et al., *Porphyre, Vie de Plotin*, vol. 1, 229–327. Paris.
Graf, Fritz. 1997. *Magic in the Ancient World*. Cambridge, Mass.
———. 2001. "Theory of Magic in Antiquity." In P. Mirecki and M. Meyer, eds., *Magic and Ritual in the Ancient World*, 93–104. Leiden.
———. 2011. "Magic and Divination: Two Apolline Oracles on Magic." In G. Bohak et al., eds., *Continuity and Innovation in the Magical Tradition*, 119–133. Leiden.
Graf, Fritz, and Johnston, Sarah Iles. 2007. *Ritual Texts for the Afterlife*. London.

Gruen, Erich. 2005. "Greeks and Jews: Mutual Misperceptions in Josephus' *Contra Apionem.*" In C. Bakhos, ed., *Judaism in its Hellenistic Context*, 31–51. Leiden.
Guignard, Christophe. 2011. *Lettre de Julius Africanus à Aristide sur la généalogie du Christ.* Berlin.
Guillou, André, et al. 1977. *Actes de Lavra*, vol. 2. Paris.
Guthrie, William K. C. 1962. *A History of Greek Philosophy*, vol.1. Cambridge.
Hadot, Ilsetraut. 2005. *Arts libéraux et philosophie dans la pensée antique*. Paris.
Hadot, Pierre. 1972. "La physique comme exercice spirituel ou pessimisme et optimisme chez Marc Aurèle." *Revue de théologie et de philosophie* 22: 225–238.
Hafner, Markus. 2017. *Lukians Schrift "Das traurige Los der Gelehrten."* Stuttgart.
Hahn, Johannes 1989. *Der Philosoph und die Gesellschaft*. Stuttgart.
Halleux, Robert. 1979. *Les textes alchimiques*. Turnhout.
———. 1981. *Les alchimistes grecs, Tome I: Papyrus de Leyde, Papyrus de Stockholm, Fragments de recettes*. Paris.
Halleux, Robert and Schamp, Jacques. 1985. *Les lapidaires grecs. Lapidaire orphique, Kérygmes lapidaires d'Orphée, Socrate et Denys, Lapidaire nautique, Damigéron-Évax*. Paris.
Harmon, A. M., trans. 1921. *Lucian*, vol. 3. Cambridge, Mass.
Harris, William. 1989. *Ancient Literacy*. Cambridge, Mass.
Harrison, Stephen J. et al., trans. 2001. *Apuleius. Rhetorical Works*. Oxford.
Henaff, Marcel. 2002. *Le prix de la vérité*. Paris.
Himmelfarb, Martha. 1983. *Tours of Hell*. Oxford.
———. 1993. *Ascent to Heaven in Jewish and Christian Apocalypses*. Oxford.
Hoffmann, Friedhelm, and Quack, Joachim F. 2018. *Anthologie der demotischen Literatur*. Münster.
Horky, Philip S. 2009. "Persian Cosmos and Greek Philosophy: Plato's Associates and the Zoroastrian *Magoi*." In B. Inwood, ed., *Oxford Studies in Ancient Philosophy* 37, 47–103.
Howgego, Christopher. 1995. *Ancient History from Coins*. London.
Hübner, Sabine. 2005. *Der Klerus in der Gesellschaft des spätantiken Kleinasiens*. Stuttgart.
Irby-Massie, Georgia L., and Keyser, Paul T. 2002. *Greek Science of the Hellenistic Era*. London.
Jackson, Howard M., trans. 1978. *Zosimus of Panopolis, On the Letter Omega*. Missoula.
———. 1990. "The Seer Nicotheos and His Lost Apocalypse in the Light of Sethian Apocalypses from Nag Hammadi and the Apocalypse of Elchasai." *Novum Testamentum* 32: 250–277.
Jacob, Christian. 2005. "'La table et le cercle.' Sociabilités savantes sous l'Empire romain." *Annales HSS* 3: 507–530.
Johnson, William A. 2010. *Readers and Reading Culture in the High Roman Empire*. Oxford.
Johnston, Sarah Iles. 1999. *Restless Dead*. Berkeley.
Joly, Bernard. 2013. *Histoire de l'alchimie*. Paris.
Jones, Arnold H. M. 1964. *The Later Roman Empire*. 3 vols. Oxford.

Jones, Arnold H. M., et al. 1971–1992. *The Prosopography of the Later Roman Empire*. 3 vols. Cambridge.
Jones, Christopher P. 1970. "Sura and Senecio." *Journal of Roman Studies* 60: 98–104.

———. 1971. *Plutarch and Rome*. Oxford.
———. 1972. "Two Enemies of Lucian." *Greek, Roman, and Byzantine Studies* 13: 475–487.
———. 1986. *Culture and Society in Lucian*. Cambridge, Mass.
Jones, Kenneth. 2005. "The Figure of Apion in Josephus' *Contra Apionem*." *Journal for the Study of Judaism* 36.3: 278–315.
Jones, William H. S. et al., trans. 1956–1963. *Pliny. Natural History*, vol. 7–8. Cambridge, Mass.
Jong, Albert de. 1997. *Traditions of the Magi*. Leiden.
Kahn, Charles H. 1979. *The Art and Thought of Heraclitus*. Cambridge.
Kaimakis, Dimitris. 1976. *Die Kyraniden*. Meisenheim am Glan.
Kaster, Robert. 1988. *Guardians of Language*. Berkeley.
Kelhoffer, James. 2008. "'Hippolytus' and Magic. An Examination of *Elenchos* IV 28–42 and Related Passages in Light of the Papyri Graecae Magicae." *Zeitschrift für Antikes Christentum* 11: 517–548.
Keulen, Wytse. 2009. *Gellius the Satirist*. Leiden.
Keyser, Paul T. 1995–1996. "Greco-Roman Alchemy and Coins of Imitation Silver." *American Journal of Numismatics* 7–8: 209–234.
Kingsley, Peter. 1995a. "Meetings with Magi: Iranian Themes among the Greeks, from Xanthus of Lydia to Plato's Academy." *Journal of the Royal Asiatic Society* 5: 173–209.
———. 1995b. *Ancient Philosophy, Mystery, and Magic*. Oxford.
Knipe, Sergio. 2011. "Sacrifice and Self-Transformation in the Alchemical Writings of Zosimus of Panopolis." In C. Kelly et al., eds., *Unclassical Traditions*, vol. 2, 59–69. Cambridge.
Kondakov, Nikodim V. 1892. *Histoire et monuments des émaux byzantins*. Frankfurt.
Kravari, Vassiliki. 1991. *Actes du Pantocrator*. Paris.
Kreuzsaler, Claudia, et al. 2010. *Stimmen aus dem Wüstensand*. Vienna.
Lagercrantz, Otto. 1913. *Papyrus Graecus Holmiensis*. Leipzig.
Lancel, Serge. 1961. "'Curiositas' et préoccupations spirituelles chez Apulée." *Revue de l'histoire des religions* 160: 25–46.
Letrouit, Jean. 1995. "Chronologie des alchimistes grecs." In D. Kahn et S. Matton, eds., *Alchimie: art, histoire et mythes*, 11–93. Milan and Paris.
Lieven, Alexandra von. 2000. *Der Himmel über Esna*. Wiesbaden.
Lindsay, Jack. 1970. *The Origins of Alchemy and Graeco-Roman Egypt*. London.
Lippmann, Edmund O. von. 1919. *Entstehung und Ausbreitung der Alchimie*. Berlin.
Litwa, M. David. 2016. *Refutation of All Heresies*. Atlanta.
Lloyd-Jones, Hugh, trans. 1994. *Sophocles: Ajax. Electra. Oedipus Tyrannus*. Cambridge, Mass.
Love, Edward O. D. 2016. *Code-switching with the Gods: The Bilingual (Old Coptic-Greek) Spells of PGM IV (P. Bibliothèque Nationale Supplément Grec. 574) and Their Linguistic, Religious, and Socio-Cultural Context in Late Roman Egypt*. Berlin.
Mahé, Jean-Pierre. 2009. "Sciences occultes et exercices spirituels." In J.-M. Narbonne and P.-H. Poirier, eds., *Gnose et philosophie*, 75–86. Quebec City.
Malherbe, Abraham. 1977. *The Cynic Epistles*. Atlanta.
Marcovich, Miroslav. 2001. *Heraclitus*. Sankt Augustin.

Markus, Robert A. 1994. "Augustine on Magic: A Neglected Semiotic Theory." *Revue des études augustiniennes* 40: 378–388.

Marrou, Henri-Irénée. 1965. *Histoire de l'éducation dans l'antiquité*. Paris.

Martelli, Matteo. 2009. "'Divine Water' in the Alchemical Writings of Pseudo-Democritus." *Ambix* 56: 5–22.

———. 2011. *Pseudo-Democrito, scritti alchemici con il commentario di Sinesio*. Milan and Paris.

———. 2013. *The Four Books of Pseudo-Democritus*. Sources of Alchemy and Chemistry, v. 1. Leeds.

———. 2014a. "L'alchimie en syriaque et l'oeuvre de Zosime." In É. Villey, ed., *Les sciences en syriaque*, 191–214. Paris.

———. 2014b. "The Alchemical Art of Dyeing: The Fourfold Division of Alchemy and the Enochic Tradition." In S. Dupré, ed., *Laboratories of Art*, 1–22. Cham.

———. 2016. "Graeco-Egyptian and Byzantine Alchemy." In G. L. Irby, ed., *A Companion to Science, Technology, and Medicine in Ancient Greece and Rome*, vol. 1, 217–231. Chichester.

———. 2017. "Alchemy, Medicine and Religion: Zosimus of Panopolis and the Egyptian Priests." *Religion in the Roman Empire* 3.2: 202–220.

Martin, Dale. 2004. *Inventing Superstition*. Cambridge, Mass.

Marx-Wolf, Heidi. 2016. *Spiritual Taxonomies and Ritual Authority*. Philadelphia.

Mavroudi, Maria. 2006. "Occult Sciences and Society in Byzantium: Considerations for Future Research." In P. Magdalino and M. Mavroudi, eds., *The Occult Sciences in Byzantium*, 39–96. Geneva.

Mecella, Laura. 2014. "L'enigmatica figura di Eliodoro e la datazione delle *Etiopiche*." *Mediterraneo Antico* 17.2: 633–658.

Meier, Mischa, and Thurn, Johannes. 2009. *Johannes Malalas, Weltchronik*. Stuttgart.

Mertens, Michèle. 1995. *Les alchimistes grecs, Tome IV.I: Zosime de Panopolis. Mémoires authentiques*. Paris.

———. 2001. "Andrée Colinet (éd.), Les alchimistes grecs. Tome X. L'Anonyme de Zuretti ou l'Art sacré et divin de la chrysopée par un anonyme." *L'Antiquité Classique*, 70: 558–559.

———. 2002. "Alchemy, Hermetism and Gnosticism at Panopolis c. 300 A.D.: The Evidence of Zosimus." In A. Egberts et al., eds., *Perspectives on Panopolis*, 165–175. Leiden.

———. 2006. "Graeco-Egyptian Alchemy in Byzantium." In P. Magdalino and M. Mavroudi, eds., *The Occult Sciences in Byzantium*, 205–230. Geneva.

Metzger, Bruce M., et al., trans. 1989. *New Revised Standard Version Bible*. Oxford.

Mitchell, C. W. 1921. *S. Ephraim's Prose Refutations of Mani, Marcion and Bardaisan*. 2 vols. London.

Momigliano, Arnaldo. 1971. *Alien Wisdom: The Limits of Hellenization*. Cambridge.

Morgan, John R. 1996. "Heliodoros." In G. Schmeling, ed., *The Novel in the Ancient World*, 417–456. Leiden.

———. 2007. "The Representation of Philosophers in Greek Fiction." In J. R. Morgan and M. Jones, eds., *Philosophical Presences in the Ancient Novel*, 21–51. Groningen.

Moyer, Ian S. 2011. *Egypt and the Limits of Empire*. Cambridge.

Nauta, Ruurd R. 2002. *Poetry for Patrons*. Leiden.

Neitzel, Susanne, et al. 1977. *Die Fragmente des Grammatikers Dionysios Thrax.* Berlin.
Nesselrath, Heinz-Günther. 1985. *Lukians Parasitendialog.* Berlin.
———. 1990. *Die Attische Mittlere Komödie.* Berlin.
Nock, Arthur D. 1986. "Paul and the Magus." *Essays on Religion in the Ancient World,* vol. 1, 308–330. Cambridge, Mass.
Nock, Arthur D., and Festugière, André-Jean. 1954. *Corpus Hermeticum.* 4 vols. Paris.
Notton, J. H. F. 1974. "Ancient Egyptian Gold Refining." In *Gold Bulletin* 7.2: 50–56.
Ogden, Daniel. 1999. "Binding Spells: Curse Tablets and Voodoo Dolls in the Greek and Roman Worlds." In B. Ankarloo and S. Clark, eds. *Witchcraft and Magic in Europe vol. 2: Ancient Greece and Rome,* 1–90. London.
———. 2001. *Greek and Roman Necromancy.* Princeton.
———. 2004. "The Apprentice's Sorcerer: Pancrates and his Powers in Context (Lucian, *Philopseudes* 33–36)." *Acta Classica* 47: 101–126.
Ogden, Jack M. 1990. *Gold Jewellery in Ptolemaic, Roman and Byzantine Egypt.* 2 vols. Durham.
Oikonomidès, Nicolas. 1984. *Actes de Docheiariou.* 2 vols. Paris.
Osborn, Eric. 2005. *Clement of Alexandria.* Cambridge.
Panaino, Antonio. 2006. "Aspetti della complessità degli influssi interculturali tra Grecia ed Iran." In C. Riedweg, ed., *Grecia Maggiore,* 19–53. Rome.
———. 2010. "I Magi in Occidente." In G. M. Cazzaniga, ed., *Storia d'Italia* 25: 49–76. Turin.
Parker, Robert. 2005. *Polytheism and Society at Athens.* Oxford.
Patai, Raphael. 1994. *The Jewish Alchemists.* Princeton.
Petit, Madeleine. 1974. *Philon d'Alexandrie, Quod omnis probus liber sit.* Paris.
Pigeaud, Jackie. 1988. *Aristote: L'homme de génie et la mélancolie: Problème XXX.1.* Paris.
Pfeiffer, Rudolf. 1968. *History of Classical Scholarship.* 2 vols. Oxford.
Poirier, Paul-Hubert, et al. 2000. *Zostrien.* Bibliothèque Copte de Nag Hammadi, Section "Textes," v. 24. Quebec City.
———. 2004. "Comment les gnostiques se sont-ils appelés? Comment doit-on les appeler aujourd'hui?" *Studies in Religion/Sciences Religieuses* 33.2: 209–216.
Poirier, Paul-Hubert, and Schmidt, Thomas S. 2010. "Chrétiens, hérétiques et gnostiques chez Porphyre. Quelques précisions sur la *Vie de Plotin* 16,1–9." In *Comptes rendus des séances de l'Académie des Inscriptions et Belles-Lettres* 154.2: 913–942. Paris.
Pormann, Peter E. 2008. *Rufus of Ephesus, On Melancholy.* Tübingen.
Preisendanz, Karl, et al. 1973. *Papyri Graecae Magicae.* 2 vols. Stuttgart.
Preger, Theodor. 1901. *Scriptores originum Constantinopolitanarum.* 2 vols. Leipzig.
Principe, Lawrence. 2013. *The Secrets of Alchemy.* Chicago.
Rackham, Harris, trans. 1950. *Pliny. Natural History,* vol. 5. Cambridge, Mass.
Ramelli, Ilaria. Forthcoming. "Clement of Alexandria's Notion of the Logos 'All Things as One': Its Background and Developments in Origen and Nyssen." In Z. Plese and R. Hirsch-Luitpold, eds., *Alexandrian Personae: Scholarly Culture and Religious Traditions in Ancient Alexandria.* Tübingen.
Rea, John. 1977. "A New Version of P. Yale Inv. 299." *Zeitschrift für Papyrologie und Epigraphik* 27: 151–156.

Reed, Annette Yoshiko. 2005. *Fallen Angels and the History of Judaism and Christianity*. Cambridge.
Rees, Roger. 1999. "Ammianus Satiricus." In J. W. Drijvers and D. Hunt, eds., *The Late Roman World and its Historian*, 125–137. London.
Reichardt, Walter. 1909. *Die Briefe des Sextus Julius Africanus an Aristides und Origenes*. Leipzig.
Reil, Theodor. 1913. *Beiträge zur Kenntnis des Gewerbes im hellenistischen Ägypten*. Leipzig.
Reitzenstein, Richard. 1904. *Poimandres*. Leipzig.
Rinotas, Athanasios. 2017. "Stoicism and Alchemy in Late Antiquity: Zosimus and the Concept of Pneuma." *Ambix* 64: 203–219.
Ritner, Robert K. 1995. "Egyptian Magical Practice under the Roman Empire: The Demotic Spells and Their Religious Context." *Aufstieg und Niedergang der Römischen Welt* 2.18.5: 3333–3379.
Rives, James B. 2003. "Magic in Roman Law: The Reconstruction of a Crime." *Classical Antiquity* 22.2: 313–339.
———. 2004. "Aristotle, Antisthenes of Rhodes and the *Magikos*." *Rheinisches Museum für Philologie* 147: 35–54.
———. 2009. "Apion Περὶ μάγου and the Meaning of the Word μάγος." *MHNH: Revista Internacional de Investigación sobre Magia y Astrología Antiguas* 9: 121–134.
———. 2010. "*Magus* and its Cognates in Classical Latin." In R. Gordon and F. Marco Simón, eds., *Magical Practice in the Latin West*, 53–77. Leiden.
Robiano, Patrick. 2003. "Maladie d'amour et diagnostic médical: Érasistrate, Galien et Héliodore d'Emèse, ou du récit au roman." *Ancient Narratives* 3: 129–149.
Robinson, Thomas M. 1987. *Heraclitus, Fragments*. Toronto.
Rolfe, John C., trans. 1935. *Ammianus Marcellinus*, vol. 1. Cambridge, Mass.
Romeri, Luciana. 2002. *Philosophes entre mots et mets*. Grenoble.
Ross, Alan J. 2015. "Ammianus, Traditions of Satire and the Eternity of Rome." *The Classical Journal* 110: 356–373.
Rudolph, Kurt. 1977. *Die Gnosis*. Göttingen.
Ruska, Julius. 1926. *Tabula Smaragdina*. Heidelberg.
Saffrey, Henri Dominique. 1995. "Histoire et description du manuscrit alchimique de Venise *Marcianus Graecus* 299." In D. Kahn and S. Matton, eds., *Alchimie: art, histoire et mythes*, 1–10. Milan and Paris.
Saffrey, Henri Dominique, and Segonds, Alain Philippe. 2012. *Porphyre: Lettre à Anébon l'Égyptien*. Paris.
Saller, Richard P. 1982. *Personal Patronage under the Early Empire*. Cambridge.
———. 1983. "Martial." *Classical Quarterly* 33: 246–257.
———. 1989. "Patronage and Friendship in Early Imperial Rome. Drawing the Distinction." In A. Wallace-Hadrill, ed., *Patronage in Ancient Society*, 49–62. London.
Sandy, Gerald. 1982. "Characterization and Philosophical Decor in Heliodorus' *Aethiopica*." *Transactions of the American Philological Association* 112: 141–167.
Sanzo, Joseph E. Forthcoming. "Imagining Illegitimate Ritual in Early Christian Literature." In D. Frankfurter, ed., *Guide to the Study of Ancient Magic*. Leiden.
Schmitz, Thomas. 1997. *Bildung und Macht*. Munich.

Schütt, Hans-Werner. 2000. *Auf der Suche nach dem Stein der Weisen: Die Geschichte der Alchemie*. Munich.
Sestili, Antonio. 2015. *Giulio Africano, Lettera ad Aristide*. Rome.
Sidwell, Keith, trans. 2004. *Lucian: Chattering Courtesans and Other Sardonic Sketches*. London.
Smith, Andrew. 1993. *Porphyrii Philosophi Fragmenta*. Leipzig.
Stadter, Philip A. 2014. *Plutarch and his Roman Readers*. Oxford.
Stausberg, Daniel. 2009. "Hell in Zoroastrian History." *Numen* 56: 217–253.
Stolzenberg, Daniel. 1999. "Unpropitious Tinctures. Alchemy, Astrology & Gnosis According to Zosimos of Panopolis." *Archives internationales d'histoire des sciences* 49: 3–31.
Stratton, Kimberly B. 2007. *Naming the Witch*. New York. 2007.
Strohmaier, Gotthard. 1976. "Übersehenes zur Biographie Lukians." *Philologus* 120: 117–122.
Strootman, Rolf. 2017. *The Birdcage of the Muses*. Leuven.
Swain, Simon. 1990. "The Promotion of Hadrian of Tyre and the Death of Herodes Atticus." *Classical Philology* 85: 214–216.
———. 1996. *Hellenism and Empire*. Oxford.
Tanaseanu-Döbler, Ilinca. 2013. *Theurgy in Late Antiquity*. Göttingen.
Tardieu, Michel. 1985. "L'Ardā Virāz Nāmag et l'eschatologie grecque." *Studia Iranica* 14: 17–26.
Tarrant, Harold. 1993. *Thrasyllan Platonism*. Ithaca.
Thomas, Christine. 2003. *The Acts of Peter, Gospel Literature, and the Ancient Novel*. Oxford.
Timotin, Andrei. 2012. *La démonologie platonicienne*. Leiden.
Tonelli, Angelo. 1988. *Zosimo di Panopoli*. Milan.
Trapp, Erich. 1971. *Digenes Akrites*. Vienna.
Urbano, Arthur Peter. 2013. *The Philosophical Life: Biography and the Crafting of Intellectual Identity in Late Antiquity*. Washington, DC.
Van den Kerchove, Anna. 2012. *La voie d'Hermès*. Nag Hammadi and Manichaean Studies 77. Leiden.
van der Horst, Pieter W. 2002. "Who Was Apion?" In P. W. van der Horst, ed., *Japheth in the Tents of Shem*, 207–221. Leiden.
Van Liefferinge, Carine. 1999. *La Théurgie*. Liège.
Vardi, Amiel. 2001. "Gellius against the Professors." *Zeitschrift für Papyrologie und Epigraphik* 137: 1–54.
Verbeke, Gérard. 1945. *L'évolution de la doctrine du pneuma du stoïcisme à S. Augustin*. Paris.
Veyne, Paul. 1976. *Le pain et le cirque*. Paris.
Viano, Cristina. 1996. "Aristote et l'alchimie grecque: La transmutation et le modèle aristotélicien entre théorie et pratique." *Revue d'histoire des sciences* 49: 189–213.
Vieillefond, Jean-René. 1970. *Les "Cestes" de Julius Africanus*. Paris.
Vlachou, Constantina, et al. 2002. "Experimental Investigation of Silvering in Late Roman Coinage." *Material Research Society Symposium Proceedings* 712: II9.2.1–9.
Volk, Katharina. 2004. "'Heavenly Steps': Manilius 4.119–121 and Its Background." In R. Boustan and A. Y. Reed, eds., *Heavenly Realms and Earthly Realities in Late Antique Religions*, 34–46. Cambridge.

Walker, David R. 1978. *The Metrology of the Roman Silver Coinage*. British Archaeological Reports Supplementary Series, v. 22, part 3. Oxford.
Wallraff, Martin. 2009. "Magie und Religion in den Kestoi des Julius Africanus." In M. Wallraff and L. Mecella, eds., *Die Kestoi des Julius Africanus und ihre Überlieferung*, 39–52. Berlin.
Wallraff, Martin, et al. 2007. *Julius Africanus, Chronography*. Berlin.
———. 2012. *Julius Africanus, Cesti*. Berlin.
Walsh, Patrick G. 1988. "The Rights and Wrongs of Curiosity (Plutarch to Augustine)." *Greece & Rome* 35.1: 73–85.
Wellmann, Max. 1928. *Die Φυσικὰ des Bolos Demokritos und der Magier Anaxilaos aus Larissa*. Teil 1. Abhandlungen der Preussichen Akademie der Wissenschaften, Jahrgang 1928, Philosophisch-Historische Klasse, v. 7, 1–80. Berlin.
Weinstock, Stefan. 1953. *Codices Britannicos. Catalogus Codicum Astrologorum Graecorum*, 9.2. Brussels.
Wendt, Heidi. 2016. *At the Temple Gates*. Oxford.
West, Martin J. 1971. *Early Greek Philosophy and the Orient*. Oxford.
White, Peter. 1978. "*Amicitia* and the Profession of Poetry in Early Imperial Rome." *Journal of Roman Studies* 68: 74–92.
Whitmarsh, Tim. 2001. *Greek Literature and the Roman Empire*. Oxford.
———. 2005. *The Second Sophistic*. Oxford.
Williams, Craig A. 2010. *Roman Homosexuality*. Oxford.
Williams, Michael A. 1996. *Rethinking "Gnosticism."* Princeton.
Winkler, John J. 1982. "The Mendacity of Kalasiris and the Narrative Strategy of Heliodorus' *Aethiopika*." *Yale Classical Studies* 27: 93–158.
———. 2006. "From Judaism and Hellenism to Christianity and Paganism." In F. Amsler et al., eds., *Nouvelles intrigues pseudo-clémentines*, 425–435. Geneva.
Yonge, Charles Duke, trans. 1855. *The Works of Philo Judaeus*, vol. 3. London.
Zago, Michela. 2010. *Tebe magica e alchemica*. Padua.
Zink, Odile. 1979. *Eusèbe de Césarée, La préparation évangélique, Livres IV - V, 1–17*. Paris.
Zuretti, Carlo Oreste. 1932. *Corpus des manuscrits alchimiques grecs*. Vol. 8. Brussels.

INDEX OF PASSAGES

Acts of Peter
   4, 5, 7–11, 13, 14, 19, 20, 23–28, 64; *31 (Lipsius)*, 64n66; *54.31–33 (Lipsius)*, 64n63; *56.23–24 (Lipsius)*, 64n63; *75.14–15 (Lipsius)*, 64n64

Aelian
   On the Characteristics of Animals (De natura animalium) Prol., 80n36; *1.38*, 56n21; *10.29*, 60n36; *17.12*, 80n35

Aeneas of Gaza
   Theophrastus 4–66, 102; *59.19–25*, 102; *62.26–29*, 102n41

Aeschines
   Against Ctesiphon 134, 137, 34n34

Alexander of Aphrodisias
   Commentary on Aristotle's Metaphysics 18.17–18, 52n3

Ammianus Marcellinus
   History 14.6.1–26, 24; *14.6.2, 14.6.7*, 24n64; *25.3.23*, 24n62; *28.3–5*, 24n64; *28.4.12–14*, 24

Anastasius Sinaita
   In Hexaemeron 8.3.2–6, 95n9; *8.3.6*, 95n10

Anaxilaus of Larissa
   Fr 1–10, 52n5, 52–55

Anonymous Philosopher
   CAAG 3.441.21, 100n32

Anthologia graeca
   6.92, 100n33; *7.7*, 81n39

[Apollonius of Tyana]
   Letters 16–17, 35n42

Apuleius
   Apology 6.1, 49n101; *25–26*, 35n42; *26–27*, 40n62
   Metamorphoses 2.28–30, 84n46

Aristophanes
   Knights 48, 12n13

Aristotle
   Metaphysics 14.1091b, 35n40, 39n61
   Meteorologica 3–4, 100n33
   On Philosophy fr. 6 Rose, 35n40, 39n61

[Aristotle]
   Problems 4.30 (880a), 30.1 (953a10–955a27), 81n37

Artemidorus
   Interpretation of Dreams 1.51.32–37, 97n20

Athenaeus
   Learned Banqueters 1 (16e–17b), 62n52; *2.12, 14n23; 2 (52d–e)*, 56n19; *4 (157b)*, 81n39; *6.8*, 62n52; *6 (234c–235e)*, 12n13; *7 (294)*, 63n54; *9.19 (376d)*, 120n8; *11 (478a)*, 66n76; *13 (584a)*, 21n53; *13 (584e)*, 55n17; *14 (642e)*, 63n54; *15 (677e–f)*, 66n76, 66n77

Augustine
   City of God 10.9, 140n89
   Confessions 5.12, 23n60
   De diversis quaestionibus 83 79.4, 140n88
   De doctrina christiana 2.20.30, 140n88

Book of the Watchers
   8.1, 132n68

Bundahišn
   34.18–19, 31n19

Cassius Dio
   Roman History 68.16.2, 71n2

Cicero
   On Divination 1.90–91, 36n45

Clement of Alexandria
   Excerpts from Theodotus 4.75, 32n24
   Paedagogus 2.8.63, 32n24, 116n90; *2.10.99*, 29n10
   Protrepticus 1.8.3, 31n22; *2.22.1–2, 28*, 32n26; *2.22.7*, 32n23; *2.34.5*, 29n10; *4.5.4*, 29n10; *4.48.4–6*, 94n3; *4.58.3*, 32n24; *5*, 39n61; *5.64.6–5.65.4*, 31n19; *5.65.1–4*, 32n24
   Stromata 1.4.25.3–4, 32n24; *1.13–15*, 31n19; *1.15.66–71*, 32n24; *1.17.87*, 31n22; *1.21.127*, 32n24; *2.2.8, 2.4.17*, 29n10; *3.2.11, 3.6.48*, 32n24; *4.7.49.3, 4.22.141.2*, 29n10; *5.5.29.5–6*, 31n22; *5.1.10.2*, 132n70; *5.14.90–5.14.91.1*,

159

INDEX OF PASSAGES

30n17; *5.14.103*, 31n18, 38n53; *5.14.115*, 29n10; *6.3.33*, 32n24; *6.7.57*, 32n24; *15.69*, 38n53
Columella
De re rustica 12.4.2, 120n8
Constantine VII
De cerimoniis aulae Byzantinae 1.163.8, 95n7; *2.581.9*, 95n11
Corpus Hermeticum
1.1, 111n69; *1.1.9–10, 1.9*, 113; *1.21, 24–26*, 113; *5.1, 9.6-7, 9.21-22*, 114n85; *12.2*, 114n83; *4.4, 5*, 113; *12.2*, 113n81; *12.21*, 114n85; *13.11.7–8*, 112n78; *SH 23.3*, 114n85; *25.8*, 114n82–83
Asclepius 8.20–21, 114n85
Cyranides
1.8.13–17, 1.161–169, 54, 56n21; *2.31.21–23*, 53–54, 56n21; *2.40.19–21, 3.13.6*, 54, 56n21

Digest
10.2.4.1, 74n16; *27.1.6.7*, 11n11, 20n51; *48.10.1.8*, 96n15
Dio Chrysostom
Orations 36.40, 35n42; *36.51–54*, 31n19
Diodorus of Sicily
Historical Library 1.39, 76n26; *1.39–40*, 76n24; *1.40*, 77n28; *1.96–98*, 39n61, 81n38; *2.52*, 100n33; *3.14*, 103n42, 44
[Diogenes of Sinope]
Letters 19 Hercher, 52n4
Diogenes Laertius
Lives of Eminent Philosophers prol., 91n81; *1.1–9*, 35n39, 39n61; *1.8*, 35n41; *6.68*, 22n55; *8.3*, 39n61; *9.7–8*, 30n16; *9.34*, 39n61
Dionysius of Halicarnassus
On the Ancient Orators 1, 17n40
Dioscorides
Materia Medica 1.10, 2.118, 136, 164, 176, 178, 3.11, 35, 65, 102, 4.33, 68, 75, 78, 127, 176, 38n53; *5, 100n33; 5.75*, 139n84; *5.87*, 86n64; *5.162*, 58n30

Empedocles
B111 DK, 33n29
Epictetus
Discourses 2.9.13, 11n11
Epiphanius
Panarion 2.5.13, 52n4, 54n12; *76.2.8–10*, 97n25
Eudemus of Rhodes
Fr. 150 Wehrli, 35n40
Eupolis
Flatterers fr. 157 Kassel–Austin, 12n14

Euripides
Iphigenia in Tauris 1336–1338, 28n8; *Suppliants 1110*, 28n8
Eusebius
Against Hierocles 2.27, 142n1
Chronography 221CE, 85n56
Demonstration of the Gospel 3.2.78.10–14, 46n96
Ecclesiastical History 6.21.3–4, 85n55
Preparation for the Gospel, 44; *4.5*, 48n99; *4.6*, 46n94, 46n95; *4.17*, 48n99; *5.10.10*, 47n90; *5.10.10–11*, 46n96; *5.10.12–13*, 48n100; *5.14.1*, 47n97; *5.14.3–4*, 48n98; *6.4*, 45n86; *10.10.16*, 60n39; *15.62.16–17*, 44n84

Firmicus Maternus
Mathesis, 98; *3.5.33*, 99n28; *3.19*, 99n29; *4.14.19*, 99n27; *4.14.20*, 98n26; *4.22.2*, 99n30

Gellius
Attic Nights 4.1, 64n65; *5.4*, 11n8; *5.14*, 60n36, 63n53; *6.8*, 62n52, 60n36, 63n53; *7.8*, 60n36; *10.10*, 63n55; *11.1.5*, 11n8; *12.11*, 83; *15.11*, 11n12; *16.7.13*, 11n8; *17.2.15*, 11n8; *17.8.14*, 59n32; *18.10.8*, 11
Geoponica
7.31, 86n63; *8.19*, 85n59; *10.14–15*, 86n61
George Cedrenus
Compendium historiarum 1.629.9, 95n7
George Syncellus
Chronography 12.13–17, 132n68; *14.2–14*, 132n67; *14.2–4*, 118n2; *14.14*, 96n13; *18–19*, 5n17; *123.11-12*, 84n47; *439.18–20*, 85n58
Gorgias
Praise of Helen 10, 14, 34n34
Gregory of Nyssa
Against Eunomius 1.38, 97n22; *1.40*, 97n23; *1.44, 1.48*, 97n24; *2.3*, 107n55

Heliodorus
Ethiopica 2.28, 76, 81; *2.29*, 76; *2.33.6*, 78, 82; *2.34*, 83n43; *2.35–4.21*, 76; *3.3*, 83n43; *3.5*, 78; *3.7.2*, 81; *3.7.3*, 79n33; *3.7.5*, 79n34; *3.7.5.1–8*, 78n29; *3.7–8*, 10, 78; *3.9*, 82; *3.10.4–5*, 81; *3.11.3*, 82; *3.11*, 81; *3.16*, 35n42, 84n46; *3.16.3–4*, 82–83; *3.17.1*, 82; *3.17.3*, 5, 82; *3.19*, 82; *3.19.3*, 76; *4.5.3*, 82; *4.6*, 75; *4.6.4*, 82, 82n40; *4.8*, 12–14, 81; *4.15*, 81; *4.15.3*, 82; *5.13.2*, 82; *5.22*, 75n20; *6.15*, 84n46; *9.2–8, 4.2*, 75n20; *10.41*, 81
Hephaistion
Introductio metrica 62.5–6, 52n2

Heraclitus
  B5 DK, B15 DK, 29n11; B14 DK, 28; B28 DK, B66 DK, 30
Hero of Alexandria
  On the Making of Automata 20.4, 59n34
Herodotus
  Histories 1.101, 34; 1.107–108, 1.120, 1.128, 33n27; 1.131–132, 33, 35n40; 1.40, 33n28; 1.195, 17n42; 2.119, 33n29; 3.61–88, 3.118, 3.136, 3.140, 3.153, 4.132, 34n31; 7.19, 37–38, 33n27; 7.35, 101n34; 7.43, 33n28; 7.62, 34n30; 7.113–114, 33; 7.189, 33n28; 7.189, 7.191, 33n29
[Hippocrates]
  On the Sacred Disease 1.7, 1.12, 18, 28n8
Hippolytus
  Commentary on Daniel 4.24.3, 116n91

Iamblichus
  De Mysteriis 3.28–31, 46n95; 5.25, 129n55; 7.5, 43n80
  Life of Pythagoras 4, 39n61; 36.267.14, 58n26
Irenaeus
  Against Heresies prol., 1.20–27, 97n25, 116n90; 1.13, 54n12, 57n25
  Fr. 8 Harvey, 116n91

Jerome
  Chronicle BCE 28, 52n4
  On Famous Men 63, 85n56
John of Antioch
  Chronography fr.191 Mariev, 94n5
John Malalas
  Chronography 16.5, 95n7
John Moschus
  Spiritual Meadow 200, 96n18
Josephus
  Against Apion 2.3, 12–14, 60n43; 20.28–32, 41, 60n43
  Jewish Antiquities 18.257–260, 60n43; 20.142, 49n102
Julius Africanus (Wallraff et al.)
  Kestoi T3, 85n54; T5a, 85n55; T7, 87n65; F2.106, 4.7, 5.3, 6.25, 9.3, 89n75; F10.48–49, 87n66; F10.50–51, 85n52; F10, 85n54, 87; F10.45–48, 88n71; F10.50–51, 89; F11.16–17, 89n75; F12.Pr, 85n57; F12.1.1–5, 89, 90n80; F12.2.53–61, 89n75; F12.2.76–87, 87; F12.2.77, 89n75; F12.6.21, 87, 87n69; F12.6.25, 89n75; F12.10–15, 87n69; F12.11.16–17, 89n75; F12.17.34–37, 88; F12.17.43–44, 89; F12.20, 85n53, 90n79;
  F17.44, 89n75; F55, 87; F61, 87, 89n75; F62.49, 89; F69–78, 87; F75, 89
  Chronography F46.53-55, 90n77
Justin Martyr
  Dialogue with Trypho 69.7, 142n1; 108.2, 46n96
[Justin Martyr]
  De resurrectione 6.11–12, 116n93
Juvenal
  Satires 1.132–136, 13n19; 2.9–10, 19n46; 3.41–48, 16; 3.58–78, 17; 3.152–159, 16n35; 3.188, 16; 5.14–23, 13n19; 5.74–75, 13n21; 5.145, 13n21; 5.156–173, 13n21; 7.36–39, 16n36

Lucian of Samosata
  Alexander 14, 59n32
  Apology (Apologia) 15, 18n44
  Double Indictment (Bis accusatus) 27, 18n44
  Lover of Lies (Philopseudes) 34–36, 67n78, 34, 67n79
  Menippus 6, 32n25
  Nigrinus 23, 20n49
  On Hired Companions (De mercede conductis potentium familiaribus) 18–19; 3, 19n48; 4, 15n29; 5–7, 16; 9, 16; 10, 64n65; 13, 15n31; 15–18, 64; 19, 11, 15; 25, 16; 27, 22–23; 29–31, 64; 34–36, 64; 35, 16n36; 40, 6n19, 22, 26n1
  On the Dance (De saltatione) 83, 23n59
  On the Death of Peregrinus (De morti Peregrini), 83n45; 13, 142n1
  On the Parasite (De parasite) 36–38, 21n54; 58, 22n55; 61, 22
  Portraits (Imagines) 10, 18n44
  Teacher of Rhetoric (Rhetorum praeceptor) 5, 24, 66; 10, 11, 23, 24, 65
  The Dream (Somnium) 9, 11n9
  Timon 45–46, 20n49
  True Stories (Verae historiae) 2.20, 81n39
[Lucian of Samosata]
  Lucius 35–36, 19n46

Macrobius
  Saturnalia 7.3, 14n23
Manilius
  Astronomica 2.750–787, 4.119–121, 109n60, 114n85
Marcus Aurelius
  Meditations 8.37, 18n44
Martial
  Epigrams 1.108, 13; 2.19, 12n17, 13n19;

3.95.10, 16n35; 5.23, 16n35; 6.9, 16n35; 10.58, 13; 11.18, 12; 11.24, 13; 12.4, 12n17; 12.31, 12n17

Martianus Capella
  On the Marriage of Philology and Mercury 3.225, 58n30

Michael Psellus
  Περὶ παραδόξων ἀκουσμάτων 13–64, 87n65; 65–90, 57n22; 70–71, 53n8

Nag Hammadi Codices
  VIII.1.3.14–1.4.1, 111n69

Nepualius (Neptunianos)
  On Sympathies and Antipathies 58, 55n18

Nigidius Figulus
  Fr. 67 Swoboda, 31n19

Nostoi
  Fr. 7 Bernabé, 28n8

Novum Testamentum
  Acts of the Apostles 13.5–12, 6–7n20; 19.19, 88n72
  Matthew 10.34, 107n55, 116n94

Numenius
  Fr. 1a Bidez, 39n61

Origen
  Against Celsus 1.16, 38n53, 42n78; 1.24, 43n81; 1.68, 67n83, 142n1; 2.52.32, 88n72

Orphic Lithica
  71–72, 41n64

P.Holm.
  2, 55; 12–14, 4n15; 866–871, 4n15

P.Oxy.
  79.5202, 60n42

P.Yale
  299, 88n72

Papyrus Erzherzog Rainer
  161, 97n19

Paulinus of Pella
  Eucharistikos 72–80, 23n60

[Paulus]
  Opiniones 5.23, 38n51

Pelagius
  On the Sacred and Divine Technique, CAAG, 3.255.9

Petronius
  Satyricon 23.3, 19n46; 35–36, 39, 120

PGM
  I.1–64, 87n67; I.42–195, 68n85; IV.2019, 95n8; IV 2083–2087, 2283–2285, 2314–2315, 138n82; IV.2443–2451, 67n80; IV.2943–2966, 88n73; VII.149–154, 68n85; VII.167–186, 56n20–21;VII.170–171, 178–179, 59n32; VII.208–209, 85n59; VII.652–661, 88n73; XIa.1–40, 68n85; XIb, 53–54, 56n21; XII.193–204, 86n60, 139n84; XII.376–397, 88n73; XII.397–400, 58n30; XII.244–245, 138n81; XIII.244-245, 138n81; XVI.12, 95n8; XIXa.8, 95n8; LXIII.4–5, 138n82; CXXVII, 56n21

Philo of Alexandria
  On Special Laws (De specialibus legibus) 3.93–104, 36n43; 3.100, 36n45, 38n53, 38n56; 3.100–101, 35n42; 3.101, 37n47–48
  On the Change of Names (De mutatione nominum) 150, 36n43
  On the Migration of Abraham (De migratione Abrahami) 38, 36n46
  On the Unchangeableness of God (Quod deus immutabilis sit) 139, 36n46
  That Every Good Man is Free (Quod omnis probus liber sit) 74, 36n46, 38n53

Philo of Byblos
  F4 FGrH 815.30–31, 816.6–7, 38n53

The Philosopher Synesius to Dioscorus
  1–2, 140n85

Philostorgius
  Ecclesiastical History 3.15–20, 97n21

Philostratus
  Life of Apollonius of Tyana, 3.19–26, 39n61; 4.25, 67n84; 8.20, 35n42
  Lives of the Sophists 1.10, 39n61; 506, 11n9; 523, 74; 524, 533, 66n77; 585–590, 74; 590.9–11, 75

Photius
  Bibliotheca 170, 96n13

Physica et Mystica (Martelli)
  3, 140n85; 13.141–142, 139n84

Plato
  Gorgias 463, 12n13; 486d, 97n25; 527, 12n13
  Laws 11.909b, 11.933a, 34n32
  Protagoras 314d–315b, 12n15
  Republic 364b–365a, 28–29, 82n40; 572d–e, 34n32
  Sophist 235a, 34n32
  Statesman 280e, 28n8; 303e, 100n33, 116n90
  Timaeus 58d–59c, 101

[Plato]
  First Alcibiades 121e–122a, 36

Pliny the Elder
  Natural History Pref. 26, 60n37, 63n57; 1.18c, 38; 1.30a.3–4, 1.30b–c, 38n55; 1.30c, 38; 1.37c, 38, 39n57; 1.30–32, 35–37, 63n58;

9.184, 59n33; 10.188, 59n32; 11.242, 39n57; 18.200, 39n57; 19.19-20, 52n6; 19.93-94, 59n32; 20.74, 21.166, 22.50, 61, 39n58; 23.54, 59n32; 24.72, 164, 39n58; 24.167, 63n53; 25.13, 39, 39n59; 25.154, 54n13; 25.106, 130, 39n58; 26.163, 85n59; 28.6, 39n60; 28.38, 55n15; 28.47, 39n58; 28.66, 55n15; 28.69, 39n58; 28.82, 55n15; 28.85-86, 92, 39n58; 28.181, 53n9; 28.188, 198, 201, 215, 226, 228, 229, 232, 249, 256, 259, 260, 261, 39n58; 28.262, 55n15; 29.59, 66, 76, 39n58; 29.102, 56n21; 29.117, 138, 39n58; 30.1-13, 39; 30.2, 39n60; 30.3-11, 39n61; 30.2.4, 38n54; 30.5-6, 39n60; 30.8.1, 38n55; 30.8-9, 40; 30.14, 39n60; 30.16, 39n58; 30.18, 60n38; 30.27, 49n101; 30.32, 100n33; 30.54, 64, 39n58; 30.74, 54n14; 30.82, 84, 91, 100, 110, 39n58; 30.140, 88n73; 30.141, 39n58; 30.145, 38; 31.22, 63n53; 32.19, 63n54; 32.34, 49, 55, 73, 115, 39n58; 32.135, 140, 55n15; 32.141, 53n7; 33.25, 103n44, 139n84; 33.64-65, 100n33; 33.84, 103n42; 33.102, 107, 86n64; 33.131, 94n3; 33.312, 96n15; 34.112, 58n29; 34.128-134, 139n84; 35.175, 54n11; 36.142, 39n58; 37.59, 63n53; 37.133, 150, 157, 159, 39n57; 37.144, 156, 39n58

Pliny the Younger
  Letters 1.9.2, 61n48; 3.3, 15n30, 23n60; 3.21, 10n6; 7.3.2, 13n20; 8.24.2, 17n39; 10.96, 142n1

Plotinus
  Enneads 1.6.5.50-53, 116n92; 1.6.9.13-16, 126n42; 1.6.9.33-35, 127n43; 1.6.9.2-5, 127n44; 2.9.14.1-11, 42n77; 4.4.26.1-4, 42n70, 42n75; 4.4.30, 41n69; 4.4.40.1-9, 42n71; 4.4.40.6-7, 42n72; 4.4.43.17-20, 42n74; 4.4.43.23-25, 42n76

Plutarch
  Against Colotes 1115a, 35n40
  How to Tell a Flatterer from a Friend (Quomodo adulator ab amico internoscatur), 61n49; 49b-50e, 14n26; 50c-d, 12n13; 58c, 16n35; 66e-74e, 14n26
  Life of Aemilius Paulus 6.8-9, 15n30
  Life of Dion 2, 73n10
  Life of Pericles 1.4-5, 11n9
  On Delays of the Divine Vengeance (De sera numinis vindicta) 567b, 110n62; 567c, 110n64
  On Isis and Osiris (De Iside et Osiride) 361b, 73n10; 367c-368b, 109n61; 377b-378a, 73n12

On the Failure of the Oracles (De defectu oraculorum) 437f, 58
  Precepts of Statecraft (Praecepta gerendae reipublicae) 806e-807a, 14n27
  Symposiacs (Quaestiones convivales) 1.pref, 71n3; *1.1*, 14n25, 71n4; *1.6.4 (624c-625a)*, 56n19; *2.1 (634c)*, 14n23; *4.5 (671b)*, 73n13; *4.5-6*, 73n11; *4.8*, 63n55; *5.3*, 73n11; *5.7*, 72-75; *5.7 (680b-683b)*, 72n7; *5.7 (680c-d, f)*, 72; *5.7 (681a)*, 72n8, 79n31; *5.7 (680f-681a)*, 79n33; *5.7 (681a5-b1)*, 78n29; *5.7 (682b10-c2)*, 75n19; *5.7 (683a-b)*, 72n9; *5.10*, 73n11; *7.3*, 71; *7.7*, 71; *7.8*, 23n59; *8.1*, 73n11; *8.2*, 71; *8.8*, 73n11; *8.10*, 72n6, 73n11
  That a Philosopher Should Converse Especially with Rulers (Maxime cum principibus philosopho esse disserendum) 776b-779c, 71n5; 778b-d, 14n28
  To an Uneducated Ruler (Ad principem ineruditum), 14; 780e, 42n76; 780e-f, 71n5

[Plutarch]
  Life of Homer 1.3-4, 81n39

Porphyry of Tyre
  Philosophy from Oracles (Smith) fr. 286-296F, 46n93; fr. 316F, 46n95; fr. 326F, 45n87; fr. 330F, 330aF, 47n97; fr. 331F, 46n95; fr. 339F, 45n86; 340F, 46n95
  Letter to Marcella 16, 126n39
  Letter to Anebo (Saffrey-Segonds) fr. 13, 45n90, 46n96; fr. 78, 45n90; fr. 100, 46n96
  De regressu animae fr. 286-296F Smith, 46n93
  On Images (Peri agalmatōn) fr. 351-360a Smith, 127n45
  On Abstinence 1.28, 1.43, 45n88; 1.57.2, 140n89; 2.33, 46n92; 2.33-34, 140n89; 2.37-44, 140n88; 2.41-42, 45n90; 2.42, 46n96; 2.43, 45n87; 2.49, 126n39; 4.16, 45n89
  Life of Pythagoras, 6, 45n89; 15, 78; 33, 41, 45n89; 12, 39n61
  Life of Plotinus 3, 69n86; 10.3-5, 45n88; 16, 4n16, 38n53, 41n68, 69n86
  Commentary on the Timaeus 16 Diehl (= 28.12-22 Sodano), 45n89

Proclus
  Commentary on the Republic of Plato 2.109-110, 38n53; 2.234.14-19, 101n37
  Commentary to the First Book of Euclid's Elements 105.16-18, 101n39
  Commentary to the Timaeus 1.43.1-21, 101n39
  The Prophetess Isis to her Son Horus CAAG 2.28-9, 132n69

INDEX OF PASSAGES

Pseudo-Clementine Recognitions
  1.5, 41n67; 2.7–15, 65n67; 4.27, 38n53; 10.52, 62n51
Pseudo-Clementine Homilies
  1.3, 61; 1.5, 41n67; 1.9–11, 61; 1.14.1, 61n47; 1.20.7, 1.21.4–5, 61n48; 2.8, 61n48; 2.15–18, 66n73; 2.18–32, 65n67; 2.22.3, 65; 2.32, 116n91; 2.32.2, 65n71; 2.33–34, 66n75; 4–6, 83; 4.4, 65n70; 4.7, 61; 4.10, 62; 5.2, 62n51, 63n56; 5.3–8, 82n40; 5.10–19, 61n48; 6.29.3, 65n70; 7.3.1, 65n70

Quintilian
  The Orator's Education 1.2, 15n30; 2.15.2, 36n43

Refutation of All Heresies
  1.2.5, 1.2.12, 1.13, 39n61, 57n25; 4.28, 31, 33.3, 58–59; 4.31.1–2, 68n85; 4.33.4, 55n18, 59n32; 4.35.3, 68n85; 5.21.1–6, 97n25, 116n95; 9.10.7, 30n14; 4.42.1, 58; 6.39, 57n25
Rufus of Ephesus
  On Melancholy fr. 73 Pormann, 81n37

Sch. [Plato], First Alcibiades
  122a (60 Cufalo), 38n53
Seneca the Elder
  Suasoriae 2.19, 23n59
Seneca the Younger
  Letters to Lucilius 88.40, 60n36, 40, 44, 66n75; 90.33, 100n33
Sextus Empiricus
  Pyrrhonian Outlines 1.46, 56n21, 57n24
Sophocles
  Oedipus Rex 387–389, 34n33
Strabo
  Geography 3.12–14, 100n33; 3.2.8, 103n42; 11.536c, 34n30; 16.2.39, 32n25
Suda
  A 559, Δ 250, 96n14; Δ 1156, 94n5, 96n14; Z 159, 38n53; Z 168, 2, 9n2, 96n14, 121n16; Π 253, 120n8; X 227, 96n14; X 280, 94n5, 96n14
Suetonius
  Teachers of Letters and of Rhetoric 17, 15n30; 25.1, 11n12; 25.3, 16n33
Suppl.Mag.
  2.76, 56n21

Tacitus
  Annals 11.4.3, 15n30; 2.27–2.33, 12.22, 12.53, 74n15

Tatian
  To the Hellenes 27, 38, 60n36
Themistius
  Orations 7.145.12–26, 101n34; 7.145.26–146.1, 101n36; 7.146.1–11, 101n35
Theocritus
  Idylls 17, 63n57
Theodoret
  Ecclesiastical History 2.28.9, 3.15.7, 97n24
Theodosian Code
  14.9.3, 23n61
Theophanes Confessor
  Chronographia 150.12, 95n7
Theophrastus
  Historia Plantarum 9.5.17, 28n8
  On Stones, 100n33
[Thessalus]
  De virtutibus herbarum prol., 13, 41n66

Vetus Testamentum
  Ezekiel 22.17–22, 100n33, 116n89; 37, 115n87
  Jeremiah 6.27–30, 100n33, 116n89
  Malachias 3.3, 116n89
  Zachariah 13.9, 116n89
Vitruvius
  De architectura 7.8.1–4, 7.9.4, 100n33

Xenophon
  Cyropaedia 1.6.2, 35n38; 4.5.14, 4.5.51, 4.6.11, 5.3.4, 35n37; 6.4, 18n44; 7.3.1, 7.5.35, 7.5.57, 8.3.11, 8.3.24, 35n37; 8.1.23, 35n36, 35n37
  Memorabilia 2.9, 12n16
  Symposium 1, 12n15

Yasna
  32.7, 51.9, 31n19

Zacharia of Mytilene
  Life of Severus of Antioch 16, 38n53
[Zacharia of Mytilene]
  Ecclesiastical History 7.1, 95n7
Zosimus of Panopolis
  MA 1, 133–137, 3n11; 1.1, 143n2; 1.2, 112n74; 1.2.20–24, 138n77; 1.4, 4n16, 112n78; 1.5, 112n78; 1.7, 107n55, 110n65, 112n78, 133n73, 138n78, 140n86; 1.8, 112n78; 1.9, 105n52, 117n96; 1.10, 4n16, 143n2; 1.10–15, 110n63; 1.11.106–107, 105n51, 117n96; 1.11–15, 113n80; 1.11.104–107, 134n74; 1.12.115–120, 135n75; 1.13.126–132, 105n52, 117n96; 1.13–14, 2n3, 110n65; 1.14.133–134, 134n74; 1.15, 112n78; 1.18, 112n74; 1.18.178–188, 138n77; 1.19, 120n10;

1.19.193–199, 121n15; *3*, 119n5; *5*, 105; *8*, 2n9, 119–120; *8.1–2*, 120n9; *8.1–20*, 119n6; *8.43–44*, 119n4; *8.62–63*, 96n16; *10*, 104–115; *10.3.69–73*, 111n71, 123n24; *10.2.17*, 111n69; *10.2.19*, 105n50; *10.2.41–42*, 104n48; *10.3.54–57*, 111n70; *10.3.63*, 105n50; *10.3.69–72*, 111n71; *10.4.75–78*, 104n48; *10.4.97–98*, 115n88; *10.4.98–99*, 112n75; *10.4.99*, 112n76; *10.5.105*, 117n96; *10.5.108–113*, 115n87; *10.7.133–135*, 112n77; *11.1.2, 2.41, 12.2.11–14, 12.2.14–18*, 105n50

CAAG *1.28-9*, 132n69; *1.84.4–11*, 136n76; *2.110.1*, 108n57; *2.150.13, 156.8, 156.14–17, 157.2, 162.3*, 112n78; *2.167.20–168.5*, 119n4; *2.169.9*, 112n78; *2.170–171*, 112n72–73; *2.175.14–15*, 112n78; *2.186–187*, 123n26; *2.188.19*, 112n78; *2.189*, 122n20; *2.189.4, 198.3*, 112n78; *2.190.5–9*, 122n21; *2.190.10–191.7*, 123n26; *2.191.7–18*, 124n30; *2.192.1–2*, 124n27; *2.192.7–9*, 125n31; *2.204*, 120n11; *2.204.9–10*, 121n12; *2.204.15–19*, 121n14; *2.216.4–9*, 115n86; *2.241.12–16, 2.242.1–3, 8–9*, 130n62–64; *2.245.19–246.1–3*, 130n65; *2.246.14–23*, 131n66; *2.246.22*, 9n1; *2.241.9–242.9*, 128n51; *2.241.19–22*, 128n51; *2.241.25–26*, 128n52; *3.255.9*, 139n84; *3.285.3–4*, 121n16; *3.441.21*, 100n32

Eighth Treatise on the Working of Tin (Syriac Cambridge Mm. 6.29) fols. 32ʳ–45ᵛ, 125n32–37; *fols. 49ᵛ–50ʳ*, 118n2, 132n67; *fols. 85ʳ–87ʳ*, 126n40

Final Abstinence (Festugière) 1.274, 127n46; *1.281 n. 7*, 130n61; *1.365.13–14*, 128n50; *1.365.21*, 128n53; *1.366.29–367.5*, 129n58; *1.366.6–367.5*, 129n56; *1.366.8-9*, 128n48; *1.366.21–22*, 128n48; *1.367.10–24*, 136n76; *1.367.24–27*, 140n87; *1.367.10–368.4*, 120n10; *1.367.13–14*, 130n60; *1.368.1*, 128n48

GENERAL INDEX

Adrian of Tyre, 74–75
Anaxilaus of Larissa, 4, 51–57, 62
Antiochus Soter, 62, 78, 83
Apion, 7, 38n55, 51, 59–63, 66, 68, 78, 82n40, 83, 90, 143
Axioms
  a nature is defeated by another nature, 99
  know yourself, 126
  like knows like, 126–127

Banquets, 21n53, 62, 64, 70–75, 78, 82, 83n43, 119–120, 122
  as setting for the use of *paignia*, 52–57
  as source of pollution, 65
  set up through the use of witchcraft or contraptions, 66–68

Calasiris (character of the *Ethiopica*), 8, 70, 75–84, 90
Charicleia (character of the *Ethiopica*), 75–78, 79n30, 80–83
Charicles (character of the *Ethiopica*), 75–83
Chēmeu (book), 5, 118, 128n53, 132–133, 141
Christ, 3n11
  as *logos*, 31, 31n22
  as sorcerer, 42, 142
  as sword (*machaira*), 107n55, 116, 117n96
  becoming everything, 134–135
  body compared to the Ark of the Covenant, 116
  compared to Prometheus, 136
  given the name of *planos*, 46n96
  name used in rituals, 42–43
  prefigured in *Ezekiel*, 115n87
  soteriological role, 105, 116–117, 135
Client scholars, 1, 5–8, 9–25
  as specialist of eastern wisdom, 88–90
  not found in sources, 9–11
  represented as flatterers and parasites (*kolakes, parasitoi*), 12–25
  represented as prostitutes, 21
  represented as sorcerers, 17, 22–23, 62, 64–69, 82–84
Color, 1, 57, 59n32, 87, 98, 102, 105, 106, 109–110, 130, 131
  blackening, 94n3
  interpretation of, 127
  of statues, 94, 125
  of stones, 99, 100n33
  whitening, 119, 122–124

Daimones
  antimimos daimōn, 135
  avoidance/protection from, 5, 28, 44–45, 105, 113, 130, 133, 141
  good or evil, 44–48, 46n95, 73
  in the afterworld, 110
  invocation/control over, 32, 32n24, 33, 42, 45, 65, 119, 133
  involved in alchemy, 112–113, 119, 129n55, 130–131, 132n71, 133–134, 136–137, 140–141
  providers of sacred wisdom, 14, 132
  sacrifice to, 5, 14, 65, 127
Democritus
  alchemical recipes attributed to, 1–5, 41, 112n72, 122, 125, 131, 137, 141–142
  allegorized alchemical texts, 118, 128, 130, 131–133, 141
  believed to be the only author to have preserved alchemical notions, 128, 144
  commenting on alchemical texts, 121, 128, 128n53
  in contact with *magoi*, 139–140
  paignia attributed to, 41, 55–56, 59n32
  theory concerning *eidōla*, 72
  theory concerning the flooding of the Nile, 76, 86n61
  work associated with *mageia*, 40, 142–143

GENERAL INDEX 167

Egg, 55, 56, 58, 59n32, 130
  compared to the universe, 120
Erasistratus, 62, 78, 83, 90
Eschatology
  in Clement, 28–33
  in Plutarch and Zosimus, 106–111
  in the *Bundahišn*, 31n19
  in the *Refutation of All Heresies*, 116
  involving the transfiguration of all matter in the universe, 102
Ethiopians, 53, 75–76
Eusebius, 44–50
Evil eye (*baskania*)
  in Plutarch's *Symposiacs*, 72–75
  in the *Ethiopica*, 78–82
  of the *phruē*, 80n35

Flatterers and parasites (*kolakes, parasitoi*), 12–25, 61, 68, 86, 97,
  related to *bōmolochoi*, 37

Gnosticism, 3, 105

Hermes, 2
  as ruler of the *magoi*, 138n82
  mentioned in an oracle of Apollo, 47
  number of times cited by Zosimus, 118n1
Hermetica
  claiming that philosophers are above fate, 134
  discussing the use of a substance called *kōbathia*, 122, 125, 131
  influence on Zosimus, 111–117
  Lithica, 41n64
  mentioning that one should not attempt to curb fate, 105, 134, 140
  Περὶ ἐναυλίας, 107n55
  Φυσικά, 112n78
Hermetism, 2–3

Julius Africanus, 4, 8, 53, 57, 60, 70, 75, 84–91

Kakotechnia, 36–37, 48–49

Maceration (*taricheia*), 104, 107, 114
Mageia
  a feature of the natural world, 41–44
  a form of divination, 36
  a technique to alter fate/control *daimones*, 44–45, 133–135, 138, 140
  associated with alchemy and Democritus, 138–140
  associated with *curiositas* and *perierga*, 47, 60, 63, 88, 90, 143

  associated with kingship, 36
  associated with *paideia*, 40, 62, 90–92
  associated with *paignia*, 49n101, 52–59
  associated with scholars, 17, 41, 49–50, 60, 68
  associated with the worship of the gods, 36
  books of, 37–41
  conceived as Persian and distinguished from witchcraft, 35–37, 39–40
  conceived as Persian and identical with witchcraft, 39
  discussion of, avoided by Plutarch during banquets, 72–75
  hinted at by Africanus, 85–92
  in the PGM, 138n82
  polysemy of the term, 6–8, 25, 26–27, 141–143
  used to refer to witchcraft, 42, 44–48
  the work of evil *daimones*, 46–48
Magoi
  according to Philo of Alexandria, 36
  as Persian officers, 33–35, 45, 47–49, 139
  associated with *paignia*, 57–59
  authors of books, 38–41, 43
  Egyptian, 70, 78–84
  in historical research, 27
  mentioned by Clement, 28–33
  role expected of client scholars, 91
  teachers of Greek philosophers, 39n61, 139–140
  term used to describe scholars, 17, 22–25, 40, 51–52, 63–68, 82–84
Metallic humans, 104, 107–109, 11, 115

Nechepso, 99n30
Neilos (rival of Zosimus), 4, 122–127, 131, 136–138, 144
Nicotheos (prophet), 4, 118
Nile, theories for its flooding, 76–78

Origen, 42–44

Paideia, 3n13, 5–6, 8, 10–11, 14–15, 17–18, 20–23, 25–26, 40, 49, 51, 61, 63, 65–66, 70, 77–78, 83–84, 88–92, 117, 119, 141, 143–145
  defined, 1
  sold, 11
  shared with Roman aristocrats, 18–19
Paignia, 90, 138, 143
  and banquets, 51–57
  attributed to Democritus, 41, 55–56, 59n32
  related to *mageia*, 49n101, 52–59
Pancrates/Pachrates, 51, 59, 66–68, 90, 143
Paul (apostle), 7, 63

Peregrinus "Proteus", 83
Peter (apostle), 61, 64
Plotinus
    comparing the soul to gold, 116
    discussing *mageia*, 41–44
    on recognizing one's divine nature, 127–128
    seeking to refute Christians, 4
    seeking to demonstrate the existence of Zoroastrian pseudepigrapha, 38n53, 41, 69
Plutarch of Cheironeia, 14–15, 70–75, 109–110
Porphyry of Tyre, 4
    and Christians in Plotinus' school, 3n13, 4, 38n53
    citing Antonius Diogenes' novel as a trustworthy source for his biography of Pythagoras, 78
    claiming that eastern philosophers taught Greek philosophers, 39n61
    claiming the title of *hiereus*, 126
    on blood-sacrifice, 140
    on *mageia*, 44–47
Prophecy, 30–31, 116–117

Refining, 100n33, 102–103, 139n84
Representations of learned sorcerers, 7–8, 11, 25, 49-92, 119, 138, 142–144

Salpe (*obstetrix*), 55–56
Scholarly patronage
    and the evolution of *paideia*, 5, 23, 90–92, 142–144
    as friendship, 10, 14, 90
    as slavery, 18–22
    perverting scholars and *paideia*, 22–23
    possibly involved in the Christianization of Roman aristocrats, 142
    potentially involving the trade of curses and divination, 22–23, 81–82, 82n40, 88
Scholarly rivalry, 57–69, 74, 122–137
Simon of Gitta, 7, 51, 58, 59, 61–68, 90, 116n91, 143
Specialists of eastern philosophies, 74, 76–78, 82, 88–90
Structor, 119–120

Theagenes (character of the *Ethiopica*), 75–76, 78, 81–83
Theosebeia (patroness of Zosimus of Panopolis), 3, 5, 9, 105, 113, 118–122, 125–126, 130–131, 133, 136–137, 141, 144
Transformation, 1–2,
    as "reversion" (*ekstrophē*), 110, 115
    in relation with mythological and historical figures, 39, 101
    of substances compared with the transformation of the self, 104–117
    of the eyes into what is seen, 72n8
Transmutation of metals into gold, 93
    in non-alchemical literature, 100–103
    possibility denied, 101

Ulpian, 74

Zosimus of Panopolis, 1–6, 8–9, 70, 92–96, 98, 103–144
    a Christian, 3n11
    client scholar, 119–122
    compared to late antique philosophers, 140
    involved in scholarly rivalry, 122–137, 141
    opposing Hermes to Zoroaster, 134, 140

www.ingramcontent.com/pod-product-compliance
Lightning Source LLC
Chambersburg PA
CBHW021759230426
43669CB00006B/126